THE LINHAY
ON THE DOWNS

THE LINHAY
ON THE DOWNS

And Other Adventures in the Old
and the New World

HENRY WILLIAMSON

ALAN SUTTON
1984

Alan Sutton Publishing Limited
Brunswick Road · Gloucester

First published 1934
This edition published 1984

British Library Cataloguing in Publication Data

Williamson, Henry
  The Linhay on the Downs.—(Sovereign)
  1. Voyages and travels—1951–
  I. Title II. Series
  910.4   G465

  ISBN 0-86299-194-3

Cover picture: detail from Winter Sunset with Barn Owl
by Raymond Booth.
Courtesy of The Fine Art Society, London

Printed and bound in Great Britain

CONTENTS

PART ONE
ENGLAND

The Linhay on the Downs	13
A Fresh Start	24
Salmon Fishers	27
The Sex-Life of Rooks	29
A West Country Trout Farm	32
Traps and Trapping	36
My Partridges	38
The Fishers	41
Science, or, Sentiment	44
Rise of a Village	51
'Some Marvels of Pond Life'	58
The Gold Fish	65
The Old Trout	68
'The Dear One'	75
Dimmit Light	78
Stag Hunting	81
Heat Wave	86
Wasps	89
August Evening	95
Harold	98
Wane of Summer	102
A London Sanctuary	105
Moonlight	110
Potwallopers' Marsh	114
The Spate	117
The Harmony of Nature	122
Hill of Winds	125
A Night on Salisbury Plain	128
Still the Drought	133
Morning Tide	136
The River Freezes	139
Flighting	142
The Yule Log	145

CONTENTS

Sea and the Wind: North Devon   149
The Glory of the Gale: South Devon   151
Ravens   154
High Peak Canal   156
Wood Fires   160
From 'The Sun in the Sands'   168

PART TWO
ESSAYS ON BOOKS AND AUTHORS

On Otters   187
Reading in Bed   197
Izaak Walton   210
A Brave Book   219
Reality in War Literature   224

PART THREE
AMERICA

S.S. *Berengaria*   265
Manhattan   267
Southern Sun   271
To England   306

ILLUSTRATIONS

Author at Home   *facing p.* 64
Windwhistle Hut
The Age of Innocence
River Scenes in Summer
August in the Estuary of the Two Rivers
Loetitia and John Williamson with Fish
Last Glimpse
River Scenes in Winter

TO
MISS LOUISE OF LE MANOIR FLEURI
(Mrs. Robert de l'Aigle Reese)

IN GRATEFUL MEMORY OF
MANY HAPPY DAYS IN THE SOUTH,
AND IN THE HOPE
THAT THE LATER PAGES OF THIS BOOK DO NOT
OBSCURE THE KINDNESS AND HOSPITALITY
SHOWN TO AN ENGLISHMAN

PART ONE

ENGLAND

THE LINHAY ON THE DOWNS

On the high down above the sea, in the corner of the last rough grazing field, stands a linhay, half fallen into ruin. It is built of boles of spruce fir, unhewn but barked, and boarded with rough wooden boards. It has a roof of corrugated iron. The roof is intact, but many of the wooden boards have fallen with the rusted nails. Those boards remaining are green and damp, and shaggy with grey lichens.

The linhay had been built with its eastern end open to shelter bullocks in stormy weather, but the gentleman farmer had sold the down with his other land after the Great War, and the new owner, a native farmer, had let it fall ruinous. Battering winds and rain straight from off the Atlantic, and the hot sun of summer, had warped and rotted the boards and opened two other walls to the weather.

On windy days buzzard hawks lie over the downs on crooked wings, watching for rabbits in the heather slope below; or turn and glide over the line of the hill. It is a beautiful and desolate place, where the spirit can spread itself wide and airy as the sea and the sky.

One morning between winter and spring I set out to picnic in the linhay with a companion. As we climbed the road to Windwhistle Cross the wind blew harder, and found cold places in our clothes. Past the beech plantation the way lay over fields, cutting across the broad and rushing gale. I was more hardened than my companion, who covered her face with her gloved hands and walked with bowed head. After awhile we reached a wall of stone and earth, tunnelled by rabbits, and fallen in gaps. The wind, seeking to level all things, was whipping up bits of stone and earth over the wall, and we had to shield our eyes. Plants growing on the crumbling riband of earth remaining on the top of the stones were pressed tightly down, guarding their leaves among the mosses from the stripping storms. White splashes marked the stones, where in still weather the buzzards had waited and watched for rabbits to lollop out of their buries in the wall.

We reached the linhay, and knew immediately that it would give no shelter for a fire as in other expeditions. The hollow was frigid in shadow and scoured by the wind. The last stone wall before the heather and brambles of the wild seaward slope stood a few strides away, and behind this we sat down and rested out of the wind. An easy matter to break the old boards with a fifty-pound slab of ironstone fallen from the wall, but not so easy to make a fire. Half a box of matches and chips sliced with a knife, however, changed the acrid smoke of deal-wood into flame, and the flame into red and black brittle embers, which wasted in sparks over the grass. The wind was too strong. There was no contentment in such a fire.

While we were munching our sandwiches in the sunshine my companion, who had been staring into the shadow-cut interior of the linhay ten yards away, asked me if I saw anything above a stone against the inner wall. Yes, I saw a pair of ears upraised, and a dark brown eye below them.

I stood up, and the ears went down flat; but the brown eye continued to watch. A rabbit was squatting there.

I sat down out of the wind, and soon afterwards the

ears were raised again. The wind tore at the flames and rocked a loose stone on the wall behind us. It was blowing harder. We moved away, spreading a raincoat before a derelict plough which old grasses had partly covered. Seagulls, shifting and slanting in swift uneven gliding, began to appear above our heads, first in pairs, and then in many numbers. The sunlight was put out, and the wind was trying to crush us with cold. I got up and looked over the wall.

I saw a grand and terrible sight. The headland which lay out into the bay, dark and puny under the vastness of sky that seemed to begin just beyond my feet, was blurred and lost. Beyond, a mile or two from the extended sands below, where hundreds of gulls were standing still and tiny as scattered whitish seeds, all was chaos. It was as though the sky was falling, as though a monstrous dark spectre had risen out of the sea and was moving to overthrow the land.

We picked up our raincoats, gathered them back from the wind, and allowed ourselves to be billowed into the linhay. The air-blows thudded against the boards of the intact side — the shippen was open west, south and east, except for the round support posts, gnawn with damp at the base, which remained upright. Wind rebounding from the single wall flung over us like a comber, dropping dust and straw-specks in our ears and the corners of our eyes. It was cold on the rough trodden floor, whereon lay flakes of frayed board and dried dung of bullocks. Slabs of stone lay against the wall, about six inches from the bottom board, and in one space the rabbit was still crouching, its ears pressed on its shoulders, its life quivering behind the staring dark eyes.

The headland was gone; the sky was falling. Beyond the forming ridges of distant waves the sea seemed to be taking on a wrinkled dull grey skin, like molten lead in a trough; and as we watched, the falling blackness was riven, and in the rift a snout arose, and spread upwards into the shape of a funnel as it travelled over the surf to the shore. It was a waterspout. We saw the tiny white seeds sprout with wings, and settle on the sands again. The open linhay trembled, and we buttoned our coats to the neck.

A ladder was fixed to the middle post of one side of the linhay, leading to the tallat, or loft, through an open trap-door seven feet above our heads. We climbed up, and were in an open space crossed by rafters under slanting corrugated iron sheets, lit at the seaward end by a window frame without glass. The floor was rotten in places. Wooden pegs of snares, some with tarnished brass-wire loops, were thrown in one corner, with a sack. The skull of a mouse, with brittle bones interlocked in greyish fur, lay on one beam, where an owl had roosted. I looked through a break in the floor; the rabbit was still beside the stone.

Wind-noises ran through the bleak tallat, coming in at the eaves, the floor cracks, the window frame stripped of putty and paint, where owls had perched. They filled the loft, like the hollow and curious voices of straying things never of the earth or its life. We stood close together, while light rapidly drained from the rafters, the floor, each other's face. We waited, a little fearfully, for the storm to reach us, awed by the mysterious noises of the wind, which were changing every moment.

The plaining voices were lost in the buffets on the iron roof. The skull of the mouse rolled on the beam, and the bones fell aslant, joining a trickle of broken straws along the floor. My companion wrapped her coat closer round her legs. I peered through an empty square of the window, and saw greyness rushing up the heather slope of the down. I saw the fire by the wall, already gutted of embers, kicked as though by an invisible foot. The charred lengths of board, flecked with yellow and red points of flame, rose up and flew yards, and fell flat, smoking violently in the grass.

Voices wailed and shrieked, seeming to dissolve the substance of the tallat in a pallor of darkness. Straw specks and mice bones whirled on the floor, suddenly to rise up and scatter. The linhay was shuddering in the wind. Would the inner core of its uprights hold in the storm? I trod a careful way to the trap-door, and the wind instantly threw up the wide skirt of the raincoat into my face.

We waited, our backs to the screaming draughts racing up the corrugations of the iron roof. Suddenly a hatch in the walled angle above the trap-door burst its wooden latch and flung half open, before wedging against the floor, and shaking on the ragged grass background of the field below. An amazing object moved slowly across the grassy rectangle cut by the lichen-frayed door! My companion also saw it, and clutched my arm.

The object moved on three thin legs, with a hop that threw its head up and down in alternate roll and flop. It paused, got its hind legs under it, and took another hop forward, dragging something on the ground. Each forward movement, which needed about five seconds to prepare, took it perhaps six inches nearer shelter. By its head and tail it was a fox — but was it a fox? The tail hung like a piece of old rope, the small head was almost without hair, the ribs showed under creases of skin muddy and stuck with tufts, through which the sharp points of shoulders and hips seemed about to break with the weight of the swelled body. I had just turned my glass into focus and seen that it was a vixen dragging the chain and iron peg of a rusty rabbit gin clamped on its foreleg when the first hail smote the roof with an immense clattering crash, and the linhay rocked with the hollow thunder of the wind. I feared it would turn over, crumple, and be carried over the stone wall immediately behind. The field space below the door was a grey blank; the day was torn up and hurtling past us. Jets of icy air were driven through the floor and up between body and clothes. The sack slid over the floorboards, reached the square of the trapdoor, jumped to the rafters, on which it moulded itself before falling. It was snatched through the hatch. I yelled in my companion's ear that it would be best to stand by that hatch, to jump clear when the linhay should buckle and rise. I took her by the hand, cold as stone, and guided her along one of the joists lest the floor break under our tread.

We had reached the eastern end when the black of the storm descended on the down. Immediately we were under a torrent. I saw alarm with the misery in the dim face beside me. The linhay was lurching under the flood. Skits blown in from the open window tasted salt on my lips. And the sea was a mile away, at the end of a downward slant of fifteen degrees!

The earth under the linhay was awash. Water moved there in wrinkled sheets prickled with rain. I could see nothing of fox or rabbit. The smashing of wood for the fire had given me warmth, but this warmth was used and gone after five more minutes in the loft. My companion was rigid, as though being enclosed in an icicle. Her teeth chattered. The wind pushed its thorns under our nails and in our jaw-bones, and drew its brambles down our ears and cheeks. Our toes were broken in glacial gins.

There was no grandeur in the elements now; imagination was disharmonized from the sun. Nature was indifferent to the sufferings of all life. I could bear the screeching icy jets with fortitude, but my companion suffered, having no dolorous background in memory to make the present ineffectual. In that background were days and nights in water and yellow clay sludge to the waist, with death above the leafless winter hedge shot stooping-high: days and nights without sleep, weeks and months without hope, without liberty — life with neither present nor future, worse than death, for death was release — life more terrible than being in a gin, for God has blessed Man with the power to reason, and the seventeen-year-old volunteer knew that if he sought release, and failed, or escaped from killing men he did not hate, nor had ever seen before, he would be caught and shot before sunrise in peace time clothes, with a bandage over his eyes and a white paper mark pinned opposite his heart still joined in spirit to the mother who bore him in pain and after-joy, and his name and regiment would be read out on three successive parades to every soldier in the British Army in that alien country. The pain as of thorns pushed under finger nails was nothing — it would pass.

The linhay withstood the storm, as it had others, held by the stout cores of its upright posts. The day began to grow again in the twilight of the loft. Old boards grew swiftly green, the battering on the roof suddenly ceased with a few lingering taps against the iron sheets. Drops falling by the empty squares of the window were white, they glittered! — and blue and white sea and sky were beyond.

Kneeling down and moving my face to a crack between the floorboards I looked for rabbit and fox. Sight was limited, so I crawled stiffly (sometimes blowing through my half-clenched hands for warmth) to the trap-door, and peered over. The floor of the shippen was like the Ypres Salient in the winter of nineteen-seventeen, seen from a low-flying aeroplane. Hoof-holes, shapeless and trodden into one another, were filled with water to their broken edges. Wind wrinkled the sky-gleams by the posts.

Against the inner wall sat the vixen, on one of the slabs of ironstone. Her back and neck were curved like a snail-shell. Her nose touched the mud. She was shivering with every breath. The foot of the broken foreleg and the gin that gripped it were in the mud. Beside her on the other slab, about eighteen inches away, sat the rabbit. It looked about it with the relaxed movements and expression of an animal at ease. I had heard of timid and preying animals sheltering together innocently during a storm, but this was the only time such a pleasing sight had been witnessed.

A sound from above, from my companion, made vixen and rabbit look up together. We kept still and they relaxed again. I saw the vixen turn her mangy head towards the rabbit, which continued to nibble its fore-paw. The narrow head began to droop in sleep, or weariness.

I watched for some minutes: until a patient voice above me begged to be allowed to get down. I had forgotten those bluish hands, rough with chilblains.

As I climbed down the ladder I saw, from the tail of my eye, the rabbit in a series of splashes crossing to the grass beyond the round posts. It disappeared. The field was a brilliant green, steaming in the hot rays of the sun.

The vixen was sitting on the stone; her mouth was open, showing her teeth. She stood on three legs placed close together, swaying to keep balance, her brush pressed against the wall. She tried to stay herself with her broken leg, but it gave no support, and each time she nearly tipped into the mud.

There used to live in the village an old trapper who nearly died of the effects of a fox's bite, which festered and made his hand swell, and his joints painful with inner corruption. This animal must have been feeding on slugs, beetles, and carrion left by magpies and buzzards — rats thrown out of gins in cornfields, broken carcases of rabbits — and its teeth were probably more dirty than those of a healthy fox. How else had it survived, limping for weeks, or months (long before clicketting time, perhaps), dragging the gin clanking on every stone, and rattling on the hard ground? I was afraid of its bite, having seen some years before a fox dead in a gin with lock-jaw. Better to kill it and so put myself out of my misery, for it was a woeful sight; and although the poor beast might have been used to its slow and crippled ways, there were the cubs soon to be born. Better to knock the vixen on the nose with my stick and bury her under a heap of stones.

My companion and I ran over the grass in the wind

and the sunshine, swinging our arms and laughing rue-
fully at each other with the pain in thawing toes and
fingers. We had a warm, dry cottage in the valley over
the down, a garden filled with vegetables, fruit trees,
stores of apples, potatoes, and wood for firing; shelves of
books to read, clothes to wear, and flowers to tend in the
coming spring and summer; we had been married less
than two years, but already we had one merry little babe
with six teeth, who watched the rooks flying over the
roof with sticks for their nests, and shouted 'Dukaduk!'
to them. So when we were warm again we returned
with a sack to the linhay, and putting it over the head
of the vixen held her easily in her weak struggles,
carried her into the field, trod on the steel spring to open
the iron jaws of the gin, and lifted out the paw. An easy
matter to snick with a knife the frayed tendons, and to
bind the stump with my tie, securing it with string.
Then the sack was pulled away, rolling over the vixen.
She kicked and scrambled on her three and a half
feet and faced us, snarling, with arched back and ears
laid flat. I tapped the gin beside her with my stick, and
she snapped at it. Pushing the end of the stick through
the spring I drew it away; she lifted the stump and made
the other foreleg rigid, as though to resist. Slowly we
walked backwards, drawing the gin over the wet grass.
She whined, holding out a quivering stump. Five yards,
ten yards, twenty yards — slowly we drew away from
her, while she watched with raised ears and shifting
feet.

We stood still. She rose and hobbled on, as though
still dragging the iron. We watched her to the grass-tied
plough under the wall. Here she smelt food, and down
went her nose, searching for scraps of bread and boiled

bacon left by us for the birds. She rolled on her back in the sunlight and then disappeared through the gateway to the slope of furze and heather.

The daffodils in the garden broke yellow and danced for weeks in the wind until their blooms were frayed; sandmartins and the chiff-chaffs came back to the headland; our baby began to pull himself, totteringly, to his feet beside my chair; rooks were sitting on their nests above the graveyard; the church was decorated with flowers and budding willow-wands at Eastertide.

When next we walked to the linhay, we saw the first swallows flitting over the seaward slope of the down. A trapper called to us from the bank, stopping his work to tell us of what he thought was a very strange thing. That morning, visiting his rabbit gins in the sandhills below, he had seen the prints of a limping fox, the marks of scurry round the gin it had sprung, and the trail leading away. How the bit of raggedy stuff had gotten in the gin he couldn't think. Raggedy stuff? Might I see it? The trapper was sorry, he had 'drowed'n away, not thinking much of it at the time; 'twas a bit of old raggedy black stuff, with yaller stripes on'n. Aiy, like a wasp!'

I knew that regimental tie.

A FRESH START

By the old quarry, now hidden by trailing brambles and humps of gorse, the blackthorn blossom opened on February the fourth. The quarry looks over the sea, where the ravens are carrying furze sticks for their nest in a cliff cranny on the north side of the headland. Old country folk used to say, When the white petals open among the leafless spines of the blackthorn, then the frosts of winter are over: as though the sun by its alchemy had transmuted rime and crystal into blossom.

This is early for the blackthorn to flower, but spring in Devon comes swiftly, rushing with the south-west winds from over the green Atlantic, and flinging rain and colour on the earth. I found the first celandine on New Year's Day, with three of its eight petals uncurled in an icy blast. Poor flower, it must have withered without seeding, for no bee was abroad under the frozen sky. On the same day I saw the red campion out, but as one may find this plant in bloom on any day of the year (although really a May flower), the sight does not stir the heart like the yellow celandine.

I am writing this in the second week of March, wishing I could go out now instead of sitting inside the cottage, with its small single casement window set in the thick cob wall, and imagining what has been seen in other years. Even when the noon sun shines, the room is dim, for the thatch is like a heavy eyebrow, shutting out direct light. The raven will have lined her nest with sheep's wool by now, and the small eggs will have been brooded a fortnight, hard-set.

Early plovers have scratched their hollows for nests in the mossy plain behind the sandhills, lined them with dry grasses, and laid their eggs; the carrion crows have found some of them, for two days ago, walking over the Burrows and meditating on my novel *The Pathway*, I found, on a hummock where a buzzard had torn and eaten a rabbit, two dark-blotched eggshells, each neatly pierced by two mandible-holes. The crow sticks the egg with his beak, holds it up, and drinks the contents, while the parent birds vainly flap and wail around the crow's head.

The first bird's nest this year was found on February the seventh, in the fork of an elm by the side of the lane. It was built by a missel-thrush, or storm-cock, locally called holm-scritch or grey thrush. I heard the male singing on New Year's Day, perched on the topmost twig of an ash, heedless of the wind and the cold. Children going to school saw the nest in the making, and in due course the eggs were taken while the birds screeched and chattered.

Outside in the orchard of Hole Farm the wild daffodils are taming the young winds of the year, and on the bank the first sweet violets are talking, gentle heads together, among the docks.

Oh yes, flowers do talk, to the spirit, even as the notes of wild birds fall upon the hearing. The trees talk, heavy with sap! The elms are a mist of reddish-brown, for the wind is shedding the sheaths of the blossom; the catkins of the nut trees are ready to break and scatter their pollen; the bluebell leaves are hiding the lowlier primroses. Larks sing over the ploughed field; gemmed with emerald are the buds of the hawthorn; the long-tailed tits have paired, and the furious tiny males fight and drop out of the holly tree like grey twirling shuttle-cocks. A redbreast sings in every hedge, and the trilling bubble-link of the curlew's spring song arises from the water-streaming hills of Exmoor and Dart-moor. Lambs frisk and leap in the meadows, rooks are excited at their old nests. It is sweet to live and see the earth grow young again!

SALMON FISHERS

On April the first the Two Rivers' season for nets began — thirty-six of them, each paying five pounds for a season's licence. The season ends with August. Actually the fishermen go after salmon every month of the year, shooting their seine nets at night when the official season has ended. They complain angrily of the Conservancy by-laws: they say that 'rod-and-line' men up the rivers are favoured by the laws, since their season begins with March and ends half-way through October. Many of the older fishermen scorn the idea of salmon spawning in fresh water, declaring that it is a lie invented by the rich for the 'keeping-down of the poor man'. They hate the water-bailiffs, who fear the fishermen. Once, on a dark night, the water-bailiffs' boat was rammed by a salmon boat, in an attempt to drown the bailiffs.

There are two main runs of fish in the Two Rivers: spring and autumn. The autumn run is the spawning-run, when often the fish come in from the sea wearing their coppery river-dress. The netsmen take all they can: and during the off-season they sell 'red hake' at the kitchen doors of many of the houses in this district occupied by the families of retired senior officers of the Navy and Army.

On April the first I walked over the Burrows, and sailed across to Appledore to see a friend. A strong wind was blowing up the estuary, and the last of the water was ebbing. I sat on a seat in the west of Appledore watching the fishermen push off into slack water with their nets piled in the boat sterns.

Arrived at their stations or fishing places, one man of each crew stood on shore with the net rope, while in the boat two men bent the sweeps, and a third paid out over the stern the black net, just like a spider drawing black silk from its pockets. They rowed in a semicircle, coming back to shore and hauling-in, a man at each end of the cork-rope, and two others at the lead-rope.

I went down on the shore and watched a crew. They made four shoots in an hour. Thrice the net came in empty, except for small green crabs and shell-crusted rocks. Silently they crushed each crab underfoot, since they were the enemies of fish-food; silently they swore at the bits of rock, which were likely to tear their nets. And the fourth time, as they pulled steadily, hand-over-hand, leaning back with rubbered feet sinking into the watery sand, something flapped and splashed in the purse or seine of the net. How their faces became taut and hopeful!

The youngest, a lad of eighteen, pulled too quickly, and was checked; the mouth of the purse reached the wavelet line, and he dashed forward, heaving a fish out by the gills. How it thrashed the sand with its tail! A royal fish, thirty pounds, beautifully streamlined and tapered, as though hammered and wrought by many waves from a bar of frosty silver.

The lad pulled out a thole-pin and thumped the base of its skull; the sand-slapping ceased, and the lovely water-thing lay still and flat among boot-crushed crabs and its own fallen silver scales glinting in the sand.

He placed it in the boat; the net was shaken and piled; and the fishers went on with the day's work.

THE SEX-LIFE OF ROOKS

ARE rooks 'civilized'? That is, in the sense that civilized man is said by some philosophers, or autobiographical musers such as myself, to be decadent? I was watching some of these birds the other day from the top of the church tower. The rookery is below; one can see into the nests. From my place of concealment behind battlements I observed what certainly appeared to be an exact equivalent of an attitude that is always present among human beings in a village.

The rooks were building their nests. One young pair, I noticed, flew home with sticks in beaks and immediately set to work to thrust them into position. They spoke to one another as they worked, uttering soft ejaculations which were apparently of happiness and *joie de vivre*.

Near them, but at different ends of the tree, were two other nests, not so far advanced in construction. The pairs of rooks making these nests were, to judge by their generally scrabby appearance, old birds.

Now each of these nests was guarded by a male bird all the time. The females flew away to distant trees, broke off top twigs in their beaks, and returned; the older males sat at home, and approved with dip-and-caw every return of their wives. But the younger, more eager pair of rooks flew away side by side; and immediately Old Rook Number One flapped to their nest, stole a stick, and returned with it to his own site.

Then Old Rook Number Two flew there, stole a stick,

and made his return, perhaps to see Old Rook Number One in the act of filching a stick from his nest. Oh, what indignation, what raucous cawing of protest to the rest of the colony!

The young birds came back, and, telling each other of their happiness as before, got on with their building. Off they flew again; and immediately Old Rook Number Two, as though determined to be wise this time, flapped and hopped to their site and stole a stick. Meanwhile, Old Rook Number One was at Number Two's nest, pulling out sticks, and letting them fall.

In spite of the thieving, or tithe-taking, the young pair worked so hard that soon their nest was completed. Such a pretty thing then was to be seen! The young female settled on her nest, and with soft throaty endearments and quivering of wings, invited her mate's love — the consummation of her life.

At first he was timid, excited, and bewildered; but so charming was she that at last, with a hoarse cry, he flew to her. Oh, the scandal!

Old Rooks Numbers One and Two, and others from nearby trees, cawed their indignation, and flying to the nest, began to buffet and peck the lovers. Had the young pair acted without some corvine religious ceremony? Whatever the cause, the rest of the rookery was deeply offended.

The young male bird crouched beside his mate, while making no attempt to peck back. Soon he flew away, followed by her. They returned twenty minutes later, she with a stick in beak, he following.

In the meantime their nest had been partly destroyed. She placed her stick, then settled on the dishevelled mass again, clearly telling him not to worry; but he would not, or could not, respond to her endearments.

Soon she ceased to call, and sat unmoving on her nest; while he perched motionless a few yards away, his feathers ruffled, his head between his shoulders, in the attitude of an older bird.

A WEST COUNTRY TROUT FARM

Travellers by rail approaching Dulverton in Somerset sometimes have a glimpse of a group of rectangular fish-ponds as the train begins to slow before the station. If you are fortunate, you may see fish leaping. Usually the sky-reflecting waters are ringed and rippled in one or another of the pits; for here hundreds of thousands of trout — Rainbow, Loch Leven, and Brown — are hatched and reared.

Come with me: I am going to order some Loch Leven fingerlings and two-year olds, with which to restock a moorland stream in May next. Mr. Hartley, the owner, will show us the cycle of the trout's life before it enters the tanks of the lorry-carrier, journeying to some lake or river, while breathing water well charged by an automatic oxygenating apparatus.

It is too early in the year to see the eggs; they will be taken in the autumn from wild fish in a lake near Taunton. The lake then is netted; the cock and hen fish separated. The ripe hens are held over a bucket and squeezed by expert hands until most of the eggs are dropped. The fish are then released, and swim away in the lake again, all passion spent. I wish I could observe the reaction in the water.

Cock fish are held over another bucket, and their milt squeezed out. Afterwards the milt is poured on the eggs and stirred gently. At the hatchery the eggs are laid either on glass rods in series, or on zinc trays, covered from the light, while water from the Barle, which has passed through filter-beds of coke and gravel, trickles slowly over them.

After a few weeks dark specks appear within the eggs, which are about the size of sweet-pea seeds, and opalescent. They are then known as eyed ova, and it is safe to send them by post, packed in wet moss in a box or tin. Some travel so far as South Africa and the United States.

Most of the eyed ova remain in the zinc trays within troughs of tarred wood. The water flows and glides gently from one trough to another. The eggs are inspected regularly for fungus disease, and infertile eggs — those which turn opaque and yellow — are removed.

One morning it will be seen that an egg-case, like a diminutive grape skin, is floating loose by the perforated zinc barrier; and an alevin, about half an inch long, with yolk-sac distended, trying to conceal itself under the eggs. Thereafter the hatching will be general. Two or three alevins in every hundred may be deformed, with curved spines. These spin round and round instead of wriggling forward into the mass crowding for conceal-ment to one or another corner of the tray.

In about three weeks the sacs shrink and become the bellies; the little fish, called fry, will begin to poise themselves in the water, head to stream, and watch for anything that passes. They are transferred, and fed on finger-pinches of powdered liver.

Later they go to the fry pits; there to await the periodical showers of larger food. Visitors to the fishery are warned against going near the pits, as the wavery, foreshortened and distorted image (the under-water view) of a human being excites them, and they dash at one another. A larger, more developed fishling may seize his neighbour and retire to the bottom to gorge him. A mite of an inch eating another three-quarters of an inch long!

They grow unevenly. Bigger fingerlings are separated. Yearlings may be from three to six inches. The two-year-olds and three-year-olds cruise violently when a human figure appears on the grassy banks: the fish-master scatters a spoonful of trout food: the surface boils and breaks; the under-water flickers in green and blue and grey: black-spotted backs and tails and flanks appear: pallid mouths open. 'Look,' he says, 'see those minnows by the grill: they've come in by the leat through the filter beds somehow; and why they aren't taken is a mystery.'

'Yes, for re-stocking rivers we usually advise finger-lings or two-year-olds. Last week an American bought a hundred Rainbows weighing about three pounds each, and having marked them with silver tags on their adipose fins, released them in the sea near Porlock, wondering if any would find their way across the Atlantic and round Cape Horn to their ancestral rivers of California. It's possible, of course.

'Otters? Once a dog-otter got in and slew several hundred pounders and two-pounders. Kingfishers come sometimes, but we don't object. Our worst enemy is the heat in summer. Warm water loses its oxygen rapidly. Algae grows in the heat, and absorbs more oxygen. Those shades help a little, but we have to look out constantly for any sign of disease. We've been singularly fortunate this summer, but a spate is long overdue. The small maiden salmon, from four to seven pounds, will be coming in soon from the Atlantic, but they won't be able to run up in this low water.' He pointed to the Barle river running noisily over the shallows below the fishery.

Sometimes at night the carrier-lorry goes to London with fish for the market. You may see some of the Rainbows I fed this afternoon in the glass tank of that restaurant off Shaftesbury-avenue to-morrow evening; you may be one of those who point at a fish and say 'I'll have that one, and be sure to fry it in Spanish olive oil, not French'.

TRAPS AND TRAPPING

SOMEONE has written to me one of those letters which every author receives periodically. It is about the cruelty of trapping in England and elsewhere.

This lady — my correspondent on this subject is usually a lady — asks me to help to awaken the public conscience. Do I not know, she writes, that in most parts of the country hundreds of thousands of little animals are caught nightly in steel gins which break and lacerate their limbs, while the darkness is filled with the screams of the hopeless little creatures? That the gins are old-fashioned, barbarous, and not so efficient as more humane traps which could replace them if only the public conscience were not so indifferent? That the gins have serrations or teeth of iron which invariably break the limbs of rabbits, causing them to struggle and pull so wildly that their eyes bulge from their heads in agony?

Yes, it is true.

During the past twenty years in North-West Devon I have collected some interesting facts about trapping. Rabbits, like rats, are destructive of much farm produce. They are tenacious and prolific. A doe has on an average possibly thirty-six young a year. Rabbits seem to be most numerous where they are trapped most. I have heard it said that many old bucks are caught in gins which otherwise would kill and eat young rabbits.

Trapping in England has become more extensive since the World War, when so many farms have been sold by the big landowners to the tenants who do not preserve game. Hares, pheasants, partridges, and foxes cannot exist where there are traps, except as strays. A hare in the district above Braunton to Ilfracombe, in Devon, is very rare; I have not heard of one for ten years.

Once I found a little kestrel dead in a rabbit gin, an egg beside her. I put the egg under a hen, and she hatched out a hawk.

Like every other industry, including the White Slave Traffic and the Wild Bird Traffic, the trapping of rabbits employs many men. It is widely organized. Trappers usually pay a farmer for the trapping rights by giving so many days' free work on the farm every year. The farmer thus rids himself of excessive vermin and gets labour for nothing.

Many rats are caught in gins. They live in the rabbit buries. Rats like to live around the farm in the winter, spending the summer holidays in the fields.

On many country stations in autumn and winter you will see wicker baskets skilfully packed with dead conies, held inverted by their feet to a transverse hazel stick. Of these about one-third will have either one or the other, perhaps both, of the forepaws missing, showing how they have escaped previously. The inventors of the modern 'humane' traps declare that such maiming is impossible with their engines. The animals are gripped and held securely until the trapper comes — perhaps twelve hours later. But would these traps prevent mental anguish?

MY PARTRIDGES

FOR five successive years a pair of partridges has nested in the hilltop field called Ox's Park. The field came into my possession in 1928 thanks to Miss Alice Warrender and her gracious gift of the Hawthornden Prize.

I had desired it for years, but had no money. Then one day it came into the market: I didn't know what to do, since my income was then about one hundred pounds a year and I had a wife, and a son, who soon would have a brother. What to do? For twelve years I had coveted the field, lain in its long grasses or walked at the edge of its wheat and watched the clouds passing over thousands of fields below. Two other villagers wanted the field; the owner was bargaining; I was desperate. While I was talking to the owner, saying sadly that I couldn't make an offer, my wife came with a letter, and opening it, I learned I had been awarded the Hawthornden Prize for *Tarka the Otter*. Hurray! Now I could make a bid for it. The owner and I had a pint of sour and bitter cider on the strength of it.

It is good soil; wheat during the War and potatoes, but grass afterwards.

The first year of my ownership it was let to the former owner for two pounds from Ladyday to Michaelmas, and in that time he took the hay which was worth nine pounds. The mowing machine also destroyed a nest of partridges.

The following year I turned farmer, and hired a man to cut the two acres one midsummer morning. Mindful of the young birds which were about, I arranged to be at the field at 6.0 a.m. I arrived at 6.30 a.m., when the mowing machine had cut three swathes; and among the fallen grasses and flowers were the chicks. Only one was alive — and it had lost a leg.

The third year the birds nested, this time in the hedge, among brambles and blackthorns. A pair of carrion crows also nested in the beech clump called Windwhistle Spinney to the north of the field. The crows found and robbed the partridge's nest.

Last year, when the eggs were about to hatch, a young man, bursting through the hedge in pursuit of an author who has a little local fame or notoriety, trod on the nest.

And now for what happened during Whitsun, when I was camping in the field with my friend John Heygate. I had flushed the bird off twenty eggs a month previously. My young dog, a merry, fierce, and incorrigible little beast of the Jack Russell Terrier breed, for which I paid five guineas in order to encourage a dog-breeding friend, had been with me then. ''Ware feather!' I had growled. He blinked, his nose flaired, and he appeared to lose all interest in the nest. The hen bird had only one leg, I noticed.

The terrier was with us at the Whitsun camping. On the Saturday afternoon the eggs were still unhatched. Addled, I thought: she had been disturbed, and they had grown cold. But on the Sunday morning, as the sun was rising above Dunkery Beacon on distant Exmoor and John and I were sluicing each other with pails of water, there was a screaking and fluttering in the hedge, with the white movement of a dog in long grasses. That terrier had remembered.

When I reached the nest he had routed among the new-hatched and wet chicks, eaten some and crushed others, while the hen was crying as she rustled in circles near the dog, feigning a broken wing and trying to draw him away.

We collected the chicks, wee, dappled, and bewildered, from their crouching places, and put them among the halves of pale brown broken shells and the five eggs which, although containing chicks, would probably perish now that the brooding was interrupted.

And would you believe such a series of disasters, but as we were cooking breakfast there was an alarm again, but a wilder kind of crying, for a weasel was among the chicks, while the hen stood with open beak as though dying, two yards away; and the terrier throttled himself in excitement by his tying-post. The weasel got away, after needling my hand in two places.

The two old birds are somewhere in the grasses as I sit in the sun, half asleep, idly writing this; for in the hot silence of the noon sun I can hear the tiny cheeping of the three surviving chicks and the discreet replies of their parents. In three days the little birds have learned to run to cover with amazing speed, and as the grass will not be cut they have a good chance of living until they learn to fly — when their enemies, including peregrine falcons and the guns of farmers and smallholders, will be ready for them.

THE FISHERS

LEANING lazily against the iron tower on the chevron-shaped pier which divides and soothes the tides of Shoreham harbour flowing in through the narrow mouth in the shingle banks, I watched two fishers.

One, an old man, had been sitting with melancholy immobility hour after hour in a boat. A little boy, probably his son, sat beside him.

The other fisher, a cormorant, was squatting on a cubic yard of wood awash with the sea and sodden and green with weed, and anchored by a chain. The bird's wings were held out as though drying. Fishtails stuck out of his long, narrow open beak. Sometimes he flapped his wings, in an effort to ease his crop, which bulged. He looked like a ruinous umbrella flung there by a wave.

Occasionally the old man in the boat glanced at the cormorant, and cursed it. The old man had caught nothing.

The tide was low, and near slack water. The bird had done all its successful fishing near the buoy — codling, pollack, and other fish probably played around the weeds streaming from the mooring chain. I had watched him paddle awhile, and then tip up and vanish; but in imagination I followed him as with oily wings pressed close to his side, he thrust with webbed feet down into the water. Trudging after the glints of fish, while bubbles streamed out of his closed beak, he would separate a fish and follow it until it was within seizing distance: and then the beak would open and the mandibles grip

41

it with their cutting edges. The fish was swallowed head first when the bird had risen to the surface.

When the fishtails had disappeared the cormorant walked off the balk of wood into the water again. He bobbed up from his submarine prowl with some sort of flatfish, which flapped and showed white. The cormorant held up his head and tried to swallow it, but the flatfish was too wide to pass its gape. Repeatedly giving a wary glance at the man with the big glinting eye on the pier two hundred yards away (I was watching him through my Zeiss monocular) the cormorant paddled up and down by the buoy, shaking his head to shift his grip on the fish. He could not swallow it. For ten minutes he paddled around, and then a gull swooped down at him, crying harshly.

The cormorant dived, while the gull hovered overhead, waiting for the cormorant to reappear. Every time the cormorant bobbed up with the fish the gull swooped; until, after half a dozen dives, the cormorant opened his black wings, flapped them along the water, and flew over the pier.

At once the screaming gull was on his tail. The cormorant, unable or unwilling to dodge, impeded by the wide fish in his beak, and perhaps scared by the nearness of the boat, dropped the fish and flew out to sea. The gull dived after the fish, but the old man saw it splash, and shouted to the boy to pull up the anchor. This the boy did, and his father rowed quickly to where the fish floated. He was so pleased that he gave up fishing, calling out to me that they were not biting to-day; and rowing ashore, he showed me what the cormorant had dropped. It was a plaice weighing nearly two pounds. The hooked beak of the cormorant had pierced it in twenty-three places. 'I don't trouble,' said the fisherman. 'It won't taste no worser for them little holes being there, 'tis natural-like, in a manner of speaking, if you understand my meaning.' 'O.K.' grinned the boy.

SCIENCE, or, SENTIMENT

I

A PAIR of ravens was in the habit of visiting a tame raven which lived a few miles inland from their cliff nesting ledge above the sea. The tame raven was in a large cage made of wire netting and posts, erected on the edge of a lawn about fifty yards from a house.

In March the wild pair came regularly for food which the tame bird used to put through the cage for them. The pair had five young in their nest made of furze sticks and lined with hair, wool, old rope, etc., in the cliff of the distant headland. They came once every day for about two weeks; and twice, and even thrice a day, as their fledgelings grew bigger.

Then in April, when their young had flown, and been driven away, the wild ravens arrived at the cage and began to dig a hole in the turf at the base of the netting.

A few years before wild ravens had visited the valley and had quickly killed another tame raven. This time, the owner waited to see what would happen. She did not interfere because she believed that the wild ravens were digging out the caged bird.

The hole was soon large enough for the passage of a raven. The wild birds were much too wary to enter the cage; and after hesitation, the tame bird crept through. He was free. The wild birds flew up, calling him, and together they disappeared westwards towards the cliffs and the sea.

Was it gratitude that made them set him free? Did he ask them to help him to escape?

If one had watched three men in a similar case one would say that the motive was friendliness, the social instinct, gratitude, God-in-man, whatever you will; and why not for ravens? They have eyes, lungs, blood corpuscles, livers, spinal fluid, as have men; they fall in love, know anguish when their young or their mates are in danger, need food, sleep, sunshine; they are born and they die mysteriously as man. Why then should they not have, or share, the fundamental feelings of human life? My own opinion is that they feel as active men feel; that they think or reason within their habits and experience.

All birds and animals have a great sense of play or fun. I once knew a raven that used to tease a spaniel chained to a kennel. The bird would steal the dog's bones and place them just outside the arc of movement made by his chain. The bird would dip and bow before the enraged dog mockingly. (*Mockingly* is the precise word.) In every way the raven was the dog's master; and after awhile the dog, when unchained, would come when the raven called. It licked the raven's feathers. It submitted, gratefully, to a search through its hair for fleas.

Thereafter the raven ceased to mock the chained dog; it would play with the dog's bones, but if it took them out of reach it would put them back again. They were friends.

After all, why shouldn't they behave as their near relatives biologically behave in a natural environment? 'Sentimentality,' cries the incipient scientist. 'Humanizing animals,' says the urban critic. Some clever scientists, indeed, accept nothing intangible as living until it is

45

dead. One's neighbour is oneself; so is the bird in the air and the animal in the forest.

Oh yes, about the raven who was dug out by the wild pair. It may be that he preferred security to adventure, for, after four days' roaming, he was found in the morning within his old cage, very hungry, and effusive in greeting to his 'owner', or human friend.

2

Some of my friends tell me I am no dog-lover; and, as they *are* dog-lovers, I do not dispute their slightly condemnatory criticism. I reply that I am a mere detached observer of animals, for the purposes of amusement and money.

One of my friends, a veritable highbrow of music, with whom I am staying as this is being written, is most derisive about my liking for good dance tunes and the crooning of Rudy Vallée and Bing Crosby. But one day I shall, unknown to him, make a gramophone record of the noises he makes regularly when addressing his dogs or his cats. He probably prides himself on his love for these animals; but why such feeling should express itself in a sort of restrained yodelling or wauling at the back of the nose late at night before leaving the animals in their special cribs, crêches, beds, etc., by the fire, I do not know.

Why do English people love animals, and dogs in particular? Not all animals, of course; very few English people love rats or mice, which rob them. When I lived in that old five-pounds-a-year cottage, at the beginning of my immoral career as a writer, the sound of rats galloping through their galleries in the thick walls at night, their squeaks and scuffles, was most pleasing. I loved, too, the noises of owls over the ceiling; as I loved washing in cold water every day of the year, and swimming in the sea. My neighbours, who had never had a bath, thought the owls — the white barn owls, now getting fewer and fewer in England — were 'dirty' birds: and as soon as I left that cottage, the landlord asked the next tenant, a mason, to wall-up the entrance hole under the thatch. He did so, and I fear, walled-up the birds, who roosted therein by day, as well. They thought me a proper fool, among other things, and often said so; although this is qualified nowadays, since a small but regular traffic of visitors to the village has been caused by various books written about the neighbourhood. Well, I'm afraid my white owls, dear totems and dream-friends of my youth, won't be seen any more floating across the churchyard on summer evenings: their bones now mingle with the hundreds of thousands of mice bones which strewed the lath-and-plaster on the other side of my bedroom ceiling.

Leaving out such things as rats and owls, we English pride ourselves on our natural love of animals, feeling probably that animals have many of the lesser virtues of human beings, without their inconsistencies or defects. They are constant in their feelings and for the objects of those feelings: they are reliable.

I have known a most inharmonious household — everyone annoying someone else and brooding on wrongs, repressions, futilities — the individual members of which became charming only when they were addressing or stroking an ugly misshapen pied cat which never washed itself.

47

The cat was reliable and inoffensive; its tail could always be depended upon to rise and curl-off with a gesture of affection, its back to arch and its throat dully to grate whenever a hand touched it, whenever a voice twisted and contorted itself into an approximation of a feline call or howl.

The white seal-like, over-fed and usually motionless fireside mass of dogflesh called Dook, or to give it its full name Dookums, lying heavily on my feet at this moment of my history, certainly has something about him which I, a mere animal observer, find myself liking.

I can prod, push, or thwack him; he simply grunts or groans, gives me a look of his pallid prize-fighter's face and remains as before, a dead uncaring weight on my pinned-and-needled feet. I curse and deride him, kick him out of the way, stand on him, shoot ink of three different primary colours from three different pens over his head and body; he never ceases to feel easy benevolence towards me, or to slog the carpet with his long and tapered tail when I reappear after an absence.

It pleases me. It makes me feel important.

Let me tell you a story about Dookums who is or was a bull-terrier.

This ancient animal disliked a kitten brought home one day. The floors and scents of the house belonged to Dook; a kitten would never do.

So the old fellow chased her; woofed her off chairs and window sills; ate her food; slobbered her milk over the rims of many saucers.

The kitten became a cat, tolerated by Dook with watchful scrutiny. One day the cat got her lower jaw across a gin, and came home mewing and maimed.

The dog saw her and was intensely interested; he walked beside the cat, observing but not chivvying her.

Thereafter, possibly seeing the attitude of the cat's owners to the cat, Dook's attitude also changed. He stared at the cat's plate; but he never did more than sniff at the food. He licked the cat's wound; he watched her gravely as the cat lay silent and unmoving on her bed, her eyes wide as she brooded on the incomprehensible terror and shock which had come upon her life.

Later, when the cat was getting better, the old dog appointed himself her guardian, and even seemed happy when she stepped daintily upon his greasy bed brought into the sitting-room at night. Indeed, they have often slept together.

It is pleasing to observe that children nowadays are not warned against dogs as were so many children in the past; for the causes of most human unhappiness arise from one thing — mental fear.

Animals, which live much by intuition, certainly know if one is afraid of them. I recall a big Alsatian that growled and loped away from and prowled restlessly around me when I first visited John Galsworthy in his Sussex home.

I was slightly scared of the animal, and did my best to appear as though I were indifferent to it. But the dog knew; and I knew that if I could, as it were, stop broadcasting the uneasy waves from my mind, the dog would become calm again, as he was before I entered the room.

I could not do it; the feeling was given out in spite of my outwardly calm attention to my friend's words of greeting. After a while, Galsworthy, who had not spoken to the dog, said to me in his very quiet and restrained voice: 'If you have a matchstick, or even better, a still smaller piece of wood, and twirl it in the dog's direction, I think he might alter his manner towards you. He would much rather play.'

So I flipped a burnt match towards the dog, which sprang up with ears set in a different way, and picked it up between his lips. He hesitated; I hesitated; then I held out my hand.

Thus we became friends; and I learned, by that slight act, one more little thing about the problem of living.

RISE OF A VILLAGE

Slowly slate roofs and corrugated sheet iron replaced thatch, which slept away after a score of years and needed relaying. Then came the Great War, and afterwards the rubber wheel began to roll swiftly where the narrow iron-hooped wooden wheel moved with leisure. The bumpy main road winding through the cottages became noisy with engines and warning horns, until, after many council meetings, it was decided to make a new road directly through orchards, gardens, and fields where no cottages existed — with the exception of one old barn.

This barn, built of cob, was owned by an aspirant to the new rising motor trade. Enamelled signs advertising petrol, oils, and tyres, were on its inner and outer walls. When it was decided to obliterate the barn for the new highway, the question of compensation arose, and with this question, a village comedy. The young owner demanded much compensation. He declared that his profits from his Garage, which soon would cease to be, were x pounds a year. The Council, or the Ministry of Transport, pointed out that after the highway was made the remainder of his land, adjoining the highway at the corner of two main routes, would be many times more valuable than before. It would be the dominating shop-site of the village. Ah, replied the young business man, but what about my goodwill and turnover during the making of the highway? My rivals, a few yards away, will have most of my trade, which is considerable, bringing me a profit of x pounds per annum. He remained firm to his claim, feeling he had a very good case: he visualized a new garage, showrooms with plate-glass windows, his name perhaps in electric lights at night. The village was opening up. It would soon be a town. He bought himself a new tweed suit, with two pairs of plus fours; he was the new, post-war type of business man. One day another man came with the arbitrators to talk about his claim. 'You say your average profit for the past three years is this sum per annum?' 'I do.' 'Very well: that is your claim, with which I have to deal only indirectly,' replied the stranger. 'I am the Income Tax Inspector, and I would like to have a little talk with you about how to fill in these three Income Tax Return forms.' 'Of course,' said the official from the Ministry of Transport, when the Income Tax Inspector had departed, 'everyone hopes to make the best bargain. It is human nature. Now can't we come to some more reasonable agreement about this corner?' To-day the old barn is gone, and the corner is shining with plate glass and paint, traffic lights are about to blink and shine above the concrete highway, and the garage proprietor is more of a mathematician and the owner of several pairs of golfing tweeds.

It is tedious to hear English people talking in a superior manner about America and its gangsters, for the growth of all human civilizations is the same. I remember the village before the highway became spotted with oil-drops from hundreds of thousands of engines passing annually on its smooth surface. Indeed, I was in a way involved in the results of the growth arising from the making of the road. Some young men set up as motor engineers in another old barn. Although I knew their experience was not large, I wanted to help them in my small way, and so gave them the job of decarbonizing the little six h.p. French car which I bought, on a wild and sudden impulse, one sunny day in London. I asked them to drain the oil from the sump, and put in fresh oil. When I called for the car, one of the partners took me for a test run. We had gone a quarter of a mile up the hill when a loud clattering of the engine told me that the big-ends had run out. It was discovered that the old oil in the sump had been drained, but no new oil had been put in. Did they offer to re-bush the bearings, to make good the damage of their carelessness? I had a bill for about ten pounds for that job; and five hundred miles afterwards the clattering came again, and the agents of the car in Exeter said that the one bearing which had not gone had been put in as though with a soldering iron. That was a further twelve pounds.

Then there was the grocer from whom I bought some bacon for Mr. Edward Garnett who was spending a holiday in a lonely cottage several miles away on the sea-wall of the estuary. He asked that the bacon should be cut thin, and I asked the grocer to do this; but he cut slices nearly a quarter of an inch thick. The grocer declared that most people liked it thick. I explained that for myself I would not have minded had it been an inch thick, or even two inches thick; but it was for a friend of mine who wanted it thin and that was why he had asked me to have it cut thin, and so I had asked in the shop for thin bacon. Immediately the grocer's face took on a sidelong, knowing expression as he suggested that as it was not for myself, surely I could 'push it off on' the other person, especially as he was a visitor. A visitor, he declared, would not like to refuse it.

Then there was the tailor who made me a pair of breeches to my measurement. When I took them back, demonstrating that they were three inches too short in the thigh, he replied to my amazement that his breeches were usually cut from a stock pattern, and that my thighs were unusually long. I felt that it was partly my fault because I had not tried them on before they were sewn up; but even so, they would already have been cut three inches too short. The tailor was a charming man, and I was surprised that he did not offer to make me another pair. He made another pair, but I had to pay for the short pair, which I 'pushed off on' a bearded philosopher on Exmoor for a Christmas present.

The new pair of breeches went round my waist almost twice, and when apprehensive of what might be interpreted as a further complaint I mentioned this to the tailor, I was gently but firmly told that I had specially asked for large breeches. I succeeded in pushing these off on another author, who pushed them off on his gardener, who flogged them to a gipsy, who later tried to push them off on to me.

I had a hut built of oak in a field. There was to be a door of oak planks and battens, with hand-forged nails on the outside — a usual pattern for an oak door. I asked the local village carpenters to copy the door on another hut eighty yards distant in the same field — a door I had made myself. Yes, it should be done. Particularly did I ask them to bore holes for the nails, as the wood was several centuries old from the ruinous mansion near Eggesford, and therefore very hard. They would make a proper job of it, I could rely on that.

Good! I offered them a glass of beer each. 'Thank you, sir, but neither my son nor I has ever touched a drop of liquor.' Would they accept a fill of tobacco? 'Thank you, sir, but we neither drink nor smoke.' A true Christian, I was informed, neither drank nor smoked. I understood: I respected their principles. And, forgive me, but it was quite clear about that door? We parted in the friendliest spirit of mutual self-esteem.

When next day I saw the door I merely told myself in despair that it was what I had dreaded and anticipated: the nails had been knocked through from the inside, splitting and breaking the wood, and the points, extending an inch or so, had been clenched over and bashed down. The carpenters promised to 'make it good'; but having received payment for their bill, that was the end of the matter.

The building of the first hut was to have started on the first day of May. 'To-morrow,' promised the builder. I waited twenty-one days staying at the inn called The Lower House; and for twenty-one consecutive evenings the builder said, 'I will come to-morrow, I'll meet you in the field'. At last he appeared, on May the twenty-second. I wanted it built like a ship, with wooden pegs. 'I'll do anything you ask. I'll till potatoes upside down if you prefer them that way'. His bag was filled with six-inch nails, called 'spikes' in the trade. 'You won't use nails if it can possibly be avoided, will you?' And as soon as my back was turned, the six-inch oak posts were spiked — some of them splitting.

Nearly three years later I wanted a further building, for the storing of wood. This also was intended to last for centuries, and English oak was again chosen. It was a larger building than the others, twenty-one feet by thirteen feet. There was to be a loft, with oak beams, joists, and planks. Briefly I recapitulated my experience to the third builder, with whom I had not dealt before. I explained that I liked oak, a noble wood; and I wanted the floor to carry a carpenter's bench and heavy cases of tools. I thought with glee that I could be sure of good work this time; the estimate had been workman-like, specifying all wood required, and its price. To my surprise, when the beams or bearers were about to go up — two lengths of wood twenty-one feet long and weighing perhaps each a quarter of a ton — I realized that they were to be fixed to and held against the upright posts only by iron bolts. If the bolts, one in each of the four posts along the side of the building, had suddenly sheared, the bearers and the joists on the bearers and the floor on the joists would have fallen — a ton or more of wood. It is unlikely that they would have sheared: but consider that principle of building!

I suggested to Carpenter Number Three that the frame should surely be interlocking, self-supporting, the weight of floor and roof bearing directly down the posts, each one of which had been cut from the heart of a small oak tree? However, it was too late to do that, and I told him I would be responsible if he would chisel four sections from each beam to correspond with and fit into four similar sections chiselled from the posts, and then pinned with oak pins. But would he please not use nails? I showed him the door of hut Number Two. No nails, please. 'You want wooden pins only, I understand?' 'Exactly!' He understood. While the carpenters were at work, the builder arrived. He gave one look, and turned away; it was obvious that he was feeling precisely as I had felt when I had realized what the iron bolts meant. 'What have you done to my posts?' he remarked unhappily. Meanwhile the carpenter had cut the sections from the posts out of line, so that much hoisting and straining and levering was needed before the beam could be knocked home. And when the next beam was hoisted up the following morning, the cuts were correctly in line but the beam was warped. Finally they were pinned; and I asked the carpenter for the fifth time, not to use nails. The joists would keep the beams tight into the posts. Returning from my lunch I saw that each projecting wooden pin was surrounded by nail-heads. 'My God!' I cried, and turned away. 'You shouldn't take the name of God in vain,' the carpenter, a small preaching man in his spare time, warned me. 'Don't you know what the Book says about hell-fire and swearing?'

'SOME MARVELS OF POND LIFE'

My uncle said to me, 'Why do you write novels? I haven't read them myself, but I'm told they're rotten. Doesn't the nature-stuff pay better?' I replied lamely that I had written more than three dozen short stories about animals and birds, and that four out of five had been rejected by every possible magazine in England and America. 'Perhaps your titles aren't good,' he suggested. 'Here's a suggestion, — although I'm not a critic, and know nothing about literature — in fact I find it difficult to read anything nowadays except the morning paper — anyhow, here's a suggestion, for what it's worth — Why not go down to that pond over there, and write about it? It's full of all sorts of life. Call it "Marvels of Pond Life", or "Some Marvels of Pond Life". You ought to be able to do it all right'. So obediently I went down to the pond, and if the result is not quite what my uncle expected (although he won't read it) posterity must blame him.

The pond was triangular and silted. It lay in the corner of the field, holding the waters of the little brook, which were dammed by a stone wall. The water worked a grist-mill in the farm behind the manor house three hundred paces below. The pond was a haunt of moorfowl and other water-birds.

As I came down the hillside I saw a heron standing at its muddy edge. The tall grey bird flapped away when I was four or five gun-shots distant. Its broad, loose wings were caught by the wind as it tried to rise, and it could make no headway; so it turned into the wind and was carried in a long glide over the next field, where it swung round again, and alighted. I could see the head on the long neck held up anxiously to watch me away, when it would return to its feeding.

I jumped over the earth-and-stone hedge, to find out what it had been eating. The mud under the broken turf had been made arrowy by its feet, as the bird had stalked from the pond's apex to the deeper water by the stone dam. After every dozen steps it had turned to peer into the pond, and at these stances the mud was much trodden; the heron had taken many steps forward to snick its prey out of the water. What had attracted it? I could see nothing.

I sat down and waited. Wind ruffled the pond's surface; wavelets lapped the margin, erasing and silting the arrowy footmarks. Very soon from the direction of the wooden fender came a noise like a duck quietly calling her ducklings; but it was a dryer, more brittle noise. A similar cry came from the bank, and then another: a chorus broke out over the pond.

I saw a rat running along with a frog in its mouth. It went into a hole in the bank continuing the stone dam. There was a well-trodden track leading into this hole, two inches wide — the path of the rats. One of the colony must have come out as the heron flew up, and seeing a frog on the bank, picked it up.

Many frogs were now apparent in the pond. Most of them were bull-frogs, smaller than the females. The glitter of the sun and the lessening cold had excited them to begin the search and struggle for mates. All things in nature have their seasons, and the males usually await the females; it is so with the bull-frog, which finding a

59

female, makes sure of her by climbing upon her broad back, and clinging there in the attitude of a jockey at the gallop. I was, all unsuspecting, to be on this afternoon a spectator of a mad, whirling, ranine romance and tragedy, thanks to my uncle's suggestion.

A female walked out of the water as I watched, and the movement drew four unattached bull-frogs. She was mounted by the quickest, but carried him six inches only before the other frogs began to muscle in on his racket. I am sorry if this American slang phrase hurts my uncle's susceptibilities, but I am no stylistic writer: my aim is always to convey to the reader what my eyesight puts into my brain. The frogs were muscular creatures; they made a racket, or noise; they were competitive, pitiless, entirely selfish. The phrase therefore is used, although it belongs to the gangsters of Chicago who have probably never heard[1] of the little pond behind the hamlet of Putsborough in North Devon.

The jockey was prepared for musclers-in. With a slow but well-judged shove with his off-hind foot he laid one on its back. Then he croaked, as though trying to get his mount to start again. She carried him forward another three inches and stopped. He dug his hands deeper under her armpits, urging her on with calf and spur. She remained motionless.

A rival greener than the jockey climbed leisurely up, avoiding the thrust of elastic hind-legs; and digging his arms in, the green rival bent his head forward and slowly arched his back, in an attempt to unseat the jockey. Their stifled croaking stirred to movement the three other frogs who had been squatting behind them. These would-be jockeys hopped forward, to receive immediate

[1] At least, until this book appears in the Penitentiary Libraries.

thrusts of feet in their faces. Two of them overturned. They got upright again, and squatted still, as though in oblivion.

The greener frog who had scrambled up was now trying to throttle the jockey. The three fingers and thumb of each hand were clenched with his striving. In other words, so offensive to my uncle, *he was muscling in.*

For nearly a minute the muscling in continued. Then the female decided to move; she took two heavy hops forward. The squeaky cries of the jockeys began again. The three also-rans moved after them. Two of them collided, and as though in despair one hopped astride the other. He was carried forward a few inches, but dismounted, and turned back. The movement of my foot had drawn him; he leapt at the toe of my shoe, fell off, and went back disconsolately towards the water, passing another aspirant who was hurrying forward, gay with a bit of weed round its neck.

Meanwhile the race was continuing. The steed was walking and hopping forward with her double load. During one of her pauses the fourth frog sprang, receiving from the green rival a quiet, sure kick in the throat which laid him out; but picking himself up, he tried again. The original jockey sat still, croaking weakly, vainly, for motion; but the green super-jockey, the line of whose back was now almost oval with the strain of throttling, kicked out again at a fresh aspirant, and missed. Immediately the aspirant gripped his leg and hung on, while the steed moved forward a few more paces. During the next interval the aspirant managed to grip the other leg of the green super-jockey, and stepping up on the wide haunches of the female, secured what may have given a satisfying illusion of superiority.

It was no longer a race; it was an omnibus. The omnibus progressed unevenly, with noises like the tooting of horns blown asthmatically. It had four pairs of protuberant headlights, the reflectors of which glinted in the sun. It appeared to have been broken down completely, so I left it, having other business with a raven's nest on the headland. I climbed over the stone dam, jumping down to a place out of the wind, pleasantly warmed by the sun.

I was now hidden from the waiting heron by a screen of ash boughs cut and laid along the top of the bank. Shoots and twigs growing upright gave cover for my head as I peered under a horizontal grey bough. The heron was still standing in the farther field, its head held high and anxious. It was doubtful if it had the sense of continuity; that it would remember I had not reappeared.

I had been standing there for about a minute when rustlings and small thumpings became audible in the bank, with the squeaks of rats. I had forgotten the rats. Were they fighting over the frog brought into the tunnels when first I had sat by the pond?

I listened, keeping still; and peering over the dam, I saw a rat running along the side of the pond, followed by two other rats. They made straight for the omnibus — still in the attitude of break-down — and through my glass I watched two rats pulling the frogs apart. The jockey, the green super-jockey, and the aspirant hung on to each other, kicking and croaking; but the rats, the zestful and murderous rats, braced their hind legs and bit and tugged. The aspirant was the first to go; he was dragged immediately along the path to the hole. Vainly the green super-jockey croaked for speed; he was nipped by a leg, but the strength of two tugging rats could not shift him. After a while, for a minute I should think, the rats ceased to pull each for himself; they appeared to organize themselves, and set about removing the omnibus as it stood. Each with a leg in its mouth, and with heads held high, they trotted along the bank, sharing the weight of muscled frogflesh.

Another rat ran to meet them, and yet another. There was squeak and scuffle, and the newcomers ran on, plainly told to mind their own affairs. They ran to the water, where, putting their heads down, they swam under like small unskilful otters.

Squeaks inside the bank told me that the rats had entered with their booty, and I remained there, hoping to get a glimpse of them, for there were many rabbit holes in the bank. Noises of tugging and thumping came with more squeaks out of a low tunnel, and tiring of my position, I stood upright again to watch the swimming rats. Long thin legs and wide grey wings upheld and dropping blurred in the retina of my eye: the heron had flown back to the pond.

It folded its wings, while raising its head and looking round for movement that might mean danger. Knowing how keen was the sight of this shy bird, I tried not to blink an eyelid, for the section of my face under the laid ash-bough was silhouetted (from the heron's point of view) against the sky.

Suddenly the heron lowered its beak. I saw a rat swimming across the pond, its whiskered head exposed with something unwieldy before it. It was carrying a frog. The heron's body, seeming so loose and thin within the shell of soft grey wings, their big flight quills tipped with black, seemed to stiffen and sharpen. It moved head and neck low and forward, an unobtrusive action against the background of its body. The rat could not have seen it, for it swam on steadily, until it was within twenty inches of the heron's sharp beak, when the beak struck and the rat was lifted out of the water. It squealed and twisted; its feet ran on air; its tail whipped its body. The heron turned round to strike it on the bank, but its beak was wedged in the rat's skull. It lifted a long leg and tried to claw it with its toes, and the weight of the rat and the wind caused it to stagger.

Then the heron saw my eyes under the bough of the ash tree, and jumped into the air with fright. It flapped and tumbled; but before I had time to clamber over the bank, it had recovered, and was steady on the wing. In the air it clawed its beak again, and the rat fell with a splash into the water. When I reached the bank opposite the splash I saw a dead rat floating in the wavelets, with a jockey already riding on its shoulders, croaking defiance to another whose head, set with glazed and bulging eyes, was poked up alongside.

Shallowford Hearth

Concrete sill, frame of English and American oak, walls of compressed straw-and-iron panels, plastered within, rough elm-board and Cornish peggie slates outside

Harold just before beating up bigger boy who turned Harold
out of Harold's pool.   Bigger boy never returned

At the first dam, made of concrete in potato sacks,
river low summer level

Beginning of spate, road and field-drain washings

The *Pinta* was clipper built, half-decked, 18-ft. long, 'stiff' in a snuffy wind.   Fate unknown

12-lb. peal taken in June with 7-foot 2-ounce rod, on dry fly and
tapered gut leader of 8-ounce breaking strain.
1 hour, 35 minutes

Last Glimpse

Peal Stone Falls (XVIII century)

Tree Pool, running into Viaduct Pool, where otters breed
every winter

THE GOLDFISH

It's dead at last.

'It died in the heat of last week,' said the fish's owner, taking a pull at his pint of beer. 'Eight year us had that fish. 'Twadden right, you know, what you'm always telling, about changing the water. 'Twas the heat that killed'n. Aiy, eight year us had thaccy fish. A record, I'm thinking.'

The goldfish was about three inches long, weighing about an ounce, when it died. A carp of, say, ten years in a lake would be perhaps ten pounds in weight at that age. A goldfish is a carp. After a generation or two of wildness, goldfish revert to the brown scales of their rootstock.

During eight years the fish had lived in a glass jar which had originally held seven pounds of jam. The jar stood on the kitchen table of the inn. Every time I went into that kitchen, usually at night for a plate of eggs and bacon that the landlord's wife cooked so excellently, I felt a little of what the fish was suffering.

Often it was at the top of the water, hanging aslant as it gasped for the oxygen which it had exhausted in its water. Where air and water met, the slightest movement absorbed a little oxygen; and this just kept the goldfish alive during those periods before the water was changed.

And how it was changed! The fish was emptied, with the foul warm water from the jar, into an enamel basin. The jar was refilled with very cold water from the well. The water stood in a pail under the sink; the slopping movements while it was being carried into the kitchen, and the bubbles during the pumping, were just sufficient to oxygenate the water.

The jar being filled, the fish was picked up and slipped into the jar, where it moved about with animation, opening its mouth rapidly as it gasped to breathe. Fish are sensitive creatures; a drop in temperature of a few degrees in a river will interfere with their normal lives. Its life after warm exhausting torpor was changed suddenly to icy palpitation.

For eight years the goldfish existed, aimlessly moving within its glass prison. Once I asked to be allowed to change its water, gradually, and to refill the jar with stream-water, which was full of natural food. Ants' eggs were poor fare for a fish, I said. Did they know that fish suffer from dyspepsia as we did sometimes? It was an effort to talk like this, for one was interfering with the affairs of others; and one dreaded to hurt their feelings — they felt affection for their fish. Might I change the water? I could assure them that the fish would benefit. Permission was given; I put some fresh water shrimps into the water, with a little cress. I explained that water from a stream which supported trout, and was therefore unpolluted, was much superior to that from a well, which was almost empty of oxygen. My hosts wanted to please me; but repeated that it had lived while other goldfish in the village died quickly: it was a favourite fish, owned by their grandson, a youth called 'Mustard', who was away trawling up by Iceland. I tried to explain again about the need for oxygen; but I might as well have been speaking Esperanto or Desperanto.

Every time I went to the inn I saw the fish in the jar, aslant the murky water, nose protruding as it palpitated with a dislustred and malformed body. Its eyes were bulbous and were probably blind. I attempted to tell them about salmon and trout in a river in a period of drought; how heat, and the floating algae which grows and spreads in warm water, takes the oxygen: how the rotting algae gives off carbonic acid gas; how in those circumstances even the strongest fish are liable suddenly to develop fungus disease, and sometimes the dreadful furunculosis, a sort of pox which may easily kill every fish in the river in a few weeks. Well, there it was, proof of the pudding in the eating; the goldfish was alive, and more no man could say.

'There 'e goes agen! I knew it! Mother, Mr. Williamson wants to reform our fish. Says it breathes like a human bein'. I've never seen a fish breathe like a human bein', and in my time I've gaffed scores and scores of salmon. Thousands I've took! And spent twenty years in Cardiff fish market, too. And you try and tell me that fish . . .' etc.

It's dead at last.

THE OLD TROUT

I

The best time to see him is in the morning about ten o'clock, any day during a spell of fine weather between April and September. He lies a few yards above the bridge, at the edge of the stream which runs over the gravel and the deeper water of the pool. By stream is meant the swifter defined course of the water moving between the river banks; for if you look at a brook or river which has its sources in moorland — and is therefore bedded with rock or gravel, and subject to spates — you will see that it seldom runs consistently. Trout usually feed in the stream or run, leading into, and out of, the deeper water which is their refuge from danger. There is seldom any food in a pool; so fish seldom feed there.

When first I saw the old trout, he was big-headed, dark, and thin. He weighed about a pound. He was old, eight or nine years. A trout is in its prime at three and a half years. He was slow; he could not compete for flies and nymphs with the more lively fish; he was probably an occasional cannibal.

When I put some Loch Leven fish into the river, I was advised to feed them for a while with the food on which they had been reared in the hatchery pits at Dulverton. Released from the confining tanks, the new bluish-green fish leapt and splashed and rolled in the cold water; while the old brown trout waggled his tail and moved into the obscurity of the pool. He was not seen again for several weeks.

Meanwhile the Loch Leven trout lived in the pool, awaiting spoonfuls of food about noon, when usually my accustomed figure appeared above the parapet of the bridge. In the afternoon and evening they took up positions in the run at the bend above, awaiting spinners and sedges which dropped their eggs before sunset. This food changed their yellow-brown spots to red, and their green-blue backs became tinged with gold.

During the first summer the old wild trout became less shy, but he would not take the artificial food. The Loch Leven fish grew quickly, developing thick shoulders and deep flanks. One grew from five ounces to a pound in two months.

When September came, and the sea-trout began to run up to spawn, the Loch Leven trout went with them. They were away two months.

The winter was mild, with little rain; and I was able to feed the returned fish about four days a week. Normally a trout feeds hardly at all during the winter; it exists in a state of semi-hibernation; frost numbs it, and food is scarce. Very soon wild brown trout and salmon parr were waiting with Loch Leven trout for the showers of artificial food. While elsewhere in the river the pools held lank and listless trout and discoloured salmon, the Bridge Pool whenever I appeared was aflip and aswirl with keen fish; native brown trout turning greenish-blue, and alien Loch Levens looking like fairer brown trout. A trout's colour and shape are determined by its feeding.

The old trout remained aloof, although sometimes he would cruise among the lively shoal, swish his tail as though excited by his daring, and then drift into deeper water again. Perhaps he had been hooked a few years before, and had not forgotten it. Trout are as timid as rabbits.

Otters regularly travelled up the river during the winter, but the trout remained. I knew when they came, because all otters left the river above the second waterfall and touched at an ant-hill, the grass of which was always killed in a dry winter. When spring came, and the otters hunted salmon in the lower pools, that ant-hill was the greenest thing in the deer park; it was a golgotha of eels' bones. Now eels are the most destructive things in a trout fishery; they eat much caddis and stone-fly creeper, and they eat the eggs and fry of trout, and the trout themselves when they can get a grip on them.

During May I bought an eel-trap, and having baited it with the head, feet, and entrails of a hen, I put it by some alder roots in the bank above the bridge.

The next morning I saw something moving in the cylinder of galvanized wire netting lying on the bed of the river, and, running down from the bridge to the bank below, I hauled on the rope. The trap came up dripping with weed. It shook with the flaps of a dark brown spotted fish within. It was the old brownie. Five other smaller trout were with him. The bait was uneaten.

The head of the trap which had lain upstream was choked with weed, and I realized that the trout had swum up through the narrow one-way funnel not for food, but for shelter. A trout loves a hole where it can hide with sufficient water passing to enable it to breathe.

I lugged the trap to the grass, and opening the door, allowed the fish to slither out. The small trout jumped about on the grass, but the old fellow, who had the head and jaws of a crocodile, began to writhe through the grass towards the river. As he seemed to need no help, I let him continue until his nose stuck in some soft mud made by the feet of cattle. Then, having wetted my hand lest the touch scald him, I eased him into the river. He swam forward, his snout tipped with mud. Having put the other fish back into the water, I ran back to the bridge, to see what the big fish would do.

A spoonful of food, and at once the water was rocking; jaws were snapping, tails swishing on the broken surface. To my surprise the old trout, hitherto so sluggish and suspicious, was quicker than the others. He raised a wave as he came downstream, he made a slashing rise as he leapt to take a piece of floating food before the opening mouth of a Loch Leven fish. I threw in more food. He cut and swirled after it. The mud was still on his snout. He behaved as a dog behaves when released from its mournful wait at the end of a chain; as a boy when released from the class-room of an inefficient master; as an innocent man reprieved from death.

Is this sentimentality, is this 'humanizing' the emotions of the fish? I saw a fish behaving as I would have behaved had I been the fish. And from that moment the old trout ceased to be shy of my presence on the bridge. He always came down with the others when he saw me, to await the exciting food showers. He had no feeling for me, of course: but the excitation had un-sluggished him, he had behaved recklessly on return to the water, taken the food, liked it, and wanted more.

As summer advanced more fish joined that little watery Band of Hope, including salmon parr and one or two small peal (sea-trout), which, escaping the thirty-six nets working two hours before and two hours after every low tide, ran up from the sea in their silver-spotted dresses during an August freshet.

How well-behaved they were! Each fish in its place, maintaining order of precedence, the old reformed cannibal at their head, where he could get (theoretically) the pick of each cast. Sometimes the cast spoonful fell short, and he came down speedily to claim his rights. He lost his dark colour; his flanks became a light golden hue, the dull red pennant of his adipose fin became a lively vermilion. His big blue-black head changed to brown, and no longer looked too big. He lay beside the fingerling trout, rejuvenated and benevolent. The fishy paradise, or millennium, had arrived.

2

Herons regularly fish the water, often from one sunrise to another at midsummer. They fly at intervals and in succession up the valley. Each heron has his particular fishing place. Some of these places are common to all. Like the trout taking his stance in the stream where the food is most plentiful, so the heron stands in shallow water on a jut of mossy rock at the tail of an eddy, where the trout await the hatching nymphs.

On many occasions as I went towards the river fifty yards distant from the park gates, the slight metallic sound of the latch being lifted would be heard and a big grey bird arise from beside the Bridge Pool.

While otters in a trout stream are, in my opinion, good for a fishery because of the great number of eels they catch, herons are almost entirely destructive. The heron is a thin, lanky creature, with an enormous appetite; he stands still for long periods awaiting the return of the fingerling trout and the fry which were scared by his great gliding wings descending and closing. He takes them with a lightning thrust of his sharp yellow beak. I have found sea-trout of 10 lbs. and more killed by herons, who cannot possibly eat them, but merely stab them for sport or devilment. Do not deduce from this that I hate herons; I like seeing them in the estuary, where there is enough food for all.

You may imagine my feelings when day after day, at intervals of about an hour or so, heron after heron came up the river and stood motionless in the shallow water at the edge of the pool where the Loch Levens were lying.

All the summer I fed the trout; they came as usual; but I noticed that the smaller wild trout and the salmon parr which had joined them were missing. One morning when I looked over the bridge I saw the old trout moving very slowly to the deeper water where the salmon lay, a strange bluish mark at the back of his head. By the aid of my glass I saw that the back of his head had been pierced in two places, about three quarters of an inch apart.

The wounds were, I judged, an inch deep. The next morning two herons flew up. I found one of the Loch Leven trout dying in the pool. Two mornings later the pair was there again; a pound-and-a-half fish lay on the sandy scour, with marks as of shears pressed on its head and flanks, where the bird had tried vainly to swallow it.

I kept watch, and learnt that at least nine herons were fishing all day and most of the night along my beat. They would take from it in one day what I might take in one year. 'Old Williamson,' I imagined

them saying, 'is all right; he's written most sympathetic-
ally about herons. Old Nog, you know, and that melo-
dramatic nonsense. Time he restocked this water again,
don't you think?'

The old trout did not feed any more with the other
fish. He grew thinner. His wound spread into a black
patch towards his tail. Once, when he came directly
under the bridge, I saw that he was becoming blind.
He was slowly starving to death. He could not take the
food I broadcast; the other fish were too quick.

Snails and slugs were collected from the garden, and
lobbed over for him. He ate some of the slugs, and seemed
a little more lively afterwards. I thought of netting him,
but that was illegal; besides, the trout-rearing pond in my
garden, where it might be possible to pension him off,
had been silted up by a neighbouring farmer's ducks.

One day, however, occurred something which can only
be described as an act of benevolent and inscrutable
Providence. As I walked around a tree by the waterfall
one of those nine herons fell down dead before me. I
skinned the bird; put part of him through the mincing-
machine; made the mince into little meat balls; tossed
them into the water, well above the old trout. He took
them slowly at first, and then with more agility. Providence was again kind to us, for the very next day another
heron fell down dead before me. The rissoles lasted for
four days. And thenceforward the big trout began to
get lighter in colour as his eyesight became clearer. In
three weeks he was strong and well again.

He remained above the bridge until the spate of
February last, after which I saw him no more. Perhaps
he went down to the sea and grew into one of those big
spotted sea-trout called pugs.

'THE DEAR ONE'

WHEN I came down the valley after trouting, the boys cried out that they had a baby Tarka. They had found it outside a field drain in the deer park, and had carried it home in a handkerchief.

A glance showed that the small, sinuous, brave-sly-eyed animal was no otter, but a stoat. The tip of its inch-long tail was dark brown, distinguishing it from weasel. It was scarcely weaned. Its milk-teeth were not yet hard. It made a shrill chattering cry. Probably its mother had been trapped by one of the keepers, and it had wandered out in its hunger.

The boys declared it to be an otter cub. Mother had said so. Farmer had said so. Their minds resisted readjustment. I said I thought it was a stoat; a little Swag-dagger, not a baby Tarka. 'Oh, I love it!' cried the elder boy, aged seven, ecstatically. 'Better put it back where you found it,' I retorted, irritable with too much to think about, which in turn had been caused by my own indolence. 'Oh, I do love it,' said the boy. Half seriously I gave it the worst character: a blood-sucker; bird-strangler; gnawer of rabbits' eyes; eater of living flesh only. 'But God made it,' retorted the seven-year-old. 'His religion,' I explained to a friend, 'comes entirely from his schooling, his parents having been impartial, non-committal, even evasive about this profound problem.' And turning to the boy, 'How do you know God made it?' 'You told me when I was four that God made trout and otters, so I thought God must

75

have made this too,' he replied. When sure that we were not laughing at him, but at me, he dared (being a very sensitive child) to ask again if he might keep it. Might he, please? Certainly, if he wanted to. He could always do what he liked.

It became for them 'the dear one'. After their bath they came down in pyjamas to peer into the inverted barrel and say good night to it, where it lay curled in cotton wool beside a saucer of milk and bread. Such a darling little thing, wasn't it, Dad? Such sweet little paws and face, hadn't it, Mum? The elder boy hugged himself with joy. The next night it nipped his finger; he looked bewildered, then he scowled with mortification at the betrayal of his benevolent feelings, and gave the stoat to his brother, aged four.

The beast did not thrive. Occasionally I saw it trying to eat. It chittered much, calling its parents. It was ill. Obviously it had been injured when they brought it home. I thought it would die soon of peritonitis; unless the Parson Jack Russell terrier, expert mouse-snapper, secret-sly chicken-slayer, got it first. The terrier, at every opportunity, and despite threats and thwacks of every kind, dashed to the inverted barrel whenever he saw a chance.

Hearing or smelling the dog, the infant stoat would raise its long flat head, the shape of a hawk's skull, and remain poised. It showed no fear (although it had fear). Weak, starved, soon to die, it did not cower or flinch, but waited with head upheld in the enemy's direction.

Seeing its plight, the elder boy reclaimed it. We fed it on warm milk from an old fountain pen filler. We wrapped it in cotton wool. He was heard praying at night for its recovery. Secretly, in the tenderest tones, while leaning cautiously over the barrel rim, he exhorted the dear one to live.

The fourth evening the terrier, whom no threat could daunt, got into the barrel. We hurried to the sounds of thumping, shoving, scrambling, chittering. He was lugged out and hurled away. There by the overturned saucer and crushed box stood the stoat, its head still upheld, but swaying on its neck. In the morning it was curled on its side, a mite hardly big enough to fill the palm of the hand, languid with the chills of approaching death. I carried it in my trouser pocket, but soon 'it was a-go', as the old people say of death in the West Country.

The seven-year-old appeared round the door, cheeks red, eyes wet with unhappiness. He would kill the dog. But why? God also made the dog. Oh did God? The boy ran away, and hid; was observed shaking his fist at the sky; told his mother he would say no more prayers.

Later when we buried 'the dear one' under a rose-tree the boy became tranquil when it was suggested that he would perhaps see his friend again in a different form, but under the same sky. And the next day all was forgotten.

DIMMIT LIGHT

Standing by the river at nightfall, one became aware of the changing water-noises. At that moment the air was cold; for windless air flows as water, and since sunset the chill air of the moor had been coming down the valley. Now it was upon the stream as mist. Star-points which had been wavering in the gentle ripples of trout-rings were dimmed immediately. Looking up beyond the black fringe of the oak-leaves, I saw that the smaller stars were gone. Silence and mist seemed one. I say silence, for my mind had obliterated the sound of the river for the past few hours, as I moved slowly upstream casting a large brown cock's-hackle fly called the Tarka Twilight.

Loud rang the tongues of the water over the stones. Mr. de la Mare's phrase from *Memoirs of a Midget* renewed itself in my head, from out that Christmas ten years ago, sitting at his dinner-table in candle-light, with his autographed copy of Edward Thomas's *Richard Jefferies* in my pocket. The meal for me was a banquet, after my year of housekeeping alone in the cottage, the faces around me were young and lovely; but I had a greater hunger, to seek some place apart where I might read about my hero in the borrowed book.

Yes, the water-voices were suddenly loud. One was aware of them in the colder air. The great oaks and sycamores which had stood through hundreds of winter spates echoed and confused them. Periodically it seemed that a new sound arose startlingly as by some new obstruction in the swift runs, or by dog or otter shaking itself, or a snag shifting and altering the set of currents. The new arresting sound grew less, and sank to an under-tone; another rose. After awhile the mind accepted the truth that the river at low summer level was flowing steadily and consistently; that all the sounds were there all the time; that the ear had selected first one, then another, as dominant.

Ten years ago I stood by trees and wandered by water during most of the twilight between sunset and dawn in summer, straining to feel in 'Nature' that which was, I believe, to be discovered if only one sought for it with all one's intensity. By intense inner aspiration Truth would be torn from the very sky. By day I read Jefferies. Despising sleep at night, I wandered for miles by cornfield path and sunken lane.

Fatigue succeeds any intensity, whether of steel, human thought, or heavenly star; time wears them; steel crystalizes, sensitivity becomes indifference, stars burn out.

The above is an attempt to answer a young poet who came to see me this morning, who came with perfervid poetry in his eyes, and who departed with scorn in them. Life exists or persists through a series of stimu-lations; but too much stimulation of one kind works in reverse, undoing one's strength instead of increasing it. He was disappointed and repelled because I did not have any enthusiasm for Art, Literature, and Communism; but instead was trying to get the three carburetters of my car engine synchronized.

The river sounds are there, but the ear selects an overtone which soon becomes an undertone, while another succeeds it. The conscious mind of man is timid and uncertain, and often persuades him that this or that is what he should do or believe; whereas the fundamental powers of his being are strong and simple, and know their own work, and do it serenely.

What does it matter — and the young poet, who was my young self, declared violently in effect and that it *did* matter — if the source of stimulation changes? Why lament, for instance, that dance music is now for the moment more audible (in the sense that a book is readable) than that of Franck? Or that Jefferies has remained unread for five years? Or that the red-shirt is now black-shirt? Or yellow-shirt? Or even no shirt at all? What does it matter? The river is flowing all the time, whether we sleep by it, lie awake by it, or never go near it. Harmony within oneself is the entire world. Apologies to the reader who has been thwarted or disappointed by the foregoing: but, seeking consciously, one finds in 'Nature' only what one puts into 'Nature'.

STAG HUNTING

THE opening meet of the Devon and Somerset Stag-hounds on Cloutsham Ball produces every August the same conflicting opinions among the thousands of people who go there, and among the hundreds of thousands who read about it afterwards. These facts about the wild red deer may therefore be of interest to the general reader.

The wild red deer, except for imported and usually tamed exceptions, are extinct in England elsewhere than on Exmoor. They are extinct because they have been exterminated. They have been exterminated by bow and arrow, wire and leather nooses, traps, guns, poison, and other devices of predatory men.

They still have many enemies on Exmoor, most of them among those farmers who do not hunt and do not like stag hunting. They are still occasionally poisoned, trapped, wired, and shot. The reason for this persecution lies in the damage they do to crops. Deer are enormously destructive, especially the stags.

The Devon and Somerset Hunt has a Compensation or Damage Fund, which pays out between one and two thousand pounds annually to farmers for damage to corn, roots (turnips and mangolds), potatoes, apples, etc. This money comes from subscriptions to the Hunt, all of which are voluntary.

Owing to the Hunt, deer have their close seasons, and only matured deer (a five-year-old stag is warrant-able, but sometimes a four-year-old) are hunted. Hinds are hunted, chiefly because they are numerous and therefore they must be kept down for the sake of the farmers. The 'Devon and Somerset' country lies over between seven and eight hundred farms.

There is no space in this short article to discuss the technique of the hunt, but Sir John Fortescue's *The Story of a Red Deer* (Macmillan) remains after nearly forty years one of the best things that has been written about the lives of the deer. It is accurate, lyrical, tender, and written in the spirit of truth. In the original edition of my own short story *The Old Stag*, his brother, the late Lord Fortescue, who also helped Jefferies with *Red Deer*, found nearly a score of errors, which were deleted in the reprint.

How is it possible, many strangers to Exmoor ask, that a man can read and esteem Sir John's story, and give it to his children to read, and then take them hunting?

Deer are charming animals, like rabbits, field voles, and red mice; but what do you do if you see a mouse in your larder? Or a rabbit or rabbits in vegetable garden, if you are, say, an enthusiastic amateur gardener? You may say that you do not put on a red coat and ride a horse in order to get rid of them; and quite seriously one might reply that that is entirely your own affair.

Deer are run to a standstill; then they are shot. The life of a deer is many times more fortunate than the life of a bullock. The deer has his freedom and pride; he roams at will, existing within an economic protectorate; he knows man for his enemy; and when his time comes, he runs, is exhausted, and dies. His flesh, called venison, is given to farmers, who cook it badly, and then eat it. An old woman, nicknamed Bloody Mary, asks for and gets the heart, whenever she is present at the kill.

As for the bullock, whose wretched flesh is also so

badly cooked all over England every Sunday, he, too, lives protected: then he is betrayed, driven on slippery roads to the legalized slaughter-house, and dies in mental terror. He dies in mental terror because he is inactive; he longs to break away, but he cannot. The stag is exhausted when killed; his life has left him, his senses whirl about him: he feels no pain: suffers no mental terror: he exists in a sort of delirium in which things are scarcely realized.

Sometimes a stag runs down the river just by my cottage; and when I see it in the water, tongue lolling as it wades slowly away from hounds, I feel overwhelming pity and protest for its plight; so do I when I see bullocks rearing and plunging wild-eyed in the abattoir, or rabbits in gins, when I hear friendly pigs screeching as they are being hauled up by their snouts tied to ropes, while the farmer's knife waits for the stretched and gurgling throat. Do you eat eggs and bacon?

The world being as it is, the deer of Exmoor will vanish with deer-hunting; and those who care for the deer know this to be true. The time may come when Exmoor is owned by the State and the deer preserved; but farmers will still be farmers, very keen men for good crops and value for their hard work.

The death of the author of *The Story of a Red Deer* must have saddened many thousands who as children in the West Country were brought up on that book. It was one of the first of the English animal stories, and it remains, and will remain, one of the best of them; a book with many pages written with that rare simplicity or clarity which is superior to the Pauline charity — since the greater includes the lesser.

Sir John died just before the publication of his auto-biography, *Author and Curator*.

> My earliest recollections are of sounds — the per-petual sound of falling water, the intermittent sounds of furious westerly gales, the annual sound of rooks cawing over nests and newly-hatched nestlings. For my home was built by a confluence of three streams, one the River Bray, flowing down from Exmoor, to the east; the second, a tiny rivulet, running from east to west, and a third, no greater, coming down from north to south and passing just to westward of the house. These last two had been turned into ponds, with a multitude of dams and overflows, and there was also a mill-weir on the Bray. Altogether within a radius of half a mile of the house there were more than a dozen little falls or cascades which made per-petual music from whatever quarter the wind might blow.

The last words I had with him were beside the Bray, by whose waters it has been my privilege to live during the past few years. I had received much encouragement and help from this man, my senior in letters; and I sensed his fatigue after the colossal labour of writing those many big volumes of the History of the British Army. Indeed, he told me the work would shorten his life by many years. Like the late Arnold Bennett, he was that rare thing — a true sensitive. The thirty years' research and compilation and analysis had worn him much. I did not know what to say to him; we knew one another, but had not many spoken words for our thoughts and feelings.

Many who have read the fine stories and sketches in *My Native Devon* must have wished for others like them: and now his last book is written — one which shall stand on the shelf with Jefferies, Hudson, Hardy, and other true countrymen.

HEAT WAVE

DURING the very hot weather of the first week in August hundreds of herring gulls were flying erratically in the air a thousand feet above the sands of Woolacombe in North Devon. Few people appeared to notice them.

I was lying on the grass above the low cliffs. It was late afternoon. An elderly lady walking past stopped and gave a faint cry. She struck helplessly at the air. A young man clad in blue coat with brass buttons and white flannel trousers hastened to her, inspected her, cried 'Excuse me,' in a very refined voice, and proceeded to strike violently at her with an artificial silk handkerchief. Terrific concern was on his face.

Other strollers gathered round. More came up. 'What's the matter?' 'Oh, look, she's covered!' 'Horrid things!' 'What are they?' 'They're on me, too!' (a small screeching noise). 'Quick, take them off!' etc.

The nuisances having been removed by the gallant handkerchief, and the little crowd having dispersed, I continued to watch the gulls imitating the swallows as they dived and turned and hesitated high in the air in the midst of millions of flying ants.

An hour later I was lying on the gravel ridge off Appledore in the Barnstaple estuary watching the ingenious gulls getting a different kind of food in another way. They were prising mussel off the rocks with their beaks, flying up with them about eighty feet in the air, dropping them, and doing the same thing again and again until the mussel shell was broken and the contents eatable. 'Marvellous!' said someone, blowing his nose loudly on an artificial silk handkerchief, I noticed, 'How Nature teaches her children!'

An old gull, I also noticed, spent his time watching the others working, and when a shell fell near him and broke, he ran forward and stole it. Then followed the usual twisting chase and hoarse cries of rage. 'Yes; marvellous,' I said to myself, blowing my nose through finger and thumb, nature's way.

Now, what were the earthy facts of these two natural processes? I tried to reason them out: only for the purposes of my trade as writer, of course.

The gulls have learned to crack up shellfish as they have learned to follow fearlessly but cautiously within a few feet of a travelling ploughshare; as we have learned to make furniture, talking pictures, or use coal (rather, *misuse*, coal). Everything in the natural world, which includes ants, automobiles, tigers, and toothpaste, has been realized or made 'real' by the principle of accident, error, and trial. This principle, with its billions of by-products, has been operating now on this planet for some millions of years; although to hear some people talking on Sundays one would think it was a matter of only a few thousand years, and that the principle were non-existent. Yes, most of the people in the village. . . .

Well, it was too hot to continue in this way of rumination, so I closed my eyes and dozed until a loud buzzing made me sit up suddenly. A humble-bee had alighted in my open mouth.

In the village which I know best — and a village is the world — I have heard it said over and over again that bees needed salt for their honey, and they got it from the sea. I believed this for years, without considering it. I have even put it out in a book as a fact. Often

I had seen bees passing over the waves when I had been bathing. They said in the village that bees went down for salt. I knew nothing about bees.

But six years later I said suddenly to myself, Why should they need salt?

Would the bee, seeing me in the water, and if it reasoned along the lines that Man reasoned, conclude that I was drinking salt water? Why shouldn't the bee be merely flying there? Why should the bee be more clever than man?

The village still believes the bee-salt idea. The village believes many more things, all bee-salt ideas. The village still strikes violently, as it were, with super-chivalry, at a few harmless ants which have alighted on an elderly lady's hat. The village still secretly fears the world.

The moral of the above is that it is an excellent world, transformable at will; a world of cause and effect, all the causes of which are logical and controllable. And the world is oneself; not one's neighbour.

WASPS

At last we said they were getting too much of a nuisance. One didn't mind the children being stung, the kitten swallowing one, the continual sight of a score of black and yellow go-getters struggling in jam, honey, or beer; but when it came to rasping away part of my copy of *The Seven Pillars of Wisdom*, I thought it time to do something.

A reward of threepence was promised for every wasps' nest located within four hundred yards of the house. One searched old books for fumacious remedies; and ended by buying three penny sticks of a saltpetre-sulphur compound at the ironmonger's — 'useful for clearing wasps, bugs, rats, and all vermin, driving rabbits for sportsmen, detecting bad drains, and other country pursuits. Made in Chile.'

As the children seemed languid about those three-pences, and as the wasps increased, the reward was raised to sixpence. Nothing happened; the children were too well fed.

Meanwhile, the greengages were attacked. For years the tree had borne little fruit; but this season of old-fashioned summer, aided by winter top-dressing of river silt, lime, dead salmon-kelts, and 'artificials', there were pounds of fruit.

At last we caught several wasps, let them gorge on mead (fermented honey), and then hitched dandelion 'clocks' to their abdomens by means of spider-threads.

It was difficult; but it was done. The game was then to follow them home.

The trail took us past a seven-barred oaken gate branded with coronet and the letter F, where several other wasps were seen busily rasping wood with their horny jaws. High over them flew the little squadron of glistening balloons. The children loved the chase and cried to each other what would be bought with the sixpences they would soon possess.

We found two nests by the river, each nest under a tuft of grass, with a rough entrance hole about the size of a penny. The children wanted to burn them at once, but it was thought wise to wait until night, when the wasps' wings would be limp in the damp air. Most of them would be in the nests, too. It was promised the elder boy, out of earshot of the two smaller children (whose cries of 'Me, too?' invariably arise when anything exciting, from a sweet to a motor-ride appears) that he would be awakened in time to see the fun.

At eleven o'clock, with Scorpio flashing red-gemmeous over the treetops, we set out. (One wondered a little sadly if one had so much enthusiasm for so little when one was young?) The sky gleamed with a pallid blue under the cloud-pine of the north-west. Trees in the deer park seemed filled with a bluish-black power of mysterious night-life. Crossing the eighteenth-century ornamental bridge we could just see the glimmer of trout rings by the bend of the river where the shrunken run moved quietly into the pool. Far away up the valley there was a faint roar, and a diminutive train, with many lighted windows, moved slowly across the sky. Did the holiday-makers from London know that we were watching their late train crossing the viaduct of the

Great Western Railway? That a heron, disturbed by the dilating play of flame on steam, cried harshly and flew downriver to pitch within three yards of our motionless selves, to walk slowly to the edge of the water, and then to shriek with terror and flap up in a great wind of his wings on our faces?

The river murmured over the shallows; an owl cried among the spruces of Bremridge Wood; and the match was struck, held shakily while wasp after wasp emerged with sleepy hostility. At last the fusee spluttered. A reddish point of light glowed dully, falteringly. Another match, and then a firm hissing as it gave off its white choking vapours. Quick, the clatt of earth on the hole! Press it down with the heel!

Silence.

We went home slowly in the thickening dimmit-light, the boy very wide-eyed as he looked at the strange tree shapes, while wondering what the nest would look like when dug out on the morrow.

2

In the morning we went cautiously to the scene of our midnight burning. A few wasps hovered dejectedly by the half-charred turf pressed over the entrance hole.

They were the workers which, for various causes — such as drunkenness and gluttony in pursuit of their duties of bringing back food for the grubs — had remained out too late to return. They buzzed valiantly but ineffectually about my ears as I struck the mattock into the turf and lifted out the nest.

This nest was about the size of a football, flimsy, greyish-brown like lichen, and easily broken by its own weight of tiers of white grubs and asphyxiated wasps. The tiers, or sections of comb, were brittle, and each one had its eggs, minute grubs, growing grubs, sealed pupae, and wasps about to hatch. Adult wasps, most of them with their stings protruding, lay in still attitude between the combs. Others were dead in the act of feeding the grubs, curiously lifelike as they remained half-in the cells.

The vapour of sulphur dioxide had caught them as men were caught by more deadly gases in the Great War; and like some men then, these few workers had, apparently, thought of their charges before themselves. Were they the females which were not barren, although not fecund like the queen their mother? For a few of the workers can lay eggs, although they have not been fertilized by a male; and these eggs hatch into males, which are stingless, and of no value to the present community. (Do not the best, or 'humanitarian' impulses, in men derive from the female, or maternal side of their natures?)

The lowest tier was the smallest, the most recently constructed from the wood-cement champed and mixed by the jaws of the workers. Here lay a wasp larger than any other. Three wasps, her daughters, lay by her head. They faced her, bowed in death. She was the great mother, who by her own efforts had made the small original nest in the springtime, seeking the mouse-hole in the river bank, enlarging it, cementing its roof, constructing the original hexagon cells, laying the eggs, feeding the larvae, watching them seal themselves behind white silken caps when they were grown, and stroking their antennae as they bit their way out as wan and languid daughter-helpers.

92

I opened some of the sealed cells, to see wasps in embryo within as white as ivory, but fragile with eyes growing a pale brown. And in one cell I found an imposter, a brown and black thing looking like a bee, but not a bee; something whose parent had crept into the nest and deposited there as an egg beside a wasp-egg; which had eaten that wasp-egg, and then food from a gentle nurse; which in turn, but for disaster and death, would lay eggs in other nests, and so continue the line of imposters called ichneumon flies.

Carrying the nest on a shovel I walked to the bridge and there I began to pull the grubs out of the cells and drop them into the water. Some of the grubs were alive, and champing their jaws hungrily. I watched them swirling in the stream below. A greenish dull flash: a Loch Leven trout had taken one. Then other flashes. Soon the water was breaking as each grub touched the surface. Grubs, pupae, young wasps — up the trout rolled for the manna dropping from heaven. The largest trout, about two pounds, waited exactly below where they fell.

I stood there for four hours while several thousand grubs went over the parapet. I grew tired of the meticulous work of separating each grub from its cell, and began to drop wads of them over. The big trout rolled up in half-turns as before. I became bored with him, and went back for a shovelful of dead wasps. Would the formic acid in their stings kill him? I did not care: my fingers were messy, and smelt of old fireworks: the sun was hot: my work left undone for months —no one would read it anyway, and Mr. Hugh Walpole was right when he wrote in *The Spectator* that 'once again it seemed there was a conspiracy to praise a sham writer, to proclaim him real when he was not real', and the sham writer of this age was myself. But, declared Mr. Walpole, he was not writing with malicious intent, but merely to say honestly that Mr. Williamson 'since *Tarka the Otter* had permitted himself to become a false, mushy, sentimental Marie Corelli kind of writer'. Now since *Tarka* these books had been written — *The Pathway, The Patriot's Progress, The Wet Flanders Plain, The Village Book, The Labouring Life, The Wild Red Deer of Exmoor, On Foot in Devon,* and the revised editions of *The Beautiful Years, Dandelion Days, The Dream of Fair Women*; and *The Star-born,* written in nineteen twenty-two, had also been published. Well, Mr. Walpole was no doubt right; and with bitter thoughts I hurled a shovelful of wasps into the water.

The old trout took more than three hundred. To-morrow, I thought, I shall see my old friend of two and a half years dead on his side in the shallows. Serve him right, if he, like Mr. Walpole, can't tell a wasp from a mayfly.

But when I went there the next day and peered over, he came up and looked at me; and if his attitude were translated into English, it would have said 'Any more wasps to-day? These smaller fish are scared of them; but I'll take all you can give me, and then some'.

AUGUST EVENING

THE sun shines and shines; can this be an English summer? The last spate was in April, and then the river was far from being bank-high. That freshet of coloured water was not even strong enough to dislodge the heaps of brambles which had been cut and thrown into the stream during January. There they still lie, dry and bleached, the old moorhen's nest two feet above the water-level. The willow branches have put out roots, many inches long, into the mass of rotten leaves and wood which has accumulated there.

The usual eddies are motionless and warm, green with algae and flannel weed, and the feeding-place of strange water-beetles. When the spate comes the contents of this and other backwaters will be carried down as pollution. It may kill fish, for it is saturated with carbonic acid gas. Litmus paper dipped into it turns red.

Those salmon and sea-trout which have not been gaffed out by poachers hide themselves marvellously during the daylight. Who would think that a fish thirty-three inches long and ten inches deep could exist, and have existed for six months, in an area of river half as big as a tennis court and varying in depth from two inches to three feet? Every inch of the bottom is lit up in sunlight; search how you will, you will not see the big fish. At dawn the prisoner thrusts himself far under the roots of an alder; you may wade and stroke him, but he will not move in his terror. A white fungus, like that which grows on old timber, has spread over his head and corrupted his tail-fin. He breathes in gulps unevenly.

At twilight, precisely as the bats begin to flitter over the water, the great sea-trout, who came up from the sea in January, sinuates slowly, as though wearily, from his refuge, and hovers awhile near the surface. Sometimes his rusty back-fin idles out. The moon lifts over the spruce firs. The fish turns, pushing a wave as he rips downstream; he rolls like a porpoise, showing a gleam of silver-gold and brown; then he leaps, falling back with a great splash that is heard for a hundred yards and more. He is trying to rid himself of the itch of fungus. Afterwards he hovers again, as he did when he was an ordinary small brown trout years ago; but the itch of maggots in his gills drives him to turn on his side, showing his taper and thickness, and rub head and flank with a flapping movement on the gravel. Afterwards, the listlessness of low warm water comes back to him, and he sinks into a torpor guarded by his senses of sight, hearing, and smell.

On the bank above the pool something moves dimly. It is a sheep, lying on its side. The wasps, seeking meat for their queen grubs, have left it; but the maggots of the blow-flies are working restlessly. This poor beast was treated with a solution of carbolic acid four days ago, but the flies returned to it, and in a short while the ivory-sweaty maggots were again tunnelling between skin and flesh. The shepherd works early and late, but is not so strong as the sun, which must appear as a benevolent god to the flies this year.

The sheep kicks convulsively, and the odours of corruption arise with the damp air moving down from the hills.

Higher up the river there is a delicious smell of honey. For nearly a quarter of a mile one smells it. It is exactly the odour of those yellow beeswax tapers which are burned for the saints in Pyrenean churches. The summer has been kind to bees as well as flies; and many swarms from hive and skep have travelled away and become wild. There are three nests somewhere under the wooden super-structure of the railway viaduct. A patch of oil from a motor car lies beside a patch of honey which has dripped from above. Yesterday I watched a war between one clan and another, for the bees of number one nest raided the honey of number two nest; food is the cause of their war.

The evening star shines over the hill, and the old arrogant cock pheasant has ceased to cry out against the fox peering and sniffing below his roosting fir. It is time to go indoors and light the lamp.

HAROLD

DURING a holiday in South Devon I have been much amused by the antics of a certain thirteen-year-old, treble-voiced individual with curly black hair, and — mark of all superior human beings — eyes self-trained in hard perception.

This lad told me that he intended to earn his living by writing 'snappy nature articles' in various papers. He did not intend to base his style on Jefferies as I obviously had, because, he informed me, 'talkies, motor cars, and wireless have speeded up human life, and what people need are facts put out like a good meal'.

I have never before had the good fortune to meet a wholly disobedient boy. Mr. Bernard Shaw once said half-seriously to a small boy waiting on a Hertfordshire railway station for the train to take him back to school: 'But if you don't want to go back, why do you? Why don't you lie down and kick? They could do nothing to you if you did.'

One understands that the whole educational principle is based on an insufficient economic structure, and it was good to meet a boy whose entire nature refused to be made in the image of parental authority or idolatry. This boy would not cause, except superficially, trouble to his parents. Superficially, yes. For instance:

Scene I — Nine o'clock. Bedtime. Harold appears at door of cottage in fishing village.

'You see, I have come back at my bedtime. I hope

you notice how obedient I am. However, as I am not tired yet, and as I like to sleep as soon as my head touches the pillow, and as, furthermore, I am hoping to secure a good tip for a race next week, I am going out again. I need the money.'

'Harold, Harold, your feet are wet! Come back this instant!'

But Harold has already vanished.

Scene II — Breakfast. Adjoining room. Next morning.
'Harold, don't eat so rapidly.'

'Excellent advice. I notice your rapid swallows, father. And I have never suffered from wind in my life.'

'Nor have I. After breakfast I want you to go to Jimmy Pidler and ask him if he has a spare ring for the rod top of mine you broke. Do you hear?'

'I'm not deaf; don't shout, please. I shall go and see old Pidler at eleven, and not a moment before.'

'You'll go now, or I'll know the reason why!'

'My reason is sound. And please don't shout; you are no longer on the parade ground,' replied the son. 'Old Pidler, from nine-thirty until about five minutes to eleven, I've noticed, wheels his daughter's children in a pram in the sun. If I disturb him between those times he will be annoyed, and I shall get no more free hooks from him. At present he likes me, so I intend to ask him at eleven o'clock.'

'You cheeky young rip,' replied the major, half laughing. ' "His daughter's children". Where's your economy of words? Why not say "grandchildren"?'

'On the contrary, I'm not cheeky; but using my wits in the right way. Old Pidler dislikes to think he's a grandfather so early in life; so always I inquire after his daughter's children. Then he gives me a couple of eel-hooks.'

'Why do you want to cadge free hooks? Haven't you enough pocket money? Sixpence a day. . . .'

'It's a meagre allowance. Besides, I'm saving up for a M.G. Midget racing car.'

This boy, at eight years, was taken by his mother to his father's study, to be admonished for some offence. He was the only one of the three to be unemotionally concerned. When the door opened, his mother said, with appropriate unhappy sternness: 'Go to your father.' As the child hesitated, she said, softening: 'It's for your own good, Harold, that you are being punished.'

'Oh, I wasn't hesitating for that,' said Harold. He bowed to his mother. 'Ladies first!'

With the village boys he was either leader or among the leaders. It was amusing to hear his mother suggesting that the influence of some of the bigger boys might be injurious to Harold.

Harold's knowledge of the reed warblers, coots, terns, duck, pike, perch, and eels of the ley is precise as his logic. The same mind directs his life. His emotions are behind his mind, poised for use in life.

Some day I may tell how he hauled in eels on crude tackle, while father fished in vain with shining reels and rods; how Harold stood up in the punt on Slapton Ley with a green bamboo pole and threshed water with spoon and spinner, alternatively terrifying father by the imminence of whizzing hooks and the wet slap of pike and perch jerked beside him. I shall tell how Harold, who couldn't swim, accepted a bet to sit on my back while I dived through breakers into deep water, how he laughed because I thought we would drown, as I swallowed pints of salt sea.

Perhaps, after all, he isn't such an exceptionable boy; but he is certainly an example of a child growing naturally, resisting domination of an older generation without mental injury.

WANE OF SUMMER

FOR days the drought wind had been blowing across the sea from Dartmouth and the north-east; for days the high waves had surged white on the shingle, filling light and darkness with a continuous rolling roar. Greenish specks bit into the nickel radiator of the Alvis car waiting on the road. The windows of the few cottages on the shore were opaque again within a few minutes of being cleaned. After the first two days all cleaning was abandoned. An open window meant papers, table-cloths, and even fragile empty coffee cups being swept on the floor. The yellow flame of the evening oil lamp trembled and wavered as the wind despaired to enter the street windows behind the billowing curtains. The aged dog called Dook lay on the carpet, or mournfully eyed the forbidden empty chairs. And at night the shift and slide and grind of a million million pebbles in the battering seas gave the illusion of darkness-movement: the cottage was a ship, and one 'lay with old sleep and quiet sadness' just above the Atlantic's dark abysm. Yes, the whole earth was moving through the strange starry ocean of time to its unknown end in twilight.

Failures, lost friends and friendships, death's dateless night, repinings, hopes, despairs, injustice — perhaps one had eaten too many blackberries, and they were the cause of sleeplessness.

In the morning light the waves reared and plunged as before; the bass-fishers gave up after an hour. The fish were beyond the arc of their casting. Baulks of wood, grey-stalked with barnacles, heaved just over the green toppling walls of water. The old white dog, biggest bull-terrier ever seen, moved himself slowly over the pebbles after his master, for his morning waterplay. Bathers lying in the white withdrawal of the waves' backwash were flung and swept sideways, or if standing were wrapped in sudden white to the knees, the gravel scooped from their feet, and spun sideways into the foam. But the old dog stood like a seal on legs; the surges covered him, and receded, and there he was still; or he turned half-round to peer with pink concealed eyes at his master, to waddle towards him, blinking slightly, as he disappeared under two feet of liquid marble. It scooped back, and there stood Dookums.

Or perhaps he was barking, like a seal, discreetly, intelligently, until a flat stone weighing several pounds was skidded into the water and he might set about retrieving it. He found it all right; and on his short stilts of legs plodded through avalanche and torrent with his burden, seeking master's feet and the immense delight of another immersion.

Later in the morning relays of human beings tripped over the shingle, their backs and legs and arms brown in the sun as they threw off towels and wraps. They walked doubtfully, hugging elbows; but one fled into the water. Do you remember, O nymph in white bathing dress, with eyes of speedwell and barley-bright hair? And you, small and bullet-head brother, whose feet were ever wet with catching those monstrous eels in the ley of brackish water behind the shingle ridge? And you, madam, whose bathing dress was filled unexpectedly with half a hundredweight of gravel after a barbarous wave had leap-frogged over you? At last it seemed that the sun would shine for ever — the sun of Florida.

But the wind, a brittle wind, like warm isinglass, grew smaller, and that was the end of summer. The old brave dog was shivering rheumatically in the lee of the boat drawn up beyond the mark of high spring-tides now that most of the visitors were gone. He could hardly lift himself over the low wall of concrete ending the shingle by the cottage doors.

Rain fell, and the waves were no longer leonine; they tumbled in like spaniel pups. Salmon leapt again a yard or so from the shore, as they sought the freshwater currents of the river Dart, and so to the spawning beds of granite sand high up between the hills of the moor.

Swallows in thousands are wheeling over the ley, or clinging to the reeds: for day and night are nearly equal: the lantern star Formalhaut lights the way to the Southern Cross and the palms of Africa: we pack our suitcases, and say good-bye.

A LONDON SANCTUARY

WANDERING through Fountain-court, which lies between Fleet-street and the Thames, one realized with a slight shock that this was the first visit for twelve years. One third of my life.

Twelve years ago it seemed to the young and brightly illusioned writer that Fleet-street was a place of terrible noise, ugliness, and strained activities all directed to purposes which were a negation of human life — human life, then, being vaguely formulated in terms of what is called the spirit. Indeed the word spirit had a capital S. In youth it appeared that the Spirit was everywhere denied or unrealized, and that those who perceived it were inevitably destroyed by commonplace thought.

Twelve years later it seemed, as I stood in the quiet autumn sunshine of Fountain-court, that the Spirit was merely one's own uncontrolled emotions, or emotionalism. I perceived it as a waste of human life, of nervous tissue. Further, that only the inharmonious dwelt on what was typified in, for example, the Crucifixion. Furthermore, that inharmony was due merely to poor parental technique with children. A little sapling well and truly planted, its roots intelligently spread, staked, and protected, and the grass kept clear so that it can grow itself direct to its god the sun, this sapling has every chance to be a sound tree. This tree will not think about Sacrifice, Sacrilege, Sacrament, and Satan. It will be itself without strain or conscious effort.

But the tree ill-planted, a cripple of salt winds or

poor soil, one of those trees seen along the Atlantic coast, does this tree dream of a future ecstasy of full foliage in some far away shining air, of strong roots carrying a sappy stream of nitrates and phosphates for its everlasting life? Frustrated and weak, does it imaginatively grow itself into the veritable Tree of Life, recording its dreams in arboreal equivalents of *The Story of My Heart, Prometheus Unbound, The Man Who Died, Tristan and Isolde, The Flax of Dream*, and all the other works of poets which the vast majority, the unpoetical, the ex-happy children, do not care about?

When I sat down this morning, I meant to write of the pigeons in Fountain-court; the leaves slipping down one after another from the trees; the sparrows robbing pigeons of crusts; the faint noises of traffic afar, and the ring of trowels as the masons pointed the brickwork of the Inner Temple houses; the postman after his round sitting on the seat by the pool and contentedly filling his pipe; myself staring at the water and discovering with joy that a dozen big Austrian carp were cruising ever so slowly through an area lit by a sun-ray; the swallow I saw fleeing towards Ludgate-circus; and of the sudden swish! as the water was turned on, leaping in a jet from the centre of the pool, scattering pigeons and startling onlookers, to fall and create a shifting sun-dog, or fragmentary colour band, from its spray.

A mere superficial description: for I was haunted, as I lingered there, by the fate of another writer, one whose talent, or life-wastage, exceeded that of normal writers, one whose distressful existence in poverty, despair, and misprision, was recalled by the sight of the birds. He was a doomed saint. Do you know Richard Jefferies' *Pigeons at the British Museum* which is in the volume

called *The Life of the Fields?* To me, the writing shines
with the very light of the sky.

Sitting at these long desks and trying to read, I
soon find that I have made a mistake; it is not
here I shall find that which I seek. Yet the magic
of books draws me here time after time, to be as
often disappointed. Something in a book tempts
the mind as pictures tempt the eye; the eye grows
weary of pictures, but looks again. The mind
wearies of books, yet cannot forget that once when
they were first opened in youth they gave it hope of
knowledge. Those first books exhausted, there is
nothing left but words and covers. It seems as if
all the books in the world — really books — can
be bought for £10. Man's whole thought is pur-
chasable at that small price, for the value of a
watch, of a good dog. For the rest it is repetition
and paraphrase. The grains of wheat were thrashed
out and garnered two thousand years since. Except
the receipts of chemists, except specifications for the
steam-engine, or the electric motor, there is nothing
in these millions of books that was not known at the
commencement of our era. Not a thought has
been added. Continual thrashing has widened out
the heap of straw and spread it abroad, but it is
empty. Nothing will ever be found in it. Those
original grains of true thought were found beside the
stream, the sea, in the sunlight, at the shady verge
of woods. Let us leave this beating and turning over
of empty straw; let us return to the stream and the
hills; let us ponder by night in view of the stars.

It is pleasant to go out again into the portico under

the great columns. On the threshold I feel nearer knowledge than when within. The sun shines, and southwards above the houses there is a statue crowning the summit of some building. The figure is in the midst of the light; it stands out clear and white as if in Italy. The southern blue is luminous — the beams of light flow through it — the air is full of the undulation and life of light. There is rest in gazing at the sky: a sense that wisdom does exist and may be found, a hope returns that was taken away among the books. The green lawn is pleasant to look at, though it is mown so ruthlessly. It they would only let the grass spring up, there would be a thought somewhere entangled in the long blades as a dewdrop sparkles in their depths. Seats should be placed here, under the great columns or by the grass, so that one might enjoy the sunshine after books and watch the pigeons. They have no fear of the people, they come to my feet, but the noise of a door heavily swinging-to in the great building alarms them; they rise and float round, and return again. The sunlight casts a shadow of the pigeon's head and neck upon his shoulder; he turns his head, and the shadow of his beak falls on his breast. Iridescent gleams of bronze and green and blue play about his neck; blue predominates. His pink feet step so near, the red round his eye is visible. As he rises vertically, forcing his way in a straight line upwards, his wings almost meet above his back and again beneath the body; they are put forth to his full stroke. When his flight inclines and becomes gradually horizontal, the effort is less and the wing tips do not approach so closely.

They have not laboured in mental searching as we have; they have not wasted their time looking among empty straw for the grain that is not there. They have been in the sunlight. Since the days of ancient Greece the doves have remained in the sunshine; we who have laboured have found nothing. In the sunshine, by the shady verge of woods, by the sweet waters where the wild dove sips, there alone will thought be found.

MOONLIGHT

THE other night, having some letters for London which must be collected by the van at 7 a.m. the following morning, I took cap and stick, meaning to walk to the roadside group of thatched cottages a mile away. It was a few minutes before midnight. I was tired, and the thought of the walk seemed wearisome. Equally wearisome appeared the idea of unlocking the garage and taking out the car. As I hesitated, the moon's horn showed by the top of a firtree on the hillside opposite. Well, it was the same sort of thing one had seen for years and years. An owl cried somewhere among the dark trees. So always they had cried. One had heard them so many times that they made no more impression on the mind than the noise of an exhaust made on the mind of a London 'bus driver.

Well, the letters must be posted, and after the hours of enforced sitting still at the desk, perhaps it would be best to walk. One didn't take enough exercise. Ah, if one could only feel about stars, moon, trees, grass, sea, as one felt about them years ago! Wordsworth had felt an identical regret, almost remorse, for the passing of similar enthusiasms.

I walked down the garden path, across the lane, and into the deer park. The air was soft and still. I passed under the great lime trees, among whose leaves in the past summer hundreds of thousands of bees had murmured, in whose thickets around the trunks woodpigeons and jackdaws had nested. How many years since one had climbed to a bird's nest? In a few moments I was on the bridge, looking down at the Bray water.

The moon was making the usual bright and broken lights on the three streams pouring from the three arches. Near the tail of the pool, where the water thinned and quickened, sudden tremulous strips of silver showed where a trout had risen. That was pleasing. Shadows of alders looked blacker than the trees themselves. The thought of that fact was wearisome, until I told myself that it was not necessary to remember it for the purposes of writing it.

Surely, I said to myself, this is a beautiful and restful scene: it is interesting, too, for see, that glimmer, just under the fall of the middle arch was surely the big trout turning over to take something, a mullhead, perhaps, that had gone down with the stream.

Your trouble, or feeling of weariness, is only that you have got into the habit of using yourself as a receiving apparatus for natural impressions, for the purpose of rendering them into words, and thus obtaining money. You feel that you can never relax, never become thought-less in the sense of letting the inner nature rise up through the enslaved mind. There are nearly a dozen people entirely dependent on you, and unless you work all the time, you will get into debt.

The camera of your mind is tired, abused by a demoni-iacal photographer. You have, in your need to rest, almost thought yourself into a nature-hater. A man does not change: Wordsworth was wrong: but a man needs change. For a change, try and do what you really want to do.

So I sat on the bridge, and shut my eyes, and thought of nothing, breathing deeply and slowly, and as slowly respiring. The night was warm for October, and after awhile I thought I would lie on the grass. What mattered if it were dew-damp? Rheumatism came from ill-feeding and drinking. I would lie on the grass. So I lay on the grass, while the distant stable clock tolled midnight.

It seemed, as I rested there, that the stars had not been seen for years. The first frost would sharpen and make them glitter; but now they shone softly, as though very peacefully.

Closing my eyes again, I let the sounds of the river flow through me until I began to feel again a serenity of earth which no conscious thought could give. How often did the activities of the brain force one away from one's true or inner or natural self. Damn the brain: a good servant, but a bad master.

I lay there until the clock tolled one, then I arose and walked happily, thoughtlessly, to the main road and the post box. Clearly the moon revealed the hour of collection, and I had brought an electric torch to make sure! Years ago the sight of anyone taking a torch for a night walk would have filled me with scornful protest.

And why go home? I was actually enjoying the walk. The windows of the cottages were all blank. The nose of the painted grotesque wooden stag's head on one of the walls gleamed where a hibernating snail had crawled. Everything was so still and quiet. My body was non-apparent. The moonlight was in me and through me. I marvelled at the cottage folk who, with one exception, had shut out this lovely air from their bedrooms. I would walk up to the moor and sleep in the heather if I wanted to, or walk on if I wanted to

Certainly I would. I went home to get my coat. Having got it I hesitated. To-morrow those book reviews must go off, and if one were tired — my breast seemed filled with the loveliness of the night, and this was the time to sleep. So I pulled my bed to the window and lay there happy, while the moon climbed far over the fir trees, until serrated by the silver fringe of thatch, and I fell away from myself in sleep.

POTWALLOPERS' MARSH

THIS morning I went with a friend to a part of Devon I had not visited for years: since the writing of *The Pathway*, indeed. Atlantic waves rolled and broke along the shallow coast which once was a forest. An area of several square miles of flat land was kept undrowned by a wall or ridge of boulders varying in size between a coco-nut and a sheep's body. All were worn smooth by wave-grinding.

Locally called pebbles, they were grey and grey-blue in colour. Surging Atlantic seas had broken them from the cliffs of Hercules Promontory a dozen miles westward. The tides had rolled them along the shallow shore, over the sand covering the ancient and sunken forest. At low spring tides, brownish stumps of trees may still be seen embedded along the shore. Bones of moose have been recovered there, the *tibia* of a wild dog, a human skull with big jaws and receding brow.

Timbers of wooden ships lie under the sand, above the roots of the ancient forest, and even I remember the wreck of a torpedo boat thrown up there; and the corru-gated shrinking corpse of a sperm whale.

The marshland behind the Pebble Ridge is owned by the Northam Potwallopers, who graze ponies, sheep, and cattle there. It is common land. Putting-greens and bunkers have been laid out, and anyone may play the Scottish game called goff, although everyone may not use the holes or disturb the flags which are the property of the Royal North Devon Golf Club.

The name Westward Ho! is a recent one, being derived from Charles Kingsley's famous book. (Kingsley, who was a parson, thought little of the adventure or action parts of his books; but the anti-Papist digressions he considered to be inspired.) Mr. Kipling's *Stalky and Co.* added to its fame. And so eventually will Mr. H. M. Tomlinson's beautiful books, *Old Junk* and *Waiting for Daylight*.

But you will be wanting to know the derivation of the word *Potwalloper*. The term, Potwallopers' Grazing Marsh, occurs in *Tarka the Otter*, and an artist who once designed end-paper maps for the book interpreted this to be golfing figures behind the Pebble Ridge. The word does not come, however, from those who wallop balls for silver championship pots; but from an Anglo-Saxon word meaning *potboiler*. Residents of Northam parish, or those who cook their food there permanently, have the immemorial right to graze stock on the saltings.

A local wit has said that the residents of the adjacent village of Westward Ho! should be entitled to graze there also, since so many of them, or their sons and daughters, are now subscribing to Schools of Fiction Writing and Journalism for Profit.

I returned to the Northam Burrows to-day; with hundreds of other tweed-clad men and women I walked on the short, strong turf, while the sun shone benevolently upon us. We were discreetly following the evolutions of the Ladies' Golf Championship. Only the murmur of voices and the hushed periods before the stroke-sounds of metal, wood, and rubber arose from the vast plain of grass and dyke and wandering sheep. All other life seemed ended or suspended. Although the sun shone in a sky of azure paling with heat to the narrow sea horizon above the thin grey line of the distant Pebble Ridge, yet we knew that autumn was but pausing before the coming of winter. Soon the cold salt rain would be driving in gusts over the burrows, the wind keening in the sharp-pointed rushes, making the ponies stand hour after hour in the hollows, their long tails blown past their hocks, standing still with their images shaken and puckered in the dull white water plashes.

Summer's grape was pressed out; nothing was to hatch or ripen; the last mushroom picked; the last cocoon formed among the rootlets of the grass. Not even one gossamer to gleam now, for every wolf-spider was hid from the glitter of the dogstar.

Summer's lease was run out; the sun at the Equinox had signed the order to quit; the tenants were all gone.

THE SPATE

By nightfall the rain was coming down in gusts from the south-west; the wind was lessening — the wind which during the day had stripped one-third of the leaves from the lime trees just inside the deer park gates. One looked anxiously for the absence of stars; for only a week of the salmon season was left: and if the rain did not come steadily now, it would come too late.

The springs were low. The river was still shrunken far under normal summer level in spite of having risen two inches by five o'clock. Risen not with spring water, however; this water had come from the road drains and was foul though clear, and had put down every trout and samlet by its dullness. It was useless water, without life, like religion taught in a school. The fish waited for it to pass away, when life would come to them again.

No real rain had fallen for six months. As I lay in bed I listened for the dull roar which would mean that the little runner at the bottom of the garden, beyond the swamp, had swollen with field-water. Then the river also would be up. I imagined the brown and turbid spate swilling bank-high; in my mind I saw sticks and branches of trees which had lain on the dry rocks for months bobbing and turning as they rolled down the valley to the big river and sea.

Now, was that the sound of water falling over the little dam of my derelict fish farm in the swamp, or was it only the wind in the Canadian willows? Torch light on the fringe of thatch revealed many glittering drops and a fine haze beyond. There was no real rain, after all. The wind was too high, the air too warm. But maybe on Exmoor. . . .

I was awake again at cock-light and dressed, and opening the garden gate as lamplight began to shine in the kitchen of the estate carpenter down the lane. I knew by the feel of the ground underfoot that the river would not have risen more than eight inches. As I passed under the big beech tree beyond the limes I saw no gleam or swirl under the alders. The lifeless road water, with its false rainbows of oil, was still moving down. Slowly I went back to the house.

After breakfast my four-year-old son, John, came to me and said 'God has sent down that rain'. Very sympathetic and understanding, this child usually accompanied me in my riverside inspections, and several times during the summer he had been observed standing in truculent attitude as he gazed upwards shouting, 'God! Send down rain! God!! SEND DOWN RAIN!!' Sometimes, I fear, he had been bluntly critical, even most abusive, about the non-appearance of rain.

'It's not a proper spate,' I replied.

'But it *is* a proper spate,' he said.

'It isn't,' I contradicted. 'It's only road washings.'

'It's high,' he replied. 'Big high 'normous spate.'

'Poof! I've seen it. You don't know what words mean.'

'I'll chuck a stone at you, you silly old water rat!' he cried, his cheeks going pink. He struck me; I gave him a banana, and immediately his eyes became impersonal.

'Truly a spate, John?'

His eyes became round and earnest. 'Yes, truly a spate, Mister Tarka. Yurr, I be coming with 'ee,' he said, as I grabbed my gum-boots.

'What did you say, John?'

'I said, "Here, I'm coming, too, sir".'

John was tactful. A few steps beyond the gates, I saw the swirling gleam of water across the grass. This water was a thick brown colour, heavy with leaves, and the scourings of ditches and field drains. The old stick-heap on the middle bridge pier was gone. The level rose as we watched. Flotsam edging of leaves, twigs, and hens' feathers were being shifted in little undulations over the drowning grasses of the bank.

Where the pit of the old burnt-out wasps' nest had been was an eddy where bubbles revolved about a corked empty medicine bottle. On the gravel ridges the docks and plants of water-celery were washed flat, and burdened with dead leaves. Within twenty-four hours, I thought, salmon from the estuary would be boring through the grey-green glissades pouring through the arches of the bridge.

Several times during the morning we went to the river, hoping to see that the freshet had become a spate. At eleven o'clock it reached its height, thereafter it began to drop back. The water was fining down quickly. One could distinguish new leaves and fragments of old leaves as they were borne down and twirled over the stones of the gravel above the bridge. Grasses which had been drowned at ten a.m. were now a foot above the water level, wet and drooping with a fine brown silt.

The young celery plants and docks on the gravel ridge making the run into the pool were bent and loaded with grasses, water-weed, and leaves. On one of the lower dead branches of an alder a dead jackdaw was hanging. The broad-arrows of herons' feet were imprinted on the sandy scours left below the washed-out wasps' nest.

Here the child, attracted by the newness of the sand, knelt with grave absorption to realize some latent dream.

I watched the scratchings and scoopings of his little hands, actions which were to him the building of a heavenly farmyard. That was a hayrick, that a shippen, that was Towser the bullock dog —

And that! — that was a salmon rolling out of the water not a yard from the boy's foot!

He was startled, and so he swore; and when I laughed, he laughed; and when I cried out, 'That was a thirty-pounder, if it was an ounce!' he tried to say the same thing, but the words got tangled, he felt inferior, and to cover his embarrassment he said it was not a salmon, but a whale that would swallow me. (His brother had been telling him about Jonah.)

'What did you say it was?' I asked, absently.

'I said it were a wh-wh-ale,' he replied; and becoming serious, 'but I think it must be a pug to jump like thaccy.'

We watched the eddy where the fish — it was actually about two-and-a-half feet long, weighing perhaps eight pounds — had rolled up, but it did not come again. It was dark reddish-brown in colour, with, I had noticed, a greenish tinge, as of algae growth, about its bony jaws. The underjaw protruded in the form of a hook over the upper jaw — it was either a very old sea trout, or a male salmon, also called cock fish, or keeper fish. By the discoloration of its scales it had been in the river since the previous January or February, when the last school of fish had run up.

We went on up the river to the Peal Stone falls. These falls were artificially made in the eighteenth century, and when a heavy stone aslant in the pool below was covered with water then the peal, or sea-trout, would be able to run up in summer. There we waited, but nothing rolled up from the white water below.

After lunch we returned there, and many times during the next day. Nothing was there. Then one remembered that throughout the summer thirty-six nets, each two hundred yards long, had been sweeping the shallow river of the estuary eight out of every twenty-four hours except during week-ends, and nearly every fish returning from the sea in its silvery coat had been taken.

Four more days of fishing left; no spate for six months; and here was the freshet fining down, grand running water; but there were no fish left to run.

THE HARMONY OF NATURE

FOR several days now this white fog has occluded the rest of the world. Occasionally the sun shows a pale silver disc overhead, giving illusion of warmth; then the drifting cold mist swirls silently over the hedge, and I must either continue to dig or put on my coat again.

The mist moves like the spirit of silence not yet dead. Rooks and jackdaws flying over the field suddenly appear, to veer as suddenly, and vanish again. A robin, bird always to appear when man is digging, flits between worm-picking pauses from one clod to another.

The temperature appears to vary much from hour to hour. Two hours ago it was surely freezing, the dead tufts of grass in the uncropped field were crisp to walk through; now the hoar is gone as it mysteriously settled.

Three hours ago, at eleven o'clock, the white owl sailed from its beech tree in Windwhistle Spinney and flew high east, presumably to its hunting. At noon it came back, with the same determined flight, fifty feet high, and settled in its usual fork. Had it gone down to the forsaken iron mines of the valley, disturbed in its day-dozing by thoughts of a mate?

Last fall a dying barn-owl was found in a rabbit gin two fields away, and this may have been its old mate. Owls appear to pair for life.

A grey squirrel has found my small plantation, for many of the tops of the various pines are gnawn off and lie scattered underneath the trees. If it be a grey American squirrel, then it is the first I have heard of in this district of North Devon.

A sleepy queen-wasp stung me this morning as I was frying my breakfast bacon. Apparently she chose the handle of my frying-pan for a place of hibernation, beside a small, terrified spider, and the warmth of the fire awoke her to action and defence.

Half an hour later, routing in my tool-shed for a sharp-pointed shovel called a backbreaker by the District Council road workers who never exert themselves unduly, I was stung by another queen wasp. Now it may be coincidence, but soon afterwards the pains in my back, due to rheumatism, ceased; and thereafter I felt more in harmony with the world.

2

Returning to this hut after an absence of several weeks, to put it in order before leaving England, I found that about three dozen rats had paid it a visit, and liking the candles, soap, old boots, musty eggs, and withered apples therein, had decided to stay there. A favourite perch was on one window ledge, judging by the picnic-litter left on it.

I noticed before unlocking the door that a brown owl or owls had been perching outside the window. This was unusual; but it appeared that they had come there to look at the rats within, drawn perhaps by the squeakings. Did the rats mock the owls behind the glass? It is not so improbable as it may seem. Rats are very curious creatures, with an extraordinary sense of fun. Fine scratches were on the paint of the window sill, marks of talons.

The horde of rats had entered the hut by gnawing a hole beside a lead water-pipe in the three-hundred-year-old oak floor planking. They had almost gnawn through the pipe itself. They were grimy brutes, leaving marks where their fur had pressed between the plaster of the wall and a table leg.

What fun they must have had! Corks were gnawn to bits. Two pounds of putty had been eaten, and what the subconscious minds directing the processes of their alimentary tracts must have thought I don't know: for two pounds of white putty had been transmuted into several neat little pyramids of white sausages.

The surface where the original lump of putty had pressed was scalloped out by the rodents. They had eaten half my hat and played hide-and-seek through the bellows. If only my young friend Harold were here with his ferret, I thought, how we would drive them back to real hard work!

Meanwhile, I fill their holes with broken glass, and sprinkle creosote in the rabbit buries whither they have fled. It is evening. I sit before the fire, drowsy after the unaccustomed working with a backbreaker.

The whooping bellows of the siren of Bull Point and the gruff roar of the Hartland Monster come through the mist. A young moon is purple-yellow among the pale, untwinkling stars. Faintly, very faintly, the drone of the tide echoes from the bare trees of Windwhistle Spinney.

I shut the door against the night's cold breath.

A thump on the roof, the noise of claws getting a grip on ridge-tiles. A hollow quavering, bubbling cry, a squealing outside the walls. A tawny owl has got one of the rats. Good; the harmony of Nature.

HILL OF WINDS

THE lingering long grasses of summer, which the frosts and rains soon will dissolve, are flattened by the gusts which penetrate my clothes. They are old clothes; the tweed coat has patches on the arms, and only tags of brown cotton remain of the buttons. No petrol shall ever take from my raggedy trousers the ancient stains of candle and cooking-pot.

I am a happy oddmedodd, a scarecrow, as I kneel to plant my thorn and beech saplings. My boots feel thick and clumsy, but they are good boots, with beech-slab soles, bought in Wigan two years ago, during a break in that long day's motoring from Argyllshire to Devon.

These roots must be spread out: the longest root towards the south-west, whence come the Atlantic gales. Then with the hands scoop the earth over the roots, a slight shaking to settle it round the webs, and the earth pressed firmly down. That's done. How neat the double row looks! Beeches outside and thorns inside: the thorns will help to hold the brown beech leaves, and so to retain a future shield for the unmade garden behind the hedge.

It is pleasant to stand up and gaze around. The larger trees in the south-west corner by the hut are shaking violently in the wind. Their trunks, however, stand firm. Five and a half years ago they were planted — ash trees, oaks, birches, larches, beeches, and three varieties of firs, *pinus insignis*, *macracarpa* and *austriachus*. Only the firs have grown well. When knocked out of their pots five years ago they were eighteen inches high and as thick as one's finger; now they are taller than a man, and their trunks are six inches thick.

They were planted wrongly, too, being put into pits with their roots not only unspread, but balled, just as they left the pots. The winds vagged them about; the rats gnawed them for two years (we thought the rabbits were to blame); the gales rubbed their trunks against the stakes, and many broke off. They were planted in April, in drought; the following winter was one of ice and snow and blizzard, when I ski-ied for days through drifts which in places covered the hedges growing on top of the earthen banks. The next autumn came the Great Gale, when thousands of elms and other trees were thrown throughout England.

The continual wind-threshing turned smooth holes in the earth around their trunks, and we tried wire stays, pegged to the ground. The wire snapped. We tried heavier, five-ply wire. The trees grew, and soon the wire was embedded in the thickening trunks. Some snapped off. So we shed the wire and let the trees fend for themselves. They should grow flat, if so they wished.

It was said that such trees, if topped, would die; they would die any way, so I topped them. And there they are to-day, thick and green and massy, consolidating themselves under the wind, and very soon the western windows of the hut will be obscured from the carter's gaze as he goes down the red ironstone lane.

The beeches and ash trees and larches hung back for four years, then I began to remove the turf around their trunks. Some I watered in the hot weather, and lo! very soon long, twisty branches with tender green leaves were feeling for the sun in the sky. Last spring a blackcap warbler actually built in one of them. One felt then that something had been achieved.

This hilltop field is protected from the northerly winds by the beech spinney of Windwhistle Cross. Water runs under the field. There is a well sunk by hand fifty-two feet down into the rock. To the south one sees, on a clear day, the blue tors of Dartmoor, forty miles away as the falcon glides. Eastward lie the smoother, greyer slopes of Exmoor. The lighthouse at Hartland Point flickers across twenty miles of sea. The lights of Instow, Westward Ho! and Appledore lie down in the blackness of night like embers glittering in the wind.

Sometimes I see the Lundy falcons sweeping overhead, travelling down wind at a hundred miles an hour; and as the sun declines with one of our marvellous great Atlantic sunsets, I see the white owl come fanning over the hedge, to drift in wavy flight over the mice runs in the grass; sometimes to hover, beating hollow wings in complete silence near my still form.

Does he know me? See; he perches on the mountain ash, four yards away. What a curious dark stare he has. Like a ghost he passes on: the ploughboy goes down the lane on his bicycle, whistling, to his supper: I collect mattock and shovel, and go to my hut, opening the door to its flamy cheer, and the sighing contentment of a kettle steaming in the open fireplace.

A NIGHT ON SALISBURY PLAIN

UNSEEN peewits were crying their wild cries in the mist somewhere. The sounds were part of the grey silence of the Plain. I could hear the last of the hot oil dripping into the engine sump, from the overhead camshaft gear. Ten yards away the long low length of the black car was part-dissolved. Mist was condensing on my eyelashes.

It was a late November afternoon. The last twenty miles had taken me two hours and a quarter. Foolishly I had relied on my petrol gauge, although known to be faulty; and now I was on my reserve tank, enough for sixteen miles in ordinary travelling, but only one-half or a third of that distance on second or third gear. I must wait until the fog lifted.

By the ruins of brickwork and concrete overgrown by grasses I recognized my whereabouts: Stonehenge was very near. This place had been an encampment for airmen and their craft during the War. Afterwards there had been what is called an agitation in the Press for the removal of the buildings. They were demolished; and once again the great circle of Stonehenge was seen from the road in outline against the northern sky, relict from the age of mammoths, sabre-toothed tigers, and skin-clad men of small stature, short age, inferior teeth, and ideas of salvation through the blood sacrifice of men other than themselves.

Stonehenge was seen clearly again, but no longer in solitude: for the hutments and hangars were broken down at the time when motor cars were beginning to increase almost in geometrical progression. A barb-wire fence was erected with a tea-house, and approach to the Sun Temple cost each visitor one shilling.

It was no use going on: the night must be spent here. Fortunately I was wearing my black leather flying coat, and there was a rug in the car. It was pleasant to sit down, to suspend oneself in the silence of the Great Plain. Here had come Hardy, and Jefferies, and Hudson, and Edward Thomas who had been killed only a few hundred yards from me at the battle of Arras sixteen and a half years before.

The mist drifted by me. I was alone. But was I alone? The place was thick with occult life. I shivered, and felt my eyes starting with tears; and I remained still, waiting, like The Traveller in Walter de la Mare's poem, which was read to Hardy as he lay dying.

What was Stonehenge? Men asked one another, How came it to be built here; and, Whence these mighty slabs of stone, weighing hundreds of tons; and, Why were they set thus and thus?

Likewise, when the sunshine and starlight of centuries have rolled away from this age and civilization, which may indeed become traceless like other civilizations save for things such as bones, shards, fragments of walling, aluminium pistons and phosphor-bronze carburettor floats, men may wonder on the scars in the chalk of Salisbury Plain which were practice trenches for firing, bombing, and bayonet-fighting; on the curious traces in the distant downs of designs which probably had some religious significance, possibly connected with the then-universally sanctified idea or ideal of blood-sacrifice, called War.

Night shut down through the greyness, and the peewits ceased to call. My footfalls among the flattened
heaps of broken bricks and iron and rotting wood seemed
strange and unreal to me. I felt myself to be another
person. I determined to prolong the strange feeling of
being strangely alone in a silent world. I collected
fragments of deal wood which had been doorposts,
lintels, and window frames, and made a fire. My car was
off the main road, and I could sleep under its tonneau
cover when so I wished. There was food and a vacuum
flask of hot coffee. There was enough wood for the fires
of a bivouacking battalion. I pretended that this was a
shattered village on the Somme, so quiet when the
Germans retreated to their Siegfried Stellung sixteen
and a half years ago.

Flames speared the mist, which gave way before the
bright thrusts. I ate, drank, took strength and comfort
from the fire. A mouse ran over the cracked concrete
whereon I sat. It took a crumb, fled away, returned for
more, fled away, came back, sat upright, stared at me,
and then crouched to a more serious feeding. It looked
to be a very old mouse, and I wondered if it could
possibly have known the time when the soldiers were
here. No; but it was strange how it accepted me and the
fire.

All over England were memorials to men who had not
come home from the War, most of them made to the
ideas of elderly non-combatants. Will the anti-
quarians of the future deduce from these memorials, with
their chaste and sometimes angelic figures holding aloft
righteous swords, torches, lamps, etc., that what to
soldiers of the line was generally tedium was to the
memorial-builders generally Te Deum? That the

memorials had no relation, even symbolically, to reality? That they helped by the fostering of illusion to perpetuate things as they were?

The mouse departed with a swelled belly, probably to sleep in its slightly mouldy bed of gnawn grasses under a pile of bricks somewhere. I threw more wood on the fire.

What of those designs, their regimental badges, cut by soldiers in the swarded slopes of the downs near Shaftesbury? Have the grasses, the trefoils, the cinque-foils, and other wild flowers — dove's-foot, crane's-bill, harebell — have they crept over the chalk again?

The White Horse, its origin lost beyond memory, is still the White Horse, for all to see and meditate: but where are the badges of those Australians, Londoners, County men, and the keen youths from the North? Of those youths who went from the rolling chalklands of the Great Plain to the rolling chalklands of the Somme, after cutting their own memorials in the hill-side under the English sunshine of 1915 and early 1916 — such things could only be done before idealism was shattered by reality, before July the first, 1916, when the New Army found its grave in Picardy — of those singing, cheering, single-minded civilian-soldiers, how many returned? None. Not one of the returning survivors was the same man. What would the future antiquarian see then as their true memorial, I wondered to myself, lying on my back, wrapped in the leather flying coat and strangely serene to feel the ancient grey earth beneath me: which would the unborn antiquarian accept, the idealistic interpretation of those who stayed at home and imagined vain things, or these old scars and cuts and brick-heaps in the chalk?

I lay there, between dozing and waking, until the sun

peered red just above the road winding over the eastern plain. The fog was gone, the plover were calling one to another forlornly, and a laden milk van was rolling along towards London. It was very cold. As I walked away there was a small shrill screeching, and a weasel bounded over the rubble, a large mouse in its jaws.

STILL THE DROUGHT

It is very strange that the river is so low. For more than a year there has been no real spate. In October we thought the springs had been filled on Exmoor by the Atlantic rains, and the river would keep its new level; but it was a false rising, and after a few days the water was down again almost to summer level.

No runs of sea-trout have appeared since last January. The river here is about a dozen wandering water-miles from the tide-head.

During the summer the water was below what is known as summer level. But in autumn, after the equinox, we said, the rains will come and the fish will run up. In October some rain fell, but it did little more than make the springs break.

Nearly all the salmon and sea-trout coming in from the Atlantic during the spring and summer and autumn of 1933 were taken in one or other of the nets in the estuary. Each net had meshes of two inch squares, the legal dimension. Only the smallest peal or sea-trout, half a pound and under, could escape the nets.

Boats shooting a draft were not permitted (a bye-law) to linger in the water; they were supposed to drop their nets in a semi-circle as they rowed from one point of the shore or gravel bank to another point up or down the tide-line. The two ends of the net were then drawn together, in watchful hope of silver forms eventually thrashing in the seine or purse of the net.

There was a weekly close-time, between noon Saturday and noon Monday, in order to give some fish the chance to ascend to the fresh water of rivers Torridge and Taw. There, on the many beats — of a total market value of several hundred thousand pounds — hundreds of fly fishermen were waiting almost fanatically for those fish.

But little or no rain fell. Salmon came in from their far feeding grounds on the unknown rocky shelves of the deep Atlantic, to return to the rivers of their birth; and finding no pressure of fresh water beyond the tide-head, they dropped back with the ebb, to come again with the next flowing tide.

Day after day, week after week, in darkness, sunlight, and by the moon's opalescent glimmer, every twelve hours they moved up and returned — very few escaped those nets sweeping the narrow waters eight hours out of every twenty-four.

Seals and porpoises followed fresh schools into the estuary, and the netsmen cursed, for they scared fish over the bar to the open sea again; but instinct drove the fish back — to the thirty-six licensed nets and many other unlicensed ones.

So when the rain came in October there were very few fish in the lower reaches of the rivers to ascend to the higher pools and runs. I saw none jumping the falls above the Peal Stone, where a year before, when there was good running water, I counted over a hundred salmon and sea-trout jumping in less than an hour and a half. 'Thousands must have rinned upalong,' said the farmer.

Now, just before Christmas, the river is almost at low summer level again. Many schools of fish have come in from the Atlantic, but few if any have passed beyond the first weirs. Contemptuous of the Conservancy Laws made for the protection of salmon in the spawning season, and therefore of their own livelihood, the netsmen fish by night during the close season almost as regularly as during the spring and summer months.

Fresh salmon is being sold now at many of the houses of Instow, Westward Ho!, Bideford, and Barnstaple, for fourpence a pound, and even less. The price in the official season, when the fish are exposed for sale on the white marble slabs of shops, varies between four shillings and two shillings a pound.

The drought continued for twelve months after this was written: two years, with scarce occasional showers.

MORNING TIDE

BLOCKS of ice are riding up and down with the tide in the estuary, and at low water the sand-banks are covered with a brittle white crust. North-east wind whips the water, and the farm-hand returning across the saltings after looking at his sheep goes bent-kneed, collar up, head down, sack on shoulders, hands in pockets. Curled breast feathers of gulls are lightly fixed on the glazing mud, whence the sea ebbed two hours ago.

Over Exmoor the sky has a curious grey-pallid expectancy, as though awaiting the visitation of some lunar icicle spirit to release its snow upon the earth. A chevron far away to the south, over the Santon Burrows, descends and assumes the shape of two eyebrows; the white-fronted geese have come down before the ice-blasts. A snowy owl has been seen quartering the marsh in daylight; perhaps a Greenland falcon may appear, stooping on duck or goose from its mile-high pitch, with the noise of the wind in its wings, barb-shut, audible half a mile away. The local taxidermist may have it on show in his window a few weeks afterwards: this was the fate of the white bird which slipped effortlessly along its two thousand mile journey to the estuary during the severe winter of 1927.

Yesterday four porpoises came up with the flood tide, pursuing a school of salmon, playing as they drove through the stream of the tide where the long string of dirty foam was beaten up by the press of currents in mid-channel. Occasionally one would curve out of the water, to fall back again bottle-head first, leaving a boil where it disappeared. Only one salmon leapt before the drive: a fish four feet long, of the type known locally as green-back. Sometimes these fish are found dead or dying in the tide-eddies, each with a bite taken near the vent. The porpoise, called herring hog, or more usually errinog, by local fishermen, tears away his bite, and chops after another fish.

Porpoises are not fish, but mammals. Their young are born in the sea, instinctively clinging to their mothers, who suckle them on milk. They are warm-blooded, and have hair under their sea-coats of blubber and hide. Their flippers or fins have decadent claws, suggesting that once these animals ran on land, like the seals, which are half-way between otters and porpoises in their adaptation to a life in water. Once a literary critic of Byron derided Byron's phrase about day dying like a dolphin — but wait until the end of this chapter.

The porpoises, probably two pairs, turned west again with the change of tide, and rolled their merry way down the fairway towards the bar and the open Atlantic. They bobbed and rolled, their feeding done; for all mammals, except some of the higher, wearier, unexercised species, restore themselves by regular play (of which the act of love is not a part).

These four errinogs had been observed when they came in with the tide; and some of the higher, but not wearier, because exercised, mammals were waiting for their return in the fishing village.

The tide was lapsing fast, it was almost the time of new moon, when the springs ran up to their limit in the arms of the land. Over the fairway buoys, leaning westwards, the water broke. Wind gave another half-knot to the rate of recession. At five knots the water pushed itself into the Atlantic again. The black and miniature whales blew sprays from their spiracles; they turned and swam on their backs, sometimes one would leap out of the water and fall back again with a smack to knock off its parasites. They travelled so swiftly that an irregular trail of foam was left behind them for half a mile.

Below Appledore Pool a boat put out. Two men rowed strongly. The porpoises sported towards the boat. Their eyes were scarcely larger than the eyes of moles (which are no more than pin-points). A third man in the bows of the salmon boat raised a gun, took aim, and fired. One of the porpoises appeared to twist backwards as it came out of the water. The other three dived deep, reappearing nearly two hundred yards away for the least respiration. It was yet morning; but the hues of a dull sunset were on the water near the boat.

THE RIVER FREEZES

In prolonged hard weather the freezing of a rapid stream is more than gradual; it occurs after several distinct changes. A writer of extraordinary imaginativeness like H. A. Manhood could make an imaginatively vivid word-picture of such a freezing: but the intensive sight of the mind's creative inner eye would not satisfy unless projected in parallel with what the physical sight has absorbed.

To any young genius who needs authentic material for a severe winter scene in his novel, I, an old market hack, offer gladly the following facts:

At the beginning of an ice period any stone or stick or root or fern which is sprayed or wetted near a fall or other obstruction slowly becomes coated with ice. Brambles which have pushed through the alders to find rootage for their young green tips, and have found instead the surface of the stream, become clubbed with ice. This ice, as in the case of ferns and roots, is made of innumerable layers of thin water. The club of ice on the bramble becomes slowly heavier, the bramble draws backward and forward less quickly from its spring of alder branches, until the ice extends it diagonally downstream. Water piles up against the moored ice-bottle, which loses its slender neck and becomes as though thickened by an inexperienced glass-blower. All living things feel some sort of pain; and if the weight of ice does not tear the bramble from its bush, or a thaw release it from torture, next spring it will hang there red and coarse, unbudding, until finally it withers and dies.

The frost holds. Brittle plates of ice form over still water by the sides of runs and eddies. Icicles, still called cockabells by some Devon children, hang under the falls where before water trickled very slowly. These seal the trickling places; and water trickles elsewhere, making newer cockabells. Rocks and obstacles lipped by water thicken with ice, and gradually the river level is raised. Pieces of ice break away and are carried down to the next eddy, where they lodge or ride slowly until welded into the local ice, strengthening it.

The slow solidification of eddies and still stretches by the shallows cause the runs to move faster, creating thereby other reactions or eddies or water-resistance; moving water is governed or has its existence by the same laws which govern all the movement called life. Life is action, movement, progress as well as reaction, resistance, conservance; but action, movement, progress alone are of the Spirit which giveth life, as the biblical poet perceived.

The plates of ice holding frost strive to convert running water, which lags thereby and weakens in its purpose for life. Grasses and rushes help to hold the ice. Towards midday the sun in a clear sky subdues the arrogance of rime, melting first the hoof-marks of cattle and deer which wander along the banks. Above the fall the water raised by the dam of ice suddenly presses a way through. Dead leaves churn with sand in the pool below. Soon the warning sound runs down with the fuller stream: the ice cracks and whimpers, some breaking away to ride down tilting and heaving. The shadowed piers of the bridge below hold the floes, while frost instantly begins to work on them, sealing them to the stonework.

Soon the sun is behind the trees, the grass droops again

as the rime settles. The weir is seen to be thicker with ice. Thin layers of water run over that ice, thickening it. If there are salmon in the pool they are scarcely stirred by the greater flow; the cold numbs them, quelling their fever to ascend for spawning.

It is very cold by the river, and now one sees passing in the water clots of semi-opaque, jelly-like substance, slightly resembling the jelly of frogs' eggs without the dark specks which are the eggs. It is like a colourless algae; but no algae grows in cold weather. The stream is filled with the slush. It is slush! Evangelical ice has conquered: the water is slowly being converted, slowly losing its joy of life, its natural brightness. The slush moves slower than the water, impeding it, striving to become static against every stone or snag, clinging to the plates of ice, which welcome it; and the running water diminishes.

At night the Dogstar is green above the south-eastern horizon: water-sounds are dulled, except where the falls roar. A mist moves over the water, becoming denser and pressing nearer the surface towards midnight. The mist of slush drags slower in the faint-hearted stream: the mist of ice-blink drags at it from the still air: only the falls roar with lessing power: and then, in one moment, the splayed glittering of the Dogstar on the water is gone. Ice lies from bank to bank.

FLIGHTING

NORTH-EAST wind has cleared the sky, which at twilight is hard and pale green, with a planet shining very clear, without rays, low in the south-west. Tide ebbed from Skern some hours since. The channels wander deep, with small runnels below their banks, glimmering with pale sky. Wildfowlers come down at this hour.

Last week the icy shear of winds made widgeon and mallard come to their feeding grounds flying low. It was good weather for sportsmen. Duck came in from the sea, where they had been resting all day, circled high round Skern Mud, and then glided down against the wind to their favourite channel. Against the pale after-hues of sunset they were seen distinct and dark. Many fell. Reports echoed flatly over the mud. Faint distressful quacking of a winged bird, the heavy pattering of a dog following; the curt commands to another dog to keep to heel.

Gulls arose from their far feeding, and crying as though with weary pain of life, flew around raggedly, so different from their calm formation flight when they had returned from the inland fields as the sun was sinking. Then each bird flew tranquilly in place, one slightly behind and above the other to avoid the turbulence of air, and all making a V whose apex was an old male gull whom they followed because he was more experienced.

Far away down the estuary sandbanks and gravel ridges curlew and redshank flew up: golden plover sped over the water with flights of dotterel and oystercatchers. Their sweet piping cries died faint in the distance. Silence settled over the bight again, except for the trickling of the runnels and the sip-sapping noises of ragworm and cockle stirring at the end of their blow-holes, where in the harder sandy layer of black leaves and ancient sea-charred turf they lived out their obscure life-spans.

A heron flapped over, throwing up his wings as he spied a gunner below: he flopped into the mud as the secondary echoes were diminishing against the distant sandhills. He was not dead, but wounded in one wing. He struggled to his feet, and began to walk away, uttering one croak of dismay. The fowler, a young boy home from school, ran after him, slipping in the mud and sitting down in the water. A dog started in pursuit. The heron screamed harshly while continuing its grave and stilted walk over the mud. It trailed a wing.

'I thought it was a goose,' cried the boy, ashamed of his mistake.

'Don't shoot low,' exclaimed the warning voice of his father. 'And look out for your eyes.'

'Shall I leave it?'

'No, you young fool. Mark over!'

Three widgeon swept over downwind, the shot whistled after them, and they disappeared into the dimmit-light.

'I can't find the heron.'

'You must find it! You can't leave a wounded bird! Why the devil do you want to shoot at a heron? It's unmistakable.'

'Well, I thought it was a goose,' replied the voice, near to tears.

'All right, I'll come and help you find it. Look out for your eyes, a winged heron's a damned dangerous thing.'

Footsteps suck and glidder in the mud, with muttered swearing.

Other shots from the western end of the bight, half a mile away: dull reports sheared by the wind. The lighthouse across the estuary blinked and swung round its yellow beam. Boys on the burrows started a fire among the marram grasses: flames ran low and swift before the wind. Dark shapes of salmon boats went down silently on the ebb to the sandbanks by the estuary mouth. Water-bailiffs might be about, but the fishermen did not care. So they had fished a thousand years before Conservancy bye-laws were made.

Darkness shut down over the mudflats. Gulls veered overhead uneasily, scarcely seen now that the lighthouse beam was brightening with the night. Somewhere in the gullet of the stream which meandered through the mud a heron was crouching, listening and peering for its enemies, condemned, perhaps, to slow starvation, dereliction, and death.

THE YULE LOG

SINCE Michaelmas the Yule log has been propped against the walling of the hump-backed bridge over the river, which runs less than a hundred yards away from my cottage door. A small spate brought the log down one day, and the boys and I hauled it out with a lasso. It weighs about one and a half hundredweight, and is of yew.

Many times have I wondered if it were not too good for burning: if that salmon-pink wood, stronger than oak, should not be reserved for table-legs.

A crack running by a twist in the stick finally decided me. There stands the Yule log, which we shall drag into the sitting-room the day after to-morrow – Christmas Eve.

The small children are excited, and have been rehearsing in make-believe for days. Only this morning Charlie the black cat ate three-year-old Margaret's yoolug — a piece of bacon rind on a string.

It is difficult to remember all the Christmastides of the past few years — there was a happy one up in Rhode Island, when in the daytime we skated on the lakes where herrings had spawned and went to a dance at Fall River at night — another with the Navvies' Battalion in Halton Park, Buckinghamshire, when the P.M.C., a major recently a sergeant-major, and a proper old buck navvy before the war, gave the Officers' Mess roast beef, saying it was good enough for anyone, and turkeys were only for fops; and he made his subalterns eat the fat,

K

too, also he knocked down defaulting privates in the guard room, but that was long ago — and yes, there was the flat and lifeless Christmas after the Armistice, when colour and movement had gone from the only world we knew.

Best of all was the strange and beautiful Christmas of 1914, when we made friends with the Saxons of the 133rd Regiment opposite us under Messines Hill; when in the frosty moonlight of Christmas Eve we strolled about in No-man's-land, talking and listening to the carols sung in German, only forty yards away and later watching with indescribable feelings the candle-lit Christmas tree they planted on their parapet. And the great white star rising from the east, over their lines, which some of us thought must be a light on a pole, it was so bright!

That time had a dream-quality for my eighteen-year-old self. Many of us, German and English, longed, and even prayed voicelessly, that its good will and kindness should extend and deepen, until no war spirit remained. Alas! it was not realizable — then.

Why should not this Christmas be the best one has known?

The children are beginning to be human beings, with their own personalities, and therefore as companions they are stimulating. Also, we are looking forward as eagerly to our guests' coming as, we hope, they are eagerly anticipating their arrival. It has been fun arranging the bedrooms, and finding odd corners for camp beds.

And the walks we shall have, whatever the weather, on the high ground of Exmoor and in the lanes, with their tall beechen hedges! The blazing of wood fires on open hearths shall greet us when we return, pleasantly tired, to sip tea made from the black iron kettle hanging on its lapping crook from the chimney bar.

I have got a spruce fir, with all its roots; it is set in an oak tub, for later planting-out in the hilltop field. The sapling shall not be murdered; it shall, after Christmas, join the company of its brethren below Windwhistle Spinney. Late on Christmas Eve, when the children are lying excitedly awake upstairs, or breathing sweetly in sleep, we and our friends will deck its branches with shimmering delights. Then into the cupboard under the stairs, until the afternoon party!

Of course everyone will hang out a stocking. And of course Father Christmas will fill each stocking, and everyone will sit at the long refectory table for breakfast. On one side the children, graded according to size, from the gipsy-dark Margaret to the speedwell-eyed Ann — on the other ourselves, the so-called adults, watching the happy faces over the table.

Afterwards a two-miles walk across park and fields to church. On the way we shall peer over the parapet of the bridge to see if any of the spawning salmon are visible.

And I shall show my friends the ant-hill beside the river where every travelling otter scratches and rolls, a small hillock very green in spring with the many fishbone fragments that nourish the root grasses.

Before the church service everyone greets everyone else in voices that are neither loud nor yet too subdued. Contrast is the salt of life; and, after the singing of the good old hymns, we shall return in an amazingly short time to see the turkey turning slowly on the jack-spit by the hearth. And what a fire! The wood for it has been selected and matured for several years. Pine for the resinous scents; oak for body; elm for its majestic white ash; alder for its charcoal — the flames of these woods will blend and be thrown out by the bulk of the yew-wood back-brand.

The twin rows of human cormorants will perch themselves along our table, I shall refuse to carve, corks will pop with bubble of grape and ginger; the lighted pudding, set with holly-sprigs, will come in, with the mince pies, to be eyed with lessening enthusiasm except by the rows of brighter faces. Who will want figs, dates, or nuts? Then for the crackers!

There will be ping-pong, skittles, bagatelle, lead-horse-racing, crown-and-anchor, and maybe (since Harold is of the party) the three-card trick. And those of us who have realized the poise and harmony between life and death will meet in my writing-room, to listen and to think as the voice of the King, symbol of our hopes for our brother men and neighbours, speaks around the earth.

Yes; this Christmas, I hope, will be proper. Windles, the eldest boy, has just come in to tell me he has seen Father Christmas's reindeer! They were going up the path to Bremridge Wood . . . or else they were the red deer from Exmoor, driven down by the hard weather. Which were they, Dad?

Quick, Windles, tell the others what you've seen! Christmas! Christmas!!

SEA AND THE WIND: NORTH DEVON

OUR coat collars were up against the north wind which cut across the estuary. We were walking on the edge of the dunes. Northwards across the half-mile of uneasy grey water the lighthouse stood small and white. Near it the brown ball was raised on its stalk; signal that the water was high enough for the passage of ketches, colliers, tugs, and other small coasting craft which used the ports of Bideford, Fremington, and Barnstaple.

Beyond the lighthouse and the burrows, beyond the sand dunes and marshy plains where ten thousand rabbits are trapped every winter, the hills showed dimly under the northern sky scarcely trailed by clouds.

In the mind one saw, beyond the indeterminate hills, the higher and incult ground of Exmoor, the Severn Sea wrinkled under wind cold from Welsh mountains: and beyond, to colder hills where white ptarmigan crouched from the stereoscopic gaze of white gerfalcon, where yellow fox-eyes stared as from snow for the limping by of Arctic hares: onwards and onwards, across ice-fields where the only movement was of sleet carving bergs glimmering in Polar twilight.

I thought of Heine's poem of the solitary pine tree in the snow which dreamed of a palm lonely in the burning deserts of the South.

We walked silently westwards along the curve of Greysands, passing the area of smooth boulders half-buried by the scouring of tides. Then the Atlantic breaking on the shoals known as the South Tail came into sight. Even the wind could not push back from our ears the roaring of the great seas.

A tramp steamer pushing full speed ahead into the narrow fairway by the bar-buoy seemed scarcely to move. Its bow pitched out of water; then it wallowed until all but the crown of its funnel was hidden beyond the upcrashing of waves.

But it was on the shoals of the South Tail that the sea was most grand. The blind force of the wind-harried sea was beautiful to watch from the shore, as the invisible sun diffused a pale pink hue to the surges.

Never before have I seen such a colouring, more delicate than the pink of apple blossom: the more lovely and life-giving, for that it was also in the face of one walking beside me.

THE GLORY OF THE GALE:
SOUTH DEVON

HERE the shingle bank faces the east. The south-west gales do not pile the water upon the shore in long rollers; the winds rush down from the hills, colder than when they come direct from the Atlantic.

It is strange to walk a zig-zag course on the shingle, coat buttoned to neck, cap pulled down over windward ear, eyes nearly closed, to the south-west gale while yet the sea is comparatively calm.

Only on a shallow coast do seas break white and afar.

The force of the wind made me stagger; and the sea was strangely calm. Gannets were fishing less than fifty yards from shore, where the water was three or four fathoms deep.

These birds, their wings spanning over five feet, swept up and down, falling and rising in gusts which wrinkled the sea below them. One saw a fish. It turned on its side, beat its wings twice or thrice, then crooked them back, and hurtled down.

The striking speed was greater than it looked; only the least splash was made; scarcely a splash, but a hiss of fine spray vanishing immediately. The birds stayed under for periods varying between one and three seconds.

When a gannet reappeared, bobbing up as though made of white celluloid tipped with black, it had already swallowed its fish.

The beak is massive, like a heron's beak, but heavier. While the heron lances its larger prey, or snicks out smaller fish with a scissor-like grip, the gannet drives a bony wedge through the big fish it has seen near the surface. Smaller fish it swallows under water.

A few weeks ago a Belgian steamer had been driven by an easterly gale on this shore; and before she could be refloated, her cargo of pressed scrap-iron was unladen. Not all of it was taken away after the ship had gone. A line of the stuff stretched for more than a mile to leeward of where it had been pitched. The scouring tides and the driving winds had scattered the shingle with rusty litter.

Over the hills a great cloud dark and hard as slate was mounting. It swiftly filled the sky. The hill line was dissolved in grey. How dark it was! I fastened all the buttons of my coat.

A sudden blue-green flash, a crack and diminutive roll of thunder, the sea changing colour as the gusts pressed it out of shape, wind singing in the jags and jumble of old iron.

It was a lovely feeling to walk on, cap pulled over two-thirds of face, while the singing of iron changed to a screaming, to a jangle as rain hissed down and the hurricane rolled and whirled scrap-iron into the sea.

My coat was one of those stout mackintosh hunt-coats that keep out even the swanshot-rains of Exmoor: let the rain beat it and slash it, I was warm and laughing, although my legs were soaked as though I had waded in the sea. The rain on my cap beat like gravel.

Turning my back I watched the storm harrying the sea. The water heaved and smoked in silence. Were those fiery balls of incandescent copper plunging into the sea, or was it green lightning: and why such small thunder? It was almost inaudible.

As though angry at its failure to discomfort me, the wind increased until even the cubes of iron weighing a hundredweight or more lurched up and trundled to the sea, wearily knowing their fate of dissolution.

The wind blew me over, whirled coat over head, and bundled me into the rasp of the backwash. It hurled scrap-iron at me. It smeared my face with wet ribbon weed. At last, I thought, the elements have become animate and playful.

A wave's icy touch fell down my neck. The sounds of the storm were pure Schönberg: the snoring suck of shingle, the jangle and chimmer of old iron, the crash of irregular, unrhythmic waves.

I loved it all. Then the sun was shining over the hills. It was glorious. So was the fire I sat by half an hour later, a cup of China tea by my side, and friends about me.

RAVENS

Edgar Allan Poe's raven, repeating *Nevermore*, was a symbol of the poet's own fateful foreknowledge; a perpetual feeling that was Shelley's also when he wrote that his thoughts, like hounds, pursued their father and their prey. But the subject is ravens; and a less abstract aspect of the word *nevermore*. For, walking round the north side of the headland, on the lowest sheep-path in the stunted furze, heather, and crippled elderberry bushes just above the cliff-edge, I put-off a female raven from her nest on a ledge on the cliff below. What seemed so strange was that the ravens continue to build on that very ledge year after year, although every spring, usually at the beginning of March, the nest is robbed of eggs.

Ravens are wise birds. They are also cunning and most cautious. Yet every January and February for the past fourteen seasons, which is the extent of my own personal observation, they have rebuilt their nest of elderberry sticks and bits of dead furze, and relined the hollow made by the female turning and pushing her breastbone against dry grasses and sheep's-wool. At the end of February the female lays the first of five small eggs; and a fortnight later they are taken by a man who drives a crowbar into the ground above, and lets himself down hand under hand while stepping backwards down the cliff face.

In what way are ravens cautious? Well, it is unusual to surprise the female on the nest as I did yesterday. The old cock bird spends most of his time, while she is sitting, hunched on the stone-and-earth wall by the topmost path above, at the edge of the oatfields. Usually a low croak of warning is given when he sees a human being approaching a mile away. He knows all about traps and gins, too. Watch him through a glass standing by while a buzzard breaks abroad a rabbit caught in one of the trapper's gins. Only when the buzzard has pulled about the carcase and dragged it from the trapping-site will the raven hop in and drive away the great screaming mottled-winged hawk. He will take the eyes, and then stand off again, letting the buzzard tear and swallow some of the flesh, before going in again and making a proper meal. Why does he wait for the hawk to be his taster? Does this raven, who may easily be more than a hundred years old, remember the days when less cautious ravens were destroyed by poisoned carcases of sheep?

HIGH PEAK CANAL

I

For days one had been walking on the tow-path without seeing a barge. There were few hoofmarks on the mud and grass. Across fields came the incessant noise of heavy motor traffic passing to and from Manchester, on the London road. The old waterway was deserted.

The water had an eastward flow that was scarcely perceptible. At first it appeared to be driven eastwards by the wind that for days had been driving the smoke of the Black Country across the dull green fields and leafless hedges of the winter countryside. A bitter wind it was, forcing back any extra hope of life or dream arising in bird and tree and wandering out-of-work: a wind that drove one into the nullity of self.

There were a few fish in the canal, but they were unseen, waiting for the sun to renew what water-life of weed, nymph-food, snail, and shrimp could endure the hot chemical pollution from the cotton mills.

I stood against a telegraph pole while a heron glided down on hollow wings, to pitch on the opposite bank a hundred yards away. He peered around before stalking, with grave pauses, to the canal side. He meditated awhile; then the head was raised again on the long plumed neck, and he stepped over yellow reeds and a weed-bed to the edge of his fishing water.

Wind made the least ripples on the surface. The ancient corpse of a dog, sunken and hairless, freed after months of underwater twilight from the weight tied to its neck by an indifferent master, its belly looking like a white rubber bladder fringed with green flannel-weed, moved in the flow at the rate of two yards a minute. No sight for the living; the thoughts it gave were worthless.

Soon the little warmth of walking was taken away by the wind.

Peering round the telegraph pole I watched this cautious North Country heron as it waited to reassure itself that nothing human was within a quarter of a mile. Its head was parallel to the water. At last it lowered its neck until the beak was pointing at an angle to the water and a few inches above it.

Before it had time to get any food its neck was raised again, the long, thin head held vertical with anxiety. Had it seen me? I waited for several minutes until it flew up and flapped away over the fields.

Behind, four hundred yards distant, a barge was slowly approaching. A lank black horse walked laboriously and with mincing gait on the tow-path, drawing an undulating rope attached to the barge. It was an experienced animal, saving itself weight and labour by keeping the rope clear of the water.

The barge was old, almost ruinous, carrying a cargo of small coal. It was long and narrow, canoe-shaped, steered by a hefty young woman with a scarf round her head. Children's voices came from the wooden house built in the stern. A rusty pipe issued smoke. The corpse of the dog swirled away in the mud eddy behind the rudder. The woman's gaze followed my line of sight. 'Lots like that in 'ere,' she said. 'We turn over all sorts — men, women, fish.' Slowly the barge diminished.

2

Here on the hill-top the wind is sharp and keen; down there the winter fields lie under the smoke drifting across from the Black Country. Factory chimneys pour their poison at the sky — the poison that is of the sun's power of olden time, transmuted into living leaf and branch and trunk, and now so woefully misused by men.

'Woefully misused?' asks another inner voice, 'it's time that pseudo-philosophical attitude about coal, machinery, and industrial civilization was abandoned. You drive a car, and enjoy its speed; you are of modern life, enjoying its conveniences — so why this attitude because smoke hangs over the factories where your car, and the other things you use and approve, are produced? Why not accept these things calmly, as inevitable and interesting phenomena of human, or, if you prefer it, cosmic activity? Why attitudinize yourself to part of the means whereby scissors, silk, ploughs, cotton thread, are made?'

The thought continued: 'I agree that what we saw down there by the allotments outside the town was deplorable; but everywhere in the world will be found irritable, frustrated men ill-treating small children. I agree that it is dreadful to hear a pale, weedy father swearing in that cold, obscene way before thrashing his pale, weedy little boy, who sobs with pain and despair, while you stand there, knowing too much to condemn or remonstrate with the wretched man.'

'Are the smoke, the mill, the polluted river, the cold sweating cobble stones, the morning bray of the factory blower, the life-slavery, alone responsible? I can show you men who have always lived here who are kind, jolly, and full of zest.'

I was standing by the millstone-grit quarries of Teg's Nose, a thousand feet above the fields, towns, and factory chimneys small and remote as though drowned under a ghostly sea. Down there the air was damp and still; up here the wind blew hard and steady, with a cutting-edge of glass. It scooped tears from my eyes. A solitary pipit fluttered into the wind, made no headway, and turning, was immediately thrown out of sight.

The sun sinking upon the iodine-brown smoke-scape was an imperfect shield against death, a shield forged in ill-shape by the crude efforts of Man, who has abused the ancient solar power in coal, wasting its virtue, poisoning its sky.

The sun in the smoke of industrial England was red and swollen, as though diseased: the source of life, like the water of the canal below, once fresh from the hill-springs, polluted by the so-called economic life of the world.

WOOD FIRES

I

'One stick can't burn
Two sticks won't burn
Three sticks may burn
Four sticks make a fire.'

THE old saying holds true to-day in most houses and
farmhouses where wood is burned; but only where wood
is not respected. A fire can be made of two sticks, if
the sticks are matured. Most of the fires on open
hearths I have seen in England have been merely an
inferior means for cooking and giving heat. Their
owners have no feeling for fire as a living spirit.

It is the same in all classes of dwelling house. One
expects to see small logs perched on top of coal in
the standardized grates of town and suburban houses,
but when one sees the same thing on the hearth of a man
whose house stands amidst great oak trees which are
young compared with the ancientness of his forebears in
that very place, it is time to write this overdue mono-
graph.

Wood stacks should be put down to mature like wine.
It is a wicked thing to burn fresh cut wood. Immature
wood hisses and bubbles and issues forth sappy steam; it
gives little heat; its embers have no body, no pleasant-
ness, and no glow. The flames sneak around the black
and wasted cores. The average wood fire in the West
Country is as poor and inefficient a thing as the hard

cider of the average farmhouse — pale yellow stuff, turned to vinegar, because it has been put into hogsheads which for years have been pickled and deadened in the bitter acids of small green apples.

One drinks a pint of this cider, and feels drunk; two pints, and one is apparently dead drunk. Beware of it, for the effects are not those of good wine, but of poisoning. You know how snakes and fish look in those bottles of alcohol, so ghastly and pallid? Good cider to be such should be 'racked off' at least twice — siphoned into fresh casks — and then bottled and kept as wine; it should be almost as exhilarating to drink as champagne.

The good fire likewise is made only with love and forethought. Every stick (even the thickest boughs are sticks in Devon) given to the slow but powerful flames should be laid with care. The good fire should burn noiselessly on the hearth, except for the least flutter of wan flammets and the little creakings of embers. Farmers will tell you that they burn green sticks because they last longest. This is not true, when the sticks are properly matured. The ordinary farmer has little foresight, beyond the idea of the rotation of crops.

The ashes of a hearth should remain on its slate or bricks or stones from autumn to spring. On a good hearth they will weigh after the season of fires perhaps more than a hundredweight. (Everywhere else but in England open hearths are built with sloping backs, thus ensuring good draught, heat thrown well out, economy of burning, absence of down-draught, and general contentment.)

On a decent hearth when the bed of ashes has grown to, say, three inches in depth, the embers will remain alive through the night: the fire will burn continuously for months. Sticks should never be rested or propped on the irons or fire-dogs. With matured wood — which burns twice and sometimes thrice as long as sappy wood — any propping up is unnecessary. The wood should consume itself almost with the gravity and surety of a good cigar.

2

On winter nights, when rain drives against thatch and window, and the wind's ghostly bombardment fills the chimney, there is ease in the contemplation of a wood fire; yet always one feels, deep under contentment's ease, a phantasm of anxiety, of insecurity, of unreality, of relief that one may recline at ease in the flamelight. Rain slants outside, the chair is snug, the elmwood settle turns the draught from the door, trees roar on the hillside, chimney holds faint thunder — so once the wind and the rain drove across the battlefields of Somme and Passchendaele.

The poignant misery of dawn begins to grow . . .
We only know war lasts, rain soaks, and clouds sag stormy.
Dawn massing in the East her melancholy army,
Attacks once more in ranks on shivering ranks of grey,
But nothing happens.

The young soldier poet, Wilfred Owen, has been dead these many years; the rain falls now, as it fell then.

Slowly our ghosts drag home: glimpsing the sunk fires glozed
With crusted dark-red jewels; crickets jingle there;
For hours the innocent mice rejoice: the house is theirs;

Shutters and doors all closed, on us the doors are closed —
    We turn back to our dying.

He was killed in the last week of the War, on the banks of
the Sambre Canal — and that was only a moment or
two ago.

Since we believe not otherwise can kind fires burn;
Nor ever sun smile true on child, or field, or fruit.
For God's invincible spring our love is made afraid;
Therefore, not loath, we lie out here; therefore were
   born,
    For love of God seems dying.

To-night, His frost will fasten on this mud and us,
Shrivelling many hands and puckering foreheads crisp.
The burying party, picks and shovels in their shaking
   grasp,
Pause over half-known faces. All their eyes are ice,
    But nothing happens.

Always there were wood fires flickering among the ruins
of the Somme villages. Acrid ammunition-box smoke
filled the German dugouts held by British troops,
wood-lined caves in the chalk wherein one could breathe
only by lying on the floor. Ah yes, and the charcoal
fires of Ploegsteert Wood in that autumn of 1914,
in miniature braziers made of Maconochie ration
tins perforated by bayonet jabs, and held by handles
of wire. How they glowed and sparkled as they were
swung round among the trees where pheasants still
roosted! The braziers could be held momentarily in
the cupped palms of one's hands . . . the balaclava
helmets, the bearded faces, the buttonless tunics,
myself, who had not yet shaved, talking in wonder with

these survivors of the Retreat from Mons, bullets cracking among the oak trees, Verey lights' pallor-shadows slanting on the mud, lost horizon. It is all outside the casement, in the wind and the rain.

It was a long time ago, and yet it was yesterday. Nothing has happened since. Perhaps something is beginning to happen now; and in future the rain will be but rain, without its wraith of dreadful greyness. Or is that wraith but waiting to drive again across the helmeted fields of Europe?

For love of God seems dying. Dreadful irony! The love of God, as interpreted by the Church in war-time, seems to imply or involve the death of youth, says the voice of the lost poet. The embers of the fire shift slightly: feathery ash stirs in the wind which now at midnight is crying its rue under the door.

How white and peak-like is the ash of elmwood: a hundredweight of elm sticks would fill the hearth with ash, equal to that of a ton of oaken logs.

One recalls the lovely gold ash of that pitch-pine wood brought from the wreck on Croyde Bay in 1921, when you — who now will live, when we are dead, as Julian Warbeck of *The Dream of Fair Women* and *The Pathway* — yes, old fellow, in those days you were translating Catullus, and I was writing those early Nature essays, Jefferies by my side always, so it seemed. How you used to mock and deride, coming home from the inns, God knows how many pints inside you to enable you to escape that world, called normal, which neither of us knew or cared about. Where are you now, haggard poet? With your bearskin flying coat, the scar on your cheek from the crash over Ervillers, when you were shot up from the ground by machine gun fire after you'd shot down that Fokker triplane, your first flamer. Was that part of the reason why you drank twenty and more pints every night in the village pub? Do you remember the poem you wrote on the coloured flames of sea-salts in the wood, likening them to the colours of the Richthofen Jagdstaffel? Why did you gnaw your nails whenever you saw those colours of copper, sodium, and iron? Or am I, sitting here while the wind drives against casement and chimney, confusing effect and cause? I just managed to get into the world of normal men and women: but you would never submit, I knew. When last I heard of you, you were on the Thames Embankment, still scornful and arrogant, with Swinburne by your side — you befriended only by the proud dead. You would not let the living be your friend, you know, old fellow.

Do you remember the ash-sticks we burned together, seeing how the charring logs cracked and became grey-barred like the breasts of goshawks?

And those pine cones we carried on sacks from Anneswell Wood, during the Coal Strike of 1921? Perhaps if I had been less self-absorbed I might have been for you the friend you desperately needed . . .

Someone came into the room a moment ago, saying, 'They said on the wireless that John Galsworthy is dead.'

One read his novels, night after night in the winter of 1918, alone in that grey asbestos cubicle of Shorncliffe Camp after mess dinner, feet on the table, cigar in mouth — Galsworthy and the first box of cigars. I was his perfect reader; he reproduced in me every shade and strain of feeling of himself when writing those books. That was when the first draft of *The Flax of Dream* was half-written: or was it called *The Policy of Reconstruction* in those days? One day, I said, we shall be friends; and ten years later we met; but we were never friends. He was kind to me, and patient; I was too egotistical, too self-absorbed, to give him anything. And that is another way of saying that I was selfish: or that the deep truths I was feeling within myself were not shared by him. He urged me to be an artist, to use my sensibility to write about things outside myself. I was a tedious monologuist, in those days talking like Maddison in *The Pathway;* not realizing then that he knew all I was saying before I said it. He was fatigued with and beyond the search for Truth; he was sad behind his quiet and imperturbable courtesy; industrious, faithful, probably without hope, and entirely charitable. He spoke softly, distinctly, he was conserving himself, he had suffered immensely in the past, he was conserving his integrity. I wanted to be his friend, but realized that friendship was based on the keeping of one's distance. Now he is dead — with Conrad, and Hudson, and Jefferies, and Hardy, and Edward Thomas, and Ewart, and Owen.

It is summer, although Orion glitters over the bare trees beyond the midnight window — it is summer, and my shoes are strung together, and I am walking on those wide sands of the Santon Burrows, passing the weed-hung wrecks of old wooden vessels sinking deep with the years — seeing the fishing boats in the bay while wavelets of high noon curl on the strand, translucent and seeming frail as the empty shells of razor-fish which break under the press of my feet — the distant white specks of the Westward Ho! houses quivering, insubstantial and darkly dissolving in the heat mirage — and in my ears I hear the hollow roar of waves breaking against the sand bars of the dreaded North and South Tails — summer, I suspended in the air and light of the vast sky — forever summer on the shore of the blessèd isle.

Yet Orion glitters hard and bright; beyond in the deer park a great tree crashed this night; the clock ticks towards one, the embers settle, and the gale rushes by the thatch with the last day of January. Summer, summer, the soundless footsteps on the grass . . . wasn't that the ending of Old Jolyon, sitting on the log in the wood, the thistle-seed motionless on his white moustache? And now you, too, J. G. When I saw you last at Bury, two months ago, you seemed away in thought, chill within yourself, wintry where before you were autumnal. 'I'm dreading the sea-journey to Sweden,' you said, in a very quiet voice, as we shook hands; and I knew then that my intuition when arriving not to congratulate you on the Nobel Award was right; for my thought was with Coleridge when he took the hand of Keats, There is death in that hand. Thistle-seeds roll luminously over the azure sea and sky to these summer sands of the Santon Burrows, borne on the lightest of westerly air currents: but from where? Labrador in the west is three thousand miles away.

The embers are grey, a mouse runs under the uneven beechwood floor, my son cries suddenly in his sleep. The wasted moon is rising. How fares it with thee now, brother? The wind raves towards Orion.

'THE SUN IN THE SANDS'

I

DAY ebbs from my writing-room, where for the past hour I have been musing on old times. A match to the candle, then to the driftwood in the open hearth. The soft light spreads, and explores the room. Looking above the chimney-piece, I see a hollow-cheeked face gazing down at me. The gaze is not personal: the hollow-cheeked man is looking far beyond. He is one of four soldiers standing at rest, during a march up to the line, on a winter afternoon. His tin hat is tilted; his hand grasping the rifle, wrapped around with a length of old puttee, is swelled, it may be with wet and the cold; his great-coat is mud-slabbed. Hollow-cheeked and wan-eyed, like one whose mental tissue has been worn, but not broken, in overmuch bombardment, the tall soldier stares beyond the lost horizon of life, where his thoughts are set. He is the sensitive type of citizen-soldier who bears the war on his shoulders, but who will do what he is told to the end; and who knows, without bitterness, but with a certain irony, that he is doomed.

Not the sort of picture that would be appraised for its patriotism during a war: but afterwards, when the spirit strays back into the past, and the still small voice arises in the ancient sunlight of the battlefields, what shall we say when we behold what we have done to our brother?

While I am wandering in reverie, there is a knock on

the door, a rattle of the loose handle, a voice asking, 'Be 'ee writing, dad? Can I come in vor tell 'ee gude night, dad?' It is my elder son, who speaks the broadest West Country dialect I ever heard.

The small white-pantalloon'd figure, road-grubbiness washed off his brown limbs, and smelling faintly of raisins and milk and puffed wheat, patters in on bare feet, and stands by my chair. One arm turns like an eccentric flywheel; breath puffs through his teeth. He is a steam-roller.

He becomes himself again, and sits still in my lap awhile. He glances around the room, lit by the sad small flame of the solitary candle, to find something interesting; his eyes rest on the face of the soldier in the Nevinson picture.

''At poor dead man, dad, what for him dead?'

Now whence did he get that idea? Perhaps from myself. What does he understand about life and death? He is only a steam-roller, after all.

Nevertheless, I am a perverse parent in the eyes of normal people, and often say things that cause slight eyebrow lifting among certain righteous folk — those, for instance, who deprecate the old English speech of my little boy (and yet will appraise the black oak Elizabethan linen-press, with its hand-cut wooden screw, in the parlour downstairs).

'Who killed 'at poor man, dad? What for did'n kill'n, dad?'

I do not turn his question aside, although I know he cannot realize what he is asking: nor do I reply that the soldier is not dead, but glorious. How easy to say even, 'The Germans killed him'. And if I were a German father, then, 'The English killed him'.

How easy to dismiss the question thus. Even so, I know the silent question will recur again; the hollow-cheeked face, symbol of old wrongs done to men by men, will still look beyond my room with its comforting hearth, beyond the lost horizon of life.

'Your father killed him, and your grandfather, and your great-grandfather, and many men a long way back. Because we all had scales on our eyes, I suppose. They were put on each man when he was a small boy; and on some the scales remained all their lives.'

'Why, dad?'

The question of this small boy, scarcely out of baby-hood, is accidental: I have asked it of myself many times before, when straying in that ancient sunlight of memory.

'Because our imaginations were not allowed to develop naturally.'

'Why were not imag-im . . . oh darn, I can't say it. You kill 'at poor dead man dad? And granfer too? Cordarn, Ah'll shute the two of you, when I'm a bigger man, Ah wull!' he declares, solemnly.

'Then it would be the same thing again,' I murmur to the fire. 'An eye for an eye, as someone once expressed it. But if when you are a bigger man, you see all the causes plainly, you wouldn't be able to shoot anyone. By "you", I mean all men in all countries, of course. I believe it is only a question of "seeing plain" — but the "plain" is hidden under such a lot of misinterpretation by sincere, but sightless, men.'

'I won't shute 'ee, dad!' he replies brightly, reacting to the tone of my voice. 'I'll give 'ee my tar-engine instead!'

The tar-engine, cherished vehicle of the moment, is a

custard tin painted black and mounted on two cotton reels. After staring sleepily at the yellow driftwood flames, he says:

'Dad, when I'm a bigger man, you'll be like that poor dead man, won't 'ee, dad? Then you'll be all the grass up at Ox's Park, won't 'ee?'

Heavens, how this child remembers! Last spring, planting out sapling beeches and ash-trees with my little boy on the hilltop field, I had told him that one day he would have to build a big fire of faggots and dry branches, and burn me at night, when my ashes would float away on the wind, and sink into the ground, and rise again as grass in the rain and the sunshine.

'And when I'm a bigger man, dad, you will be right up in the moon and the stars, won't you? With granfer, and that poor dead man, won't you, dad?'

Did I tell him that, too, in a moment when I believed it? (For I do not find it possible to lie to this child: and he does not lie to me. If ever he does, I shall have failed.)

'I don't know,' I confess.

'So don't I know, dad,' he confidently replies.

Thereafter our conversation becomes more truly two-sided, the subject being tar-engines, steam-rollers, trains, tenders, and cement-mixers; until the candle-flame suddenly bends with the opening door, and his mother has come to take him to bed.

While I am dreaming of my ultimate dissolution in the elements again, being all the grass up at Ox's Park, his mother returns, and sits down on the log box, in a contented, relaxed attitude that tells me that the baby sleeps, and that the little boy is happily in bed. Indeed, on opening the other door, which reveals the twilit garden, we can hear him singing to himself about a tar-engine.

'Does he say his prayers when he goes to bed?' I ask.

'He is so very young: do you think he would understand?' his mother counters, never quite sure of the trend of my remarks. She stares into the fire, thinking of the beauty of a child kneeling with its head in its mother's lap. Her eyes are gentle and child-like in the light of the sea-wood flames, and a slow smile begins on her lips. 'And prayer is a good thing, isn't it?'

'He was talking about "the poor dead man" to-night', I say, and although I know it is not good to be bitter, I add: 'All is well with mankind; once and for all time God has been appeased for the innumerable "sins" of a countless mankind by the torture and murder of His "Only Begotten" Son, nearly two thousand years ago in Palestine. Teach the child to believe that, and he will be saved — saved from thinking, saved from developing within himself the clarity of Jesus of Nazareth. Colossal stroke of irony: this primitive and barbarous idea of sacrificing Innocence to save Ignorance, exposed and discredited by Jesus, and then settling on his name after his death, making him its supreme example!'

'But surely prayer isn't a bad thing?' she gently says.

How can such simplicity be answered? For I know that feeling and aspiration towards better conditions for humanity, towards the freeing of human imagination into a fuller life, constitute prayer. How can a little child understand this? It is a man's function.

'Would you like him to be taught nothing about God,' says the mother of my little boy.

'Well, I know that I have had to unlearn all I had been taught about God as a child; as a boy at school memorizing, with desperate frowns and fingers plugged in ears, certain sections of the New Testament, for repetition in examinations; as a young soldier listening — as all of us untried soldiers did in the fervent early days of nineteen fourteen — to the Bishop who was our chaplain making a Holy War appeal.'

'It must have been very difficult in those days,' she murmurs.

'Well, perhaps the English Bishop compromised in his philosophy, as he compromised in his dress: he was wearing military uniform and rank-badges of a colonel, with a clerical collar. He had a charming smile, and was sincere and kind: but did he know what he was saying? Why, even after the war, he forbade his clergy to officiate at the marriage of divorced people — of even the so-called "innocent party". And why? Because once, long ago, when some mean little-minded clerico-lawyer had asked a catch-question about the Jewish Marriage Law, Jesus had replied, "Whom God hath joined, let no man put asunder" — a profound and simple truth, also a superbly witty and evasive answer, for no one can part those who are truly spiritually married. Whereas, two thousand years afterwards, the Bishop interprets it as 'Those who have undergone a Church service'.

'What do you think we should teach a child about God, then,' asks the young mother, after a pause.

How can this be answered in words? How may feeling be described by words?

There are the birds, the fields, the sparkle of running water, the stars over the hills, and the sunshine. Let these be the foundation in the child-mind, the rock-foundations of the house of Christ which every man must build for himself. The natural foundations. Then, in time, when he grows to manhood, he will understand what Jesus of Nazareth meant — Jesus, whose mind had grown on natural foundations — Jesus, who was a mighty genius, striving to make all men great-minded — Jesus, who was destroyed by the ungrown little minds. And whose Way of Life has been destroyed by the little ungrown minds in every sect and denomination ever since. In Germany, when, for example, the German Christian clergy preached in justification of the war: and the English clergy did likewise: and the clergy of Tsarist Russia did likewise. The English clergy were only doing the duty of their holy church, for the Thirty Seventh Article of the Church of England says, *It is lawful for Christian men, at the commandment of the magistrate, to wear weapons, and serve in the wars.*

But what are words, even of the Articles of the Church of England, to a mother's vision of a little child kneeling with its head on her lap?

I take from the bookshelf beside me William Blake's *Marriage of Heaven and Hell*, and I find this passage, reading it aloud:

> The Ancient Poets animated all sensible objects with Gods and Geniuses, calling them by the names and adorning them with the properties of woods, rivers, mountains, lakes, cities, nations, and whatever their enlarged and numerous senses could perceive.
> And particularly they studied the genius of each city and country, placing it under its mental deity.
> Till a system was formed, which some took advantage of and enslaved the vulgar by attempting to realize or abstract the mental deities from their objects; thus began Priesthood.

174

Choosing forms of worship from poetic tales. And at length they pronounced that the Gods had ordered such things.
Thus men forget that all deities reside in the human breast.

And because I hope that the most powerful or useful of the many human deities — the Khristos or Christ-feeling, which is not charity, but *clarity* — will arise in my children when they are grown, uncorrupted by any idolatrous teaching, I, their human father, will not stand between them and the light of the sun.

2

Across the autumn sky flew the last swallow, very fast in the wind from the Atlantic; it flew desperately fast, and after it flew a larger bird, with sharper wings and sharper flight. This bird was a hobby falcon. They passed so near to me that I could see the blue back and yellow cere and marvellous fierce eye of the little falcon, which followed every movement of the swallow, every turn and twist through the sapling trees in the south-west corner of the field until

the hobby seemed to dash above the swallow, only three feet above it, and then to stoop upon it from that little height faster than a man could strike with his hand; and missing the swallow, the hobby dashed above and cut down upon it again, and again, and yet again.

It was marvellous to watch. Three stoops and three points made in about one second of time. I heard the air triple-roughed by the friction of stiff feathers.

From each stoop and talon-snatch the smaller bird

shifted, then the hobby, which had lost distance by about a yard, set himself to fly down his quarry. In the south-eastern corner of the field the chase ended in a buffet, a check, a few feathers in the wind, a descent to the withering grasses.

As I ran over the field the hobby rose almost leisurely, its blue wings seeming longer than before; and with the swallow held in its yellow feet it glided over the hedge, looking in silhouette like a small racing seaplane with a single float.

Then it seemed there was a greater loneliness under the sky. Dully over the hill moved the grey clouds from the south-west.

Why had not the swallow flown south weeks before, with the others of his spirit? This bird was of the sun; his food declined with summer. He was weak; and he had fallen. Had he remained for the sake of the young of a late brood? Had he lost the instinct of migration, which was the way of life?

Down below, five miles to the south, I saw the rain filling the hollow over the estuary, a slow drifting greyness shutting out the villages of Appledore and Instow, and the hills beyond Bideford. I went back to my hut, and sat by the fire, and wondered where a man might go, what he might do, to break from the slow entombment of self which had been closing upon him for the past few years.

A writer has to take root in a place, or series of places, before he knows them; and when he knows them, and has forced himself to empty himself of his impressions in the arduous making of ten books about those places . . . if only one could follow the sun as a swallow!

Swallow flights lived in the present, not in surview

of the past, or in dreams of the future. I had exhausted this country, or it had exhausted me. I had stayed here too long. Faces, glances, words, thoughts — they had worn out one another. Yet this book must be written before departure; and I had come to this place to write it, weeks since; and nothing had been done about it. In my book I would recreate out of the past years this walk and that walk, faces, glances, words, thoughts; my book should be a book of sun and moon and friendship and sea and happiness; of those years before this country became static. I promised myself to finish the book by Christmas: it must be done, so that I might catch up with myself, and write farewell, and be free to follow the sun to Florida of my dreams, and California, there perhaps to assume a new spirit, a new life, of one who had shed the past's mortifications.

With this intention, I went to live in my field, with its wide and aerial views, when first the butterflies were beginning to hide away in winter sleep. The gales of the equinox roared through the beech-clump, stripping the green-rusty leaves; and there remained, while trees grew black, and November was nearly ended, and nothing written, except of plaint and repining; and then it was December, and Christmas was nearer and nearer, and one had come and gone from this hilltop again and again, to see salmon which had been nearly a year in the river dying lean and coloured as a mire of dead leaves, with yellow patches of fungus on frayed tails and fins and heads.

These fish, weakened by spawning and the months in fresh water without food, were lying in the eddies, sometimes in water ice-fringed a few inches deep beside the bank, their tail-tips and back-fins in the air. I touched and even lifted some out of the water before the life came back to them from their farawayness of the spirit. Others were dead in the frost, or struck by beaks of herons which had killed for the lust of killing. That was something to see, to quicken one with interest, although it was a sad thing; and the New Year came, another year so swiftly and bewilderingly gone, and the sick kelts were dead and many of the silver spring-running fish snatched out by poachers' gaffs, and in the frosty weather not even a fingerling trout was to be seen from the bridge. To-morrow, one would go for a long walk — yes to-morrow — and to-morrow the book should be begun. One knew in advance what the critics would say about it; no matter, it should be begun, continued, and ended. Other work too — health and happiness lies in the balanced employment of mind and body. There was that three-legged cricket table to be made, from yew-wood thrown in the deer park eight years before, and now seasoned and of a lovely salmon pinkness and smooth hard grain; oak sticks for the hearths to be sawn; the floor which was dry-rotten in parts to be repaired. And walks, too, on Exmoor. Walks? One knew every tree, stone, lane, bird . . . so one saw nothing. To-morrow the book must be begun, at 9.30 a.m., and in the afternoon a return should be made to the carpenter's bench neglected for months and months.

To-morrow, and to-morrow, and to-morrow.

Years ago, a youth came to Devon who used to go for walks every afternoon — no, that is not quite true: when first he came to Devon he walked all the morning, all the afternoon, all the evening, and most of the night. He walked with an eager purpose, in search of wild birds — hawks, finches, cuckoos, pipits, owls — or rather the nests they made or used — and in particular the eggs that might be in those nests — not to take them, so much as to find them.

In youth the earth was not round or circumscribed; the earth extended for ever and for ever, mysterious, marvellous, enthralling. That was ended abruptly in August, 1914.

The war also ended abruptly. After a further period of disintegration, he returned to these fields and lanes. He walked at sunrise and sunset, in moonlight and the clear darkness of stars. After awhile he went farther afield, using a motor-cycle to get there and leaving it in the hedge all day — usually returning home without lights from some village inn on the moor or by the sea. One evening the police sergeant at Woolacombe said, in effect, 'I shall have to summon you if you continue to leave here night after night without lights. I know you are probably the only vehicle on the roads hereabouts at night, but the law forbids lightless travelling.' An acetylene lamp was bought, and the travels continued awheel and on foot.

It may have been the wheel, or what it symbolized, that caused the earth to become round, to be circumscribed by what a man made for himself of it; a place in which a companion was needed. The search was no longer for falcons or finches or owls, but for her who would care equally for these wild things and their wild places; and who would love and cherish and be of one flesh equally. One day it seemed that the search, hitherto so despairful, was over. Since boyhood he had known what Blake, writing one hundred and thirty years before, had known.

Never seek to tell thy love
Love that never told can be;
For the gentle wind does move
Silently, invisibly.

I told my love, I told my love,
I told her all my heart,
Trembling, cold, in ghastly fears —
Ah, she doth depart.

Soon as she was gone from me
A traveller came by
Silently, invisibly —
O, was no deny.

The two wheels of the motor-cycle sufficed for some happy months to transport the new companion, who was to share the earth, the new earth which her appearance had indicated.

The two old wheels became three new wheels; and after certain work and lapse of months wherein three wheels became insufficient for the transport of spaniel dog, wife, and infant son, it so happened that the wild birds and animals observed in the fervours of boyhood and youth were as good fairies bringing a fourth wheel to our household.

In other words, *Tarka the Otter* was awarded the Hawthornden Prize for 1928, and shortly afterwards a second-hand six h.p. Peugeot motor car was purchased.

A year later the four French-made wheels were exchanged for slightly bigger wheels of British workmanship; and after another year they were superseded by wheels considerably larger and better. These good wheels turned at a great rate; and that land which immediately after the war had seemed as remote almost as the coral islands of the Pacific became a little place which could be traversed from east to west in less than an hour.

The birds were still there, in their bright places; although some of these bright places had become even brighter with pink roofs. The birds were still there, except those which were flattened on the roads being made wider and wider for the succession of ever swifter wheels.

As for the particular four wheels, they carried the companion of birds and wild places and her offspring on occasions that became fewer and fewer. The offspring were beginning to explore the world for themselves. And while they were charming and well-beloved, yet somehow a low-swept sports car packed with children and spades and pails and bottles of milk and baskets of food was an improper, even an irritating, sight. Surely this was mere selfishness: so come on, everybody! Oh look, sea-sands, sea-sands! piped little John in excitement, as with bright eyes he glimpsed the sandbanks of the river just before coming into the town. One was glad the children were there. 'The children are all my life,' said their mother. Yes, of course, so it should be: and oneself being no companion . . .

the mornings went by, the afternoon passed, evening fell unseen, the stars at night were just a sign that one need not put up the hood when leaving this movie-show or that drinking party at the club. To be sure, the wheat taken into the granary of the mind was not yet gone, although sometimes it seemed that a famine was imminent. The brain tried to still the inner voice by declaring, Must a man like forever the same things? Must his interests be fixed? You who were once stimulated by the watching of birds are now absorbed in the watching of running water and of trout in glides and eddies, and in wondering whether the sea-trout have run up yet, and if the roots of the water buttercup, brought from the Avon at Salisbury, will withstand the floods of this gravelly stream which hurries fast and noisy from the hills of Exmoor.

Even so, the passing of the old expeditions was lamentable; even the few walks were long since abandoned. There was nothing to do. Neither were there any games. One had forgotten what it was to bestride a horse, to hit a ball. Occasional short walks were merely animated mental problems. The boat in the estuary lay at its moorings with green weed streaming on its keel for a hundred tides without a crew.

The Gold Falcon was written with its Old Testament theme of the search for God in a modern setting, an entirely objective and deliberated work, as was *Hamlet, Jude the Obscure*, and *Lady Chatterley's Lover*: the falcon was honour, or the soul, or God, awaiting and finally claiming the pilgrim whose life was search, however vain and wayward, for integrity or truth. Because of its theme, the book must be anonymous; but most critics declared in effect that the anonymity was decided by mental fear, and dismissed it as merely scandalous, superficial, decadent, incoherent, 'a great oozing slab of self-pity, bearing the wet trade-mark of Henry Williamson,' in the words of one who is probably the most successful prose stylist in contemporary English letters.

It is beautiful on this high hill, overlooking thousands

of square miles of earth and sea, and the far sky over all. Westwards, beyond the sunset, Labrador is the nearest land.

In the year I was born, Thomas Hardy wrote:

Down there they are dubious and askance: there nobody
   thinks as I,
But mind-chains do not clank where one's next neighbour is the sky . . .
Down there I seem to be false to myself, my simple self
   that was,
And is not now, and I see him watching, wondering
   what crass cause
Can have merged him into such a strange continuator
   as this,
Who yet has something in common with himself, my
   chrysalis.

One day, I think to myself, one day I shall see the earth again as a child sees it, but without the perplexities and restraints of childhood. Gather up the papers, and lock the door; beyond the Atlantic lie the orange groves of the South, the sun in the sands of Florida.

PART TWO

ESSAYS ON BOOKS AND AUTHORS,
GOT TOGETHER WHILE
AWAITING PASSAGE TO
AMERICA

ON OTTERS

A LADY writer and rider to foxhounds, reviewing *Tarka the Otter* in a weekly, complained that the style was 'far from being simple', that 'the Devonshire dialect lays traps for the unwary', that a 'too flowery pen leads the author into many statements which, to put it mildly, are rather rash,' and then she goes on to say it would appear that the author has never 'known an otter intimately and personally, but has written from otter-hunting experience, and so on.' The critic complains further that Tarka is made 'far too "Hail fellow, well met" with all the other otters on the river,' and then proceeds to say that 'never shall I forget the fury of my old friend Madame Moses when I tried to introduce a dog-cub'. Madame Moses was apparently a tame otter about which a book had been written; and the behaviour of the tame otter made the basis of criticism of the treatment of wild otters I had observed in their native waters. The lady writer and fox-hunter concluded by saying that the description of the last hunt was for her 'the most unpleasant of many vivid descriptions'.

It was an interesting criticism, and set me wondering on how dialect could lay traps, and what was the distinction between knowing an otter intimately and knowing it personally, and what the significance of the words 'and so on', and why a truthful and precise description of an otter-hunt, written with an unobtruded and as it were reserved pity, should be unpleasant to a fellow writer. Could it be that one whose style was

made up of *clichès*, or stereotyped expressions, had
obviously not yet grown to know the pleasures and the
art of using, and therefore of appreciating in the work
of other writers, one word after another word with
deliberate intention and accuracy?

There were many criticisms like the above, some of
them adding that one day the author, when he had
learned to use the English language properly, might
even write a minor West Country classic. Meanwhile 'a
correspondence was being conducted in the columns' —
to use a weedy pen for a change — and as it was interesting then, it may be interesting now. The author began
with the following letter.

FEEDING HABITS OF OTTERS

Sir,—The feeding habits and tastes of otters are, in
my experience of both wild and tamed kinds,
various. I have seen, in daylight, a bitch skinning
frogs for her cubs near the clay-pits on Lord Clin-
ton's estate at Merton, as I have described in my
book *Tarka the Otter*. On another occasion I watched
an old dog otter chewing a frog whilst lying on his
back in the water, and joyously flacking his rudder.
Sometimes an otter will hold a fish in his paws and
chew it with his head on one side, while standing in
shallow water — returning for more when the tail
has vanished; or chew while treading deep water
and clutching the fish, exactly as a seal will. Each
otter seems to have his own particular habits.

Those of your readers who are more conversant
with tame otters may be interested to know that a
partly tame otter which accepted me as her friend

188

in 1921 (her mother had been trapped, and I rescued the cub from a drain) ate roast beef and batter pudding, eggs, cooked cauliflowers and potatoes, bread soaked in milk or bacon fat, sausage skins, custard tart, and many other things. In early life this otter's chief joy was the sucking of an infant's bottle filled with warm diluted cow's milk. She would suck it long after the milk was swallowed, and mew if the bottle was taken away, and run after it. She liked to sleep with the bottle under her neck.

I knew another tame otter who was fond of beer; and another who would drink water only of a particular running tap. After drinking, she would roll on her back, and try to clutch the rope of water with her paws, and bite it.

To this the lady reviewer replied:

Mr. Williamson's interesting note on the feeding habits of the otter illustrates well the fact that captive otters unable to obtain sufficient proper, otherwise natural, food, will eat almost anything — I have seen Zoo otters munching peanuts thrown them by onlooking children! But the taste for such fare is, of course, a morbid one, arising from hunger and the craving to fill their stomachs with something.

As far as the question of an otter skinning frogs is concerned — Mr. Williamson's belief that he saw one doing so is probably based on a misapprehension of what he actually observed. If he will obtain a frog, kill, and try to skin it, he will then understand why (apart from knowledge of otter habits and characteristics) I am so sceptical about this old story. Plenty of people firmly believe they have seen an adder swallow her young, yet every scientific naturalist knows it is a physical impossibility for the young to survive in such a refuge. But the survival of the belief is interesting as showing how apt we are to be deceived. Now with regard to the otter seen by Mr. Williamson, would he kindly say how far he was from her, and give us full particulars of her actions? It would be highly interesting if he would do so.

Then came a letter from Arthur Heinemann in West Somerset, an old Master of the Eton Beagles and also of the Cheriton Otterhounds ('The Two Rivers Hunt'), an original sporting 'character' — a cider-making, midnight-hornblowing, badger-digging and cub-training fellow, a bohemian of wild life, a sage of Exmoor, goodhearted, poetical, misjudged, generous spendthrift, and a charming writer who was never really appreciated. He is dead now, and so I can write like this about him: and one day I hope to edit a book of his writings. Arthur Heinemann wrote to *The Nation* (for that was the name of the weekly):

. . . . To review a reviewer is a somewhat thankless task, nor do I hold any brief for Mr. Henry Williamson, the author. But for the benefit of 'those that come after', and in the interests of accuracy and correct statement, I trust you will allow me . . . This lady ridicules Mr. Williamson for making his otter-hero skin frogs, declaring in her original review that otters gobble them up 'whole even to their little toes', and doubting the possibility of an otter being able to skin a frog even if in not too great a hurry to devour it. When I was hunting the Cheriton Otter Hounds above Kismeldon (Kissington Bridge) on the River Torridge, hounds were busy on the trail of an otter that led them to an island in mid-stream. Here they dwelt revelling in the scent, and on wading across I saw the remains of *several frogs skinned back to the eyes* like a glove peeled off one's hand. True, I did not *see* the otter do this, but there is very strong corroborative evidence that this was the work of an otter. It is never safe to say what a wild animal will do under various circumstances and in various counties, as they adapt themselves and their habits to their locality or as necessity of food, sex, or play arises. It is all very well to observe otters or other animals tame in confinement or in their natural surroundings, but to dogmatize on their behaviour is dangerous work, and often leads to one's undoing. . . . Both author and reviewer do not appear to have noticed that the otter's greatest delight is to 'flirt' with running or falling water. Wild otters love to shoot the falls, and tame otters revel if a tap is turned on them, and will go wild with joy, even rolling on their backs in ecstasy, if sprinkled by a watering-pot. Nor does author or reviewer appear to have noticed how an otter will rub on the ground a slimy prey — fish or toad — to clean it apparently, and before eating it wash it off in the water. Having kept tame otters myself and hunted otter packs, both in Essex and Devon, beside following many other otter packs for many years, you will perhaps permit me to throw my tongue on the true trail?

A fortnight later the author, with a pen still inclined to weediness because this was a letter to the scholarly and distinguished (now extinguished) columns of *The Nation*, replied as under:

> With regard to Mr. Arthur Heinemann's letter in your issue of December the seventeenth, in which he states that he has found the remains of several frogs skinned back to the eyes, I would like to confirm his conclusion that this was the work of an otter; and to add that it was probably the work of a bitch otter. One summer day I watched a bitch with cubs playing on the bank of one of the derelict clay-pits on Merton Moor in Devon; and after the play, I watched her catching frogs in the water, and flaying them on the bank. I was lying on the opposite bank, about twenty yards away, and she was aware of my presence, but after a stare and a swim half-way across the pond to inspect me, she swam back and paid no more attention to me.
>
> So far as I could see, her way of skinning the frogs was to stand on them, nip the skin, and then lift up her head. While she was doing this with a frog, a cub sneaked one off the pile, and dragged it away and began chewing. Whether it managed to eat any of the frog I do not know. The cubs were quite small, about nine inches long, excluding the rudder, or tail.
>
> Mr. Arthur Heinemann probably knows as much about wild otters as anyone in the West Country, and what he says about the infinite variations in

behaviour and action in wild animals generally, is entirely borne out by my own experiences of them. I would go even further, and say that in their emotions and feelings they are very near to us indeed. Mr. Heinemann, I remember, once had a tame badger that got caught in a gin set by a chicken farmer; and the farmer came to him in a great rage and told him to come and see it killed. When the badger saw its friend it jumped up and hugged his arm, and *cried*. It clung there, and the farmer was so moved that he declared he wasn't going to kill it: let someone else do it, he wouldn't. The farmer's intuition, on that occasion, ruled his thought.

Now Mr. Heinemann says that I have made no mention in *Tarka the Otter* of the otter's delight in running water. If he would read the book again he would see that this joy in the water-life is one of the underlying themes of the story. The sliding down icy mud into the river, etc., is fully described. As for falling water, this description occurs in the book: 'Tarka ran back to the river, and after eating fish, he played with a rope of water twisting and un-twisting out of a drain, trying to catch it between his paws and bite it as it plattered on his face and chest.'

READING IN BED

AMONG the presents for my thirtieth birthday were four books about 'Nature', by four different authors; one a French savant, another a Swiss Doktor and scientist with many letters after his name, the third by an enthusiastic amateur, the fourth by a friend of mine who was also my doctor. Being ill in bed for a few weeks, I read them all, meanwhile thanking the donors for their most interesting gifts, which, I declared falsely (with one exception) were just what I wanted. Actually three of the four were given away as soon as possible; and my private opinions about the books were as now follow:

1 By the French savant, a translation, with the captivating title of *How Animals find their Way About*. There were one hundred and twenty-nine pages in this book, most of them very difficult to read. At the end the author appended a list of the seventy-one books used for reference in making his own volume, and to the list he added a note.

> This list of references contains, of course, only the works it had been thought necessary to use in order to set forth this summary. A complete bibliography of the subject would comprise a veritable volume.

I should call it a dreadful volume myself: for what did most of these volumes of fact, these 'records of orientation in the invertebrates and vertebrates' of which the present book was nearly typical, prove? Usually they were

written in an abominable style, which wearied the mind
so that it repeatedly slipped away from the printed page.

May the time come soon, I cried, while reaching
for the thermometer, when all the jargon of 'scientific
nomenclature' and general emptiness of interpretation
shall vanish with the dreary biographies and history
books which used to bore and torture us in the stuffy
class-room.

> By the mind, without instruments, the Greeks
> anticipated nearly all our thoughts; by and by,
> having raised ourselves up upon these huge mounds
> of facts, we shall begin to see still greater things; to
> do so we must look not at the mound under foot,
> but at the starry horizon

wrote Richard Jefferies.

> For I sit on the thrown timber under the trees and
> meditate, and I want something more; I want the
> soul of the flowers.

There was no one like Jefferies.

This book lying on the counterpane contained only
about a dozen pages of simple, interesting writing which
justified the simple title. Setting out to be strictly
scientific, sternly to shed his human equipment, mental,
sensory, and psychic, lest it colour or subtly change the
strict scientific attitude, our learned author achieved
nothing until, abandoning this unnatural attitude and
freeing his natural genius, or imagination, he succeeded
in lighting, in a few rare pages, the age-long obscurity
made and festered by the scientific attitude.

Even then one merely learned that the limpet,
unsealing itself from its hold on the rock at the rising of

the sea, found its way to and from the places of its grazing much as a man shut in a conical shell and equipped as a limpet would proceed — by feeling its way, and remembering the path, or as our author would say, orientating itself with the aid of tactile clues predominating incontestibly in the path of the mollusc's return.

Likewise the carrier pigeon, declared the scientist, found its way home over great distances by sight and memory, and not by 'sixth sense'; it got home as a man in an aeroplane without compass or map would get home, when flying over remembered country in clear weather. It was not instinctive, like migration.

Even so, what is migration, he asks. Permit me, an uneducated and unscientific amateur, to tell you, M. le Professeur. Migration is independent of the senses to-day, but it was not always so. Once upon a time birds, or their skin-winged fore-runners, chanced to fly along certain routes and found food, and, remembering the way, flew there again and again until the custom became a habit, and in time the habit was inherited; that is, an instinct.

All progress is memory, and they die that remember not, inferred the French Professor, lifting his eyes in an unscientific moment from his mound of facts to the starry horizon.

> Whether one envisages a mollusc, an insect, a mammal, or man himself, one really perceives no essential difference among them in this respect.

Hurray! Your next book might be readable! Remembering the ultimate words of *The Marriage of Heaven and Hell*, the triumphant creed of the poet, 'For everything that lives is Holy', one might almost believe that at last the streams of Science and Poetry are about to mingle and flow together to the unplumbed sea . . . and so on and so forth.

2   The next book, in two volumes, was almost heavy enough to use as ballast in my eleven-foot sailing dinghy, if only the accursed germ would leave me, and I could get into the sun again. It was a monumental work on Ants, by a distinguished Swiss authority on Ants. The social instincts of the ants had, he declared, taken millions of years to 'crystallize'; each species came into existence to do its special work, and among each species were born individuals equipped mentally and physically for special jobs. This learned Swiss Doktor of medicine hinted that a similar social instinct might crystallize in the human species, all varieties of which were capable of inter-breeding, he declared. It might be, indeed, that it was appearing, incompletely — the instinct, not the inter-breeding — in various individuals of the human species, irrespective of nationality or local customs. Was the ant, millions of years ago, an individual?

The Herr Doktor did not know. He speculated; and he was careful to say that he was speculating. His book was an incomplete encyclopaedic condensation of nearly all that had been printed about the many thousands of ant species, amplified and illustrated with observations of his own.

His book, work of a lifetime, called *The Social World of the Ants*, abounded with records of experiments, made by himself and other naturalists. He had proved, for instance, or helped to prove, that ants recognized one another by their sense of smell, and that their antennae were their sense organs. He had cut off these, and proved that ants lost the sense of direction; and, more significantly, that with the loss of the sense of smell ants of species with blood-feuds fed and lay down together like Blake's lion and lamb. Then by varnishing their eyes (which he declared a cruel experiment) and watching them falter, lose direction, and finally cower in misery and bewilderment, this learned scientist proved, apparently, that some ants cannot find their way about without sight.

An example or moral, he suggested, might be drawn from the ants; or perhaps his philosophical enthusiasms, which recurred in paraphrase through the book, might be merely political opportunism; but it was certain that ants led, from our human point of view, a terrible life. Every kind of human thought and impulse seemed to have been made manifest in the ant world. There was an unlimited variety of work and strife and horror, from the civilized human view-point of myself lying in clean sheets under a roof that leaked only in one corner.

There was humour, too — perhaps the most amusing fact about ants was that some patriotic individuals of a species living in deserts transform themselves into immense barrels, swelling many times the size of their fellows, and lie up in cellars, side by side, ministering during the long months of idle rotundity to the lean and thirsty workers. It was only a poor, rude Williamson-joke, I knew — my temperature, taken by myself every half-hour, was now nearly normal — but the thought would persist that when the ideal Socialist State, the arrival of which had been his life's hope, was established, Mr. G. K. Chesterton would surely be prepared for his brave new world duties.

There were Amazon ants, I read uneasily, a swift and terrible race which organized for raids by sending out scouts to reconnoitre neighbouring nests of farming ants. The scouts returned with information that, transmitted along antennae, excited and vitalized the assembling columns, which then advanced and surrounded the attacked nest, forming 'customs barriers', through which their porters, laden with the nymphs to become their slaves, together with the unresisting farmers, were allowed to pass. Those which resisted were killed, pierced through the head by a single bite of the Amazonian jaws. The columns returned, and the Amazons were fed by their slaves, which were economically their masters, for the feeding instinct of the Amazon was corrupt after so many generations of disuse! These ants were never cowed or dispirited, as were the 'inferior' or peace-loving ants in adversity. With the Amazons it was certainly death or glory; they appeared to be more stupid than any other kind of ant, often slaying friend and foe alike in the excitement of battle.

Ants had their drug-traffickers, such as the beetles familiar to children, the book declared. These parasites crept into the underground streets, and when accosted by the nearest police ants they raised certain hairs which possessed a fascinating odour, and, caressing the antennae of the ants, the beetles induced them to drink cocktails. When the police were soothed, the beetles crept away to corrupt the honour of the workers, stealing from their mouths the honey-dew which was to nourish the growing ants, or nymphs. It laid its eggs in the nursery, and its offspring fed on the eggs of the ants. Colonies where these beetles were numerous were usually physically degenerate, owing to the absorption of the dope, which rendered ants lethargic, and eventually destroyed them. I began to wonder if I were reading of men or ants; and came to the conclusion that it was a very good book.

Some species grew mushrooms in underground vaults, making the beds of a mulch of manure and leaf-mould; others bred and tended cattle, milking them of the honey-dew (these were the green-fly on my roses which I drenched periodically with poison), others raided and stole; others harvested seeds, taking them to dry in the sun to prevent germination after rainy weather.

Then there were the ghastly visiting ants (O euphemism!) which hunted in tropical forests, while all things from caterpillars to tigers fled before them, more terrified than by fire. They bred their soldiers with many times the weight, in armour, of the butchers and porters; they built roads like the Romans, which were lined by blind warrior cohorts, their great jaws held out to menace any marauders. Their queens were gigantic egg-laying machines, thousands of times the weight of a worker: year after year they laid eggs at the rate of thirty-thousand a day.

I could read the book for ever, and never finish it. It was an awful book. Had it been written by an ant or a man, or both? What was the secret of the ants' 'progress'? Had they developed cycles of centuries beyond us, or were they alternate and lower forms of cosmic energy, exploring another stratum of life? The Herr Doktor himself would call any speculation of that question a vanity of the false science of metaphysics. I wanted to agree, but found it impossible, since the Herr Doktor had said it first; so I argued with my wife.

I had had enough of the book: all seeking after knowledge was but a variant of the cross-word puzzle; and so in the Herr Doktor's own cautious scientific spirit I admitted only that his book was the recapitulated labour of a life-time, and of plagiarized selections from the life-labours of others who had observed and experimented with ants; and that the two volumes of his masterpiece were very heavy for their size, royal octavo; the first was but two inches thick, yet it weighed four pounds.

I gave the Ant book to Dr. F. R. Elliston Wright, whose eyes brightened when he saw it. Meanwhile I had to stay in bed, where I was writing the ninth version of a wearisome book about an otter.

Book No. 3 was about Gilbert White, by one of his modern admirers. Knowing nothing about the subject, I considered this an apt moment to acquire some real literary knowledge. It appeared that on July the eighteenth, 1720, the Rev. G. White was delighted to learn that Mrs. John White, his daughter-n-law — a guest at the Vicarage, and awaiting in the second-best room an important event — was delivered of a son, and that he might reasonably expect that his grandson would grow into as fine a man as himself, fearing God and the King. In this hope the small-faced infant was duly baptized and awarded the name of his grandfather, Gilbert.

Now, more than two hundred years afterwards, according to the earnest author, there seemed to be some doubt about that grandson, although not for a moment would he have it thought that Gilbert White was without a very proper regard for those things with which all right-minded Englishmen have ever been concerned. Nevertheless, facts must be faced, and the author feared he would have to admit that the criticism was sometimes passed that the immortal Gilbert was self-centred, and took no interest in

> stirring national or international events — wars, revolutions, talks of reform, release of slaves, or religious revivals. The Conquest of Canada, the Seven Years War, and the American War of Independence, it is alleged, scarcely moved him, and he makes no reference to Clive, Pitt, Washington, Wilkes, Burke, Warren Hastings, or John Wesley.

Now this was alarming; for my story of the otter, lying in loose sheets all over the counterpane, had no reference to the Irish war for Independence, no mention of stirring national events like the growing *Daily Mail* circulation and the Football Association Cup Tie, and as for names, neither Lloyd George, President Hoover, Aimèe McPherson, the Oxford Group, nor Horatio Bottomley were mentioned. I would in time be worse off than White, for here was a book by White's defenders who had spent hundreds of hours accumulating and cataloguing every detail and object mentioned by the master, including irrefragable proofs that he was not deficient in patriotism. Did not White, he declared, once write to Robert Marsham,

> I myself, in the year seventeen fifty-six, set off with a party at two o'clock in the morning to see the Hessian troops reviewed on a down near Winchester,

and was it not on record that he mentioned the 'incredible damage' caused by 'the blowing up of the powder mills at Hounslow'?

Again, in seventeen seventy-five, stated the defender, Gilbert White noted that America 'is at present the subject of conversation'. He saw Burgoyne's Light Horse about to embark, and wrote (here his naturalistic training stood him in good stead), to his nephew Samuel:

> The Atlantic is no small frith for cavalry to be transported over.

There were many other references, cried the devoted disciple: to Cook, to Rear-Admiral Sir Samuel Hood, with eight ships of the line; to Lord Cornwallis's Advice sloop *The Swallow* arriving in rough weather from Madras in seventeen ninety-two; to a review of troops at Bagshot Heath. 'Not a bad list for a naturalist's diary,' exclaimed the triumphant advocate.

And furthermore, he continued, White doubted whether the French Revolution would 'turn out to the benefit or advantage of old England'; and his comment on that 'strange commotion' surely revealed the very quintessence of the English character; the comment being, as the disciple faithfully notes,

> God only knows.

And later, declared the author, White wrote to his friend Marsham,

> You cannot abhor the dangerous doctrines of republicans and levellers more than I do!

Everything that White ever mentioned in his writings was commented on and explained in this book. Every detail of White's simple interest in the natural world about him — as simple as the interest of hundreds of

thousands of other ordinary countrymen — had passed
with careful assimilation into the author's mind, to
emerge with the true disciple's interpretation. Listen to
this parasitical stuff:

> At every turn of his life White loved to obtain his
> knowledge at first hand. He observed, registered,
> and deduced. To ascertain the diet of wood-cocks
> and snipe he opened their stomachs and made his
> own inspection. By the same simple method he
> proved convincingly that the nightjar does not
> injure but is beneficial to, the goatherd and the
> grazier. He hears the Duke of Richmond possesses
> a female moose, and he hastens to Goodwood to
> examine the animal. Unfortunately, it had died
> before, and was found slung up by ropes in an old
> greenhouse. The odour of the decomposing beast
> was almost insupportable, yet White measured
> it carefully, described its body, legs, ears, lips, and
> nostrils, and was finally debarred from completing
> his work only by the extent of the putrefaction.

It was no good, one couldn't be serious about such
writing, and I found myself writing extra paragraphs in
parody.

> It is an ill wind that blows nobody good, and all of
> us who are naturalists have to take the rough with
> the smooth; had fortune been less unkind, had, for
> instance, the motor car been invented earlier, White
> might have had an opportunity to ascertain at
> first hand some data outside that old greenhouse.

4   Then I came to the last book, which my doctor
had given to me, with the words, 'You are quite foolish

enough to want to waste money on buying such a thing, so I will prevent you'. He had written, illustrated, and paid for the book's publication himself. Immediately after inspecting it I wrote to the *Western Morning News*, asking to be allowed to review it, without payment. I knew then there was a chance of an article of mine being accepted. It was. Here it is reprinted; hardly doing justice to the small blue-covered book which the author gave me in the little bedroom of the cottage in Ham village seven years ago.

NATURE STUDY IN NORTH DEVON

One signpost, at least, pointing the way to the largest village in England, spells it by its name of Branton. Who changes the names of places, and why? Branton is now Braunton, Ham is Georgeham, Santon is spelled Saunton, Wooda Bay is Woody Bay, Woolcombe is Woolacombe, Cryde is Croyde. I have heard it said that a local painter of signposts, being paid a penny a letter, made the alterations, which were faithfully copied by the Ordnance Surveyors.

I have also heard it said that every species of British wild flower grows on the Santon Burrows — that wide and beautiful region of sandhills bound by marram grasses, of mossy hillocks and level plains, of dykes and marshes, which lies, with its low ragged outline, a ruddy-purple in the Atlantic sunsets, between Taw and Torridge estuary and the hills sloping up to Exmoor.

Neither saying is true; but I can understand why so many of the summer golfers at Saunton — Santon as a name is gone, like the Red Kites which used to soar over Down-end, and the Great Sea Stocks on the Burrows — continue to repeat the wildflower legend. The loose saying may have been started by one of the old writers of guide-books, many of whom when they weren't obviously copying from one another, were writing, out of their poor dark civilized minds, such descriptions of one of the loveliest wild tracts in England, as 'Let us now hurry from Santon to Westward Ho!, leaving the dreary wastes of the Branton Burrows as quickly as possible'.

In future, there will be no excuse, either for the golfer-fiction of 'every kind of British wild flower', or for any guide-book writer to remain mute about the Burrows. He can buy this book and paraphrase its contents. It is a neat little volume, and its author, Dr. F. R. Elliston Wright, exactly describes its contents by the sub-titles,

> A few Nature Notes. With lists of flora, macro-lepidoptera, and birds known to occur in the district.

The phrase 'known to occur' is important; it means that each entry has been found and identified by the author, who probably knows the Burrows, that is its wild life, better than any man alive. Some there are, perhaps, having helped to put most of the rarer visitors in glass cases — bittern, Greenland falcon, hobby, hen-harrier, spoonbill, glossy ibis, Egyptian goose, great bustard — who may dispute this claim for Dr. Wright; but this book will be read when moth and worm have eaten them.

It must not be thought that the lists make all the book. To me, personally, the *Few Nature Notes* are of the greatest interest. I read them as I read the books of

W. H. Hudson — the detail is truly scientific. Listen to
this:

> The Buzzard is treated by gamekeepers as a hawk,
> and is usually called a 'Buzzard Hawk'. On
> examining a great number of excretory pellets of
> these birds, the evidence of their food is chiefly
> earth worms, mice, and lizards. They eat snakes,
> and under the nest after hatching has occurred,
> pieces of snake about three inches long, which
> have been dropped down, are found.

And this:

> Walking homeward in the evening, bees are often
> noticed resting on the flowers of Carline thistles
> and other large composite flowers. They will so
> spend the night, probably knowing that the tempera-
> ture of these blossoms, where much active vitality
> is going on, is five or six degrees warmer than the
> surrounding atmosphere.

Readers of *Nature in Downland* will recall Hudson
suggesting that late bees cling to thistles because they
are drunk on honey. How does Dr. Wright know that
the blossoms are five or six degrees warmer than the
surrounding air? Because he has had a special thermometer made. Incidentally, he can tell when caterpillars
are dead, by the higher temperature; when living, they
are colder than air.

People sometimes ask, What are those curious plants
like little green bamboos growing in the marshy ground?
Here is the answer:

> Both in the burrows, as well as in the marshes, we
> see great numbers of horsetails. These horsetails

are very ancient plants, which are plentifully represented in the fossils of the carboniferous period. When their vegetable substance is destroyed by maceration it is possible to produce complete silicious skeletons of these plants, maintaining their erect form. The ash of horsetails contains half its weight of silica. The horsetails are useless as fodder, and are even avoided by cattle, but they have a great local reputation here for fattening horses, being locally known as 'tidy pipe'. This reputation probably depends on the fact that often they grow where there is good rich grass.

This is what our author has to say of the rarer con-volvulous hawk moth which appears in numbers every September,

The action of their wings can be heard on a still evening certainly fifteen yards away. They start coming to the flowers at dusk, and at intervals right through the night until light comes again. They will even drink from blossoms held perfectly still in the hand, when the enormously long tongue (one I measured was three inches) can be watched extending like a whip and thrust down the long tube of a flower. It will be noticed that these flowers which are visited specially by moths which feed while hovering on the wing have no sort of landing stage, like the lipped flowers of peas, orchids, etc., which are for insects to settle on.

These extracts, made at random, will show the worth of the Notes, of which there are sixty pages (I wish there were sixty more). It is not possible to indicate the quality of the illustrations, drawn by the author; they must be seen in the book to be appreciated. I think they are extraordinarily good. The frontispiece of a con-volvulous hawk moth, reproduced in its natural colours, appears almost to be walking across the glossy surface of the art-paper. It was shown to some village children, placed at the back of a white cardboard box, and not one would dare to put a hand in and touch it!

Braunton: A Few Nature Notes, by F. R. Elliston Wright. Published in the High-street of Barnstaple, by A. E. Barnes, at four shillings and sixpence.

IZAAK WALTON

WHAT new thing can be said about Izaak Walton or his fishing book at the present time? Why is the book still read? Because a few people want to read it. What makes a classic? Is it a minimum sale of five hundred copies a year? five hundred being the minimum number which can be printed from type or plates without economic loss?

To the ordinary Englishman the word 'classic' has a slightly chilling significance. During the process called education he has too often been bored by 'classics', usually in those languages called dead. The fruits of the minds of rare men were offered to the immature consciousness. Offered? Well, as our brother of the angle offered his barbed hook to the frog. In the same spirit the frog accepted the offer; and possibly in a Ranine paradise he forgot the exactitude of the experience, and declared that it made a frog of him.

A classic is usually a work of art that is read from one age to another; and, in its proper function, it is read by those who want to read it.

While there are fish in England there will be men who dream of catching them, and of the environment of fish-capture; and so *The Compleat Angler* will continue to be a classic of fishing. For modern reading — I do not refer to the scholar interested chiefly in it as a period piece — much of the book is tedious and pro-longed, especially the earlier chapters, where the author, with his material still massed and appalling in his mind, has not got into his authentic stride. As a piece of writing it is entertaining, but for a reason other than that intended by Walton; the apologia of each of the three ambulating gentlemen — Fisherman, Falconer, and Hunter — is quaint and stuffed with facts and information which the author could assemble from his various sources. Much of the book is what to-day would be called hackwork. Of course it was written for money.

Walton must have made copious notes. Like most writers of any age or civilization, all was fish that came into his net. He plagiarized; he adapted; he borrowed without asking. No blame or destructive criticism is intended in these remarks; the job of writing, like that of existence for a trout, is a voracious one, and Izaak Walton in several instances acknowledged his ablations by adding names or initials of their authors. Many authors would not do even that; they would merely re-dress or paraphrase their material, and put it out as their own. Occasionally old Walton does this; and in the process he paraphrases sufficiently to lose the exactitude of the 'fact' he would convey. For example, a Mr. Barker published *Barker's Delight, or The Art of Angling*, in 1651, three years before the publication of *The Compleat Angler*, and in the earlier book the trout fisher-man is bidden to 'let the fly light first into the water' — which Walton renders as 'let no part of the line touch the water, but the fly only'. This, to modern eyes, appears strange advice, especially as he bids the novice stand on the lee bank of the river on a windy day. It raises doubt about the extent of the author's experience of fly-fishing. This doubt may reveal only the limitation of my own English fly-fishing experience, which directs the above criticism; for it may have been customary three hundred years ago to drop your fly on the water from the fifteen-foot or eighteen-foot rods they used ordinarily, with a fixed short line. The 'casting it (the line) into the water' may not have implied what the term would imply to-day. On second consideration, and study of the text, it appears that the criticism, which was suggested to us by a senior brother of the angle, a fortunate owner of fishing on the Test, is unjust; for Izaak writes:

> And when you fish with a fly, if it be possible, let no part of your line touch the water, but your fly only; and be still moving your fly upon the water . . . you yourself being also always moving down the stream.

Even so, the trout he caught like this must have been tame, and used to the sight of men.

Walton was a poet, and a poet who lives successfully beyond the age of thirty cares more for precision and exactitude in what he does than the man of lesser perceptions; and if he had been a true dry-fly man he would never have been so explicit and complacent about the ways of taking trout by means of night-lines and lob-worms. But enough of this ill-humour against so gentle and sweet a man.

Let us suppose that the form and style of the book were such that we could lose ourselves in it. (Even in boyhood, poring over an old copy of the second edition, to discover some potent bait for the carp in the Long Pond, we could not do that.) Let us pretend that we believe, as we read, in the talk and walk of Venator, Piscator, and Auceps; in the Milkmaid and her mother and Coridon and Peter. What sort of world is it, then, what sort of human nature?

It is a world of polite discourse and gracious leisure. Never did Master have such a willing Scholar. Such patience, such enthusiasm maintained despite the thousands of facts bombarding the consciousness! Every fish ever heard or read of comes into the verbal net. At the beginning Venator, Piscator, and Auceps bombard one another; the bombardments are gracefully received, and a similar weight of wordy projectiles returned. What a chance to show knowledge! Even that tiny flyer the bee is dragged in by Auceps:

> There is also a little contemptible winged creature (an inhabitant of my aerial element), namely, the laborious bee, of whose prudence, policy, and regular government of their own commonwealth I might say much, as also of their several kinds, and how useful their honey and wax are both for meat and medicines to mankind; but I will leave them to their sweet labour, without the least disturbance, believing them to be all very busy at this very time amongst the herbs and flowers that we see nature puts forth this May morning. And now to return to my hawks, from whom I have made too long a digression.

A charming way to fill up a book! It does serve, however to break up the masses of facts about fishes. There is little action in the book; one could have wished for more accounts of actual fishing — for, as has been said often among otter-hunters, the next best thing to otter-hunting is reading about it. While we digress, in the manner of the Master, let it be said that modern otter-hunters would not care much about the seventeenth-century methods of hunting otters.

> Now Sweetlips has her; hold her, Sweetlips! . . .
> come bring her to me, Sweetlips. Look, 'tis a
> bitch otter, and she has lately whelped . . .
> HUNTSMAN Come, gentlemen . . . here's her young
> ones, no less than five; come, let's kill them all . . .
> now let's go to an honest ale-house, where we may
> have a cup of good barley-wine, and sing *Old Rose*,
> and all of us rejoice together.

The last advice would meet with approval everywhere:
is not the river Taw known as the Gentleman's River,
owing to the number of inns along its banks, placed
as though for the reception of weary otter-hunters?
But Sweetlips, she must have been an extraordinary
hound to be able to retrieve an otter, even a small
twelve-pound bitch, from the worry. As to the cubs —
a bitch with cubs is not generally hunted nowadays.
Otters are bound to be slain; farmers and water-
bailiffs with shot and trap have no mercy; the otter-
hunters are the only protectors of the species in England,
with the exception of a few rare individuals. In Walton's
day, if he be trustworthy, it was apparently jungle-law.
I do not care very much for otter-hunting myself; but
I dislike the callous and unknowledgeable things said
about otter-hunters and others; and I confess I am relieved (and yet regretful) when one is killed on my own
water, where at the moment the trout are small and
scarce. Sometimes it seems that the natural world of
hunters and hunted is better than our civilized world:
in the natural world are zests, appetites, stimulations,
and contentments rarely known by civilized man.

A fisherman knows a little of the delights of the natural world of his forefathers when he fishes, and, may I add (thus betraying an inclination toward prejudice), particularly the dry-fly fisherman. When I am in good form, that is well and happy, and fishing in the Bray, I enter another world — the natural world — where senses and instincts are harmonious and co-ordinated in one purpose. The consciousness is no longer a house divided against itself. Nowadays too many of us are going the way of Hamlet — to the wilderness. We desire, and act not, and breed pestilence: we are, metaphorically and too often literally, scant of breath. We have not enough true action. That is why the sensitive brain-worker, who must escape or perish, and who by chance is initiated a brother of the angle, becomes the kind of enthusiast that old Izaak was. When the stream is in spate, and the alders stand bleakly against the sky, we take him to our hearts, and listen to his friends the Milkmaid and her mother singing with all the charm and poise of two of Mr. C. B. Cochran's Young Ladies.

Our author's desire to scoop all and any fish into the net of his book leads him occasionally to what the good folk would call errors of taste. Do we seriously believe that this gentle ironmonger (for that was his job in life), this scholar-poet, who does not like, as he confesses, killing anything, do we believe him when he describes for us how to make sport with ducks and pike, by tying a line with live-bait lure for pike to a duck's legs, and 'she chased over a pond'? Piscator does not appear to be easy about it, for 'time will not allow me to say more of this kind of fishing with live baits', although he has apparently, eternity before him.

The Compleat Angler is, taken by and large — I am

considering it now as though it were a new book, for modern reading — a jolly book, a book with which, after the uneasy display of encyclopaedic knowledge is passed (in those days they wrote *Histories of the World:* now all they dare are *Outlines of Possible Histories*), we can feel at home. The inclusion of occasional verse is heartily approved. Who would miss the inexperienced Milkmaid's song:

> Come live with me, and be my love
> And we will all the pleasures prove.

And the answer of her experienced mother,

> If all the world and love were young,
> And truth in every shepherd's tongue,
> These pretty pleasures might me move
> To live with thee, and be thy love.

And the magnificent variation by Doctor Donne, mighty man and lover and inspired Dean of St. Paul's, the friend of our gentle angler, who was, from the evidence of the poem, vainly brought to the pleasures of the angle:

> Let others freeze with angling-reeds,
> And cut their legs with shells and weeds,
> Or treacherously poor fish beset,
> With strangling snares, or windowy net:
>
> Let coarse bold hands, from slimy nest,
> The bedded fish in banks outwrest:
> Let curious traitors sleave silk flies,
> To witch poor wandering fishes' eyes:

For thee thou need'st no such deceit,
For thou thyself art thine own bait:
That fish that is not catch'd thereby
Is wiser far, alas! than I.

What can the critic say in conclusion? That Mr. Walton will write a better book when he learns the art of selection, the art of compression, the art of construction? That it were better if his anthology of poems were not lost in piscatorial technicalities? If his fishing treatise were not spoiled by poetical excrescences? That when he learns to trust himself, and write of what he knows, he will have better chance of success? Surely not: let us leave that sort of thing to the superior, the cool, the barren literary gentlemen. We know already the opinion of our distinguished contemporary Mr. Richard Franck, the celebrated and successful sporting critic and authority on fly-fishing, himself author of the best-selling *Northern Memoirs*. Mr. Franck writes recently (about 1656):

> Mr. Walton lays the stress of his arguments upon other men's observations, wherewith he stuffs his indigested octavo; so brings himself under the angler's censure and the common calamity of a plagiary, to be pitied (poor man) for his loss of time, in scribbling and transferring other men's notions.

What can we say when so cool an authority has pronounced judgment? Dare we suggest in a whisper to the reader that Mr. Franck is of course quite right — but, well you know there is something rather unusual about the book — anyhow, let the reader keep his first edition (small duodecimo for the pocket, price one shilling and sixpence) in good condition. One day it may be a valuable item on the library shelves of his twentieth-century descendant.

SHALLOWFORD,
    24th March, 1931.

> (*The river very low, the wind south-east, and the brown trout in the Bray trying to ease their hunger with caddis grubs, each belly and gut full of little stone fragments.*)

A variation of the above was written for the edition of *The Compleat Angler* illustrated by Mr. Arthur Rackham, published by Messrs. Harrap, to whom thanks for permission to include it in this book.

A BRAVE BOOK

> Our very God existed in the plains and forests that
> we had known, and which were now to be taken
> away from us forever. Our Indian religion taught us
> that the Great Spirit existed in all things — in the
> trees, the animals, the lakes, rivers, and mountains.
> And when we wanted to get close to the Great Spirit
> and pray we went out alone . . . to the things in
> which he lived.

So writes Buffalo Child Long Lance, a chief of the
bloody Band of Blackfoot Indians in his autobiography,
which deals with his childhood on the plains under the
Rockies, at a time when he had not seen his first white
man.

Is it possible? For Chief Long Lance cannot be very
old; he was a captain in the Canadian Corps during the
World War, and was awarded various decorations for
bravery on the Western Front. After the War he became
a writer, selling stories to the highly paid American
magazines. Before the War he was a graduate of
Carlisle and Manlius, winning scholastic and athletic
honours at both colleges; and a cadet at West Point,
which he had entered on a Presidential award.

In an age when much is fake and sensation, it is
perhaps understandable, although discreditable, that
one was prepared to disbelieve the authenticity of the
book; but very soon shame was felt for suspicion. Suspicion is a poor feeling anywhere; especially near the
reading of this book *Long Lance*, which is simple,

truthful, and magnanimous. Even when the author, in describing the epic 'rebellion' in the 'nineties of Almighty Voice, could with justice employ irony or even satire, this simplicity and great-mindedness moves through his narrative as naturally as water flows.

It is a good book, and I shall give it to my sons as soon as they are old enough to read beyond *The Cock, the Mouse and the Little Red Hen*: when they are matured enough to appreciate *Bevis* and *Huckleberry Fin*.

The Indian boys of Chief Long Lance's boyhood, among the last tribes to encounter white men — 'the region is the Far North-West: northern Montana, Alberta, Saskatchewan and British Columbia' — were brought up to be natural warriors. That age is passing from the face of the earth. Machine-made warriordom is passing, too, we hope: I believe that Hitler, through his poetic or moral power will lead Europe to the new age of sunshine and peaceful strength.

The Indian boys were brought up to despise mosquito bites and itching, pain, comfort, lying, and meanness. They submitted to being whipped every morning, after which — unless frost had struck deep into the rivers — they plunged into water, sporting like otters. They burned themselves with pine-cones, lying still and silent until the embers were ash.

In early manhood came the supreme trial of endurance, which, if passed, earned the young man the title of Brave, and qualified him to go on the warpath and fight his hereditary enemies in other tribes. This trial was held at the great Annual Sun Dance, when all branches of the Blackfeet gathered at a certain plain in the prairie, and held their games and feasts. The breast muscles of the young man were pierced and threaded with thongs of raw hide; then he danced round a pole, with others.

> Sometimes they danced for hours without being able to free themselves. If the young man lasted all this time without fainting the medicine-man would order a warrior to come into the lodge on a pony, and he would untie the thong from the pole and fasten it round the horse. The warrior would then race round and round the lodge, dragging the young man behind him in an effort to release the flesh. We children would run in and jump on and off the young man's back as he was dragged around, to increase the weight. If this did not free him the warrior would . . . send his horse forward with a sudden rush . . . and the young man would get up, if he could . . . a Brave.

One wonders mildly if this really was necessary, and how many were maimed by it. Sometimes they held foot races over a non-stop course of two hundred and forty miles, which began at dawn and ended by sunset of the next day. Seven days' fasting when on the warpath (inspired by revenge), was not an unusual feat of endurance. But the most impressive writing in the book is that describing Chief Carry-the-Kettle, who survived until 1923, dying at the age of one hundred and eight years. He treated his enemies as he treated himself, and bitterness was unknown to him; when he made peace it was always with a large gesture, without false modesty, without hyperbole.

In every tribe, during the revels that followed a peace pact, there were patriotic or revengeful spirits among the warriors who sought by treachery to kill or massacre their new friends; in the various cases mentioned these die-hards were frustrated by their wives, who promptly reported them to their chiefs. Would that it were as simple a matter in Europe to-day.

Because of its epic quality, the story of Almighty Voice deserves to be widely known. Almighty Voice was a Brave who one day towards the end of the nineteenth century shot a steer belonging to the Government that had ousted the Indians. He was not a thief; he thought it was a wild bison. He was arrested and chained to a big iron ball. The mounted policeman on guard jokingly told him he would be hanged. Made desperate at the prospect of this dishonour, the young Indian escaped, became an outlaw with his girl wife, grew more desperate, was tracked for some months, and finally to avoid arrest and what he still believed to be his fate by hanging, shot a half-breed scout.

After two years of outlawry in his own country, Almighty Voice was cornered in a small wood, and he and two boys with him killed several policemen, who, in the best Victorian traditions of bravery, made a frontal charge upon them.

What happened then may sound incredible until one remembers the scenes of stupidity and hysteria in England, France, Russia, and Germany in August 1914, when Boy Scouts tracked 'spies', church crypts were said to be full of enemy machine guns, and every hard tennis court was a secret hostile gun emplacement.

That night the Mounted Police ball at Regina two hundred miles away was interrupted at its height by the band suddenly striking up *God Save the Queen*. People looked at each other in amazement: and soon after midnight a force consisting of twenty-five men with field guns and maxims left under the command of Inspector McDonnell (now Commissioner for Boy Scouts for Western Canada). Hundreds of volunteers were recruited; a labour battalion was specially raised to dig trenches and saps — 'this in case they should not be able to exterminate the Indians by shell-fire'.

For two days Almighty Voice was shelled, while lying without food and water in a little cubby-hole in the wood, his thigh shattered. His mother stood on a knoll nearby and shouted encouragements during the salvoes of fifteen pounders. At the end of four days they still heard his voice shouting back. By this time over one thousand armed white men were waiting for the preparatory bombardment to lower the enemy's *morale* before the grand charge. This is, alas, no exaggeration. It is history — one thousand armed white men and artillery, against a wounded Indian and two little dead boys. No wonder the Great War occurred in Europe twenty years later.

And at night, 'You have done well, but you will have to do better', cried the voice of Almighty Voice. Later, between midnight and dawn they heard him chanting his death song.

The next morning the bombardment began again, and soon after noon the assault was launched, to find the rebel lying dead in his hole — but before leaving for the Hunting Grounds of his ancestors this youth had carved on a near tree an epitaph to the three policemen whom he had shot five days before. In Cree syllables it said, 'Here died three Braves'.

REALITY IN WAR LITERATURE

I

A MOTOR CAR suddenly slowing down in the lane outside my window made a downward droning sound, and instantly the sunlight was put out, and I was in deep sucking mud, helplessly pulling the reins of a mule, laden with machine-guns, lying on its side on a slough of shell-holes. The vast negation of darkness, in hopeless travail with the dead weight of human and animal misery, was scored by white streaks arising in a semi-circle before us; burdened men, charred tree stumps, overturned limbers, sunken tanks, were wavery with shadows homeless in the diffused pallor of everlasting flares. To avoid the timber track, broken and congested with a battalion transport which had just received several direct hits, I had led the file of pack-mules across the morass, and one had fallen into a shell-hole; the foundering beast snorted and groaned, while the water glimmered behind its ears. High explosive shells burst in salvoes around us, with ruddy glares and rending metallic crashes; bullets, arising in richochet from the outpost-line nearer the flares, moaned and piped away overhead. I stood, hot and sweating, clogged with half a hundred weight of mud. Somewhere near the voice of a young colonel was cursing in high overwrought screams, for one of the mules had been hurled by a shell-blast among his men. They were coming out of the line after relief. Cries of horses mingled with the cries of men. Suddenly yellow-forked narrow flames rose to a great height in front, as though one of the poplars once lining the road were recreated in fire. One of the tanks going up to their jumping-off points for the morrow's battle had been hit. Within a minute the enemy harassing fire was concentrated on the road, and the flaming poplars rose, one beyond the other, into the rainy night. Then a soft downward slurring sound, followed by a dull thud; another, and another, and another. Gas shells! My box-respirator, at the alert position across the chest, was treble-weighted with mud. I could hardly discover my face, so heavy and monstrous were my arms. While I was struggling to fit the mask the brutal whine of five-nines began again along the track, and a salvo dropped in our midst.

The light of my ordnance torch, through the misty panes of the gas-mask (raving mentally that my batman should be court-martialled for neglecting to treat them with anti-dimming paste) projected a weak shine upon arms and legs tangled and twisted with shreds of a waterproof cape in a heap of dark red slime. A leather-covered trace heaved under the mass, and tautened; a stricken mule reared up gaping, and sagged, and with Driver Frith sank into the slough.

Ten hours later our remaining mules, with their ears drooping, were standing, mud to fetlocks, along the picket line with its gnawn wooden posts. The rainy sky quivered with gun-fire; five miles eastwards, beyond the much-trodden brick-and-mortar heaps of Ypres, the infantry were going over — those who had got as far as the tape-lines, and had not been killed by the night-long shelling. A minor attack, one of a dozen scarcely mentioned in the official reports during the five months of the Passchendaele offensive; it failed. As for our night's work, it was the ordinary night job of any front-line transport. Afterwards those journeys seemed enviable, compared with the November shell-hole outposts in the rain and the frost.

The noise of a motor car suddenly slowing in the lane outside my window in this year of grace nineteen twenty-eight puts out the sunlight for an instant; I admit that I encourage the visitation of old scenes of the war. The sunlight, an agent of life, is often stronger than the haunting wish to be back again; firelight darkness in the best medium, with winter rain flat and quivering on the window. Yet I have sat for hours in the afternoon summer sunshine on Rockham beach near Morte Hoe in Devon, shooting, from a boy's catapult, small irregular pebbles at a round boulder, for the psychic pleasure of hearing them rise whizzing and piping, and fall with the chromatic whining of spent richochets. And when it was time to swim, or to have sea-weed battles with my friends again, an ex-officer of Tanks took the catapult from me, and flicked pebbles in their upward crying flight, and I knew that he too was thralled in deep, dreadful night.

One smell of smoke from a wood fire — it must be deal wood, of which the ammunition and ration boxes were made — and I am back again in the German dugouts above the Ancre valley at Baillescourt farm, with smarting eyes. The memories and visions that return at the smell of a fire of bits of deal plank or boxes would alone fill a hundred pages; but would they truly recreate the past? or would they betray reality by an overplus of melancholy and sadness? For that appears to be the predominant of my psychic make-up. It would seem that only by concentrating on certain incidents, and recreating them as monoliths out of Time, and link-ing them in a book or series of books, can one recover a fragment of the power of the past.

Sometimes, but very occasionally, I find a book with which I can shut myself away, locking the door of my writing-room, earthing the aerial of the wireless set, and cursing (old Salient habit) when my gentle wife comes to say it is time for tea, or supper, or bed, and that it will make me so tired and irritable again . . . no use, a dead fire, 3 a.m. or 4 a.m. again, the world empty and grey.

Wilfrid Ewart's *Way of Revelation* stirred and held one in that way; and perhaps it was as well that the book was not printed in its original length, which was twice that of the published novel. Or it may have been better, for one would have gone to bed at a sensible hour. The publishers compared it to *War and Peace*, but it needed no such bolstering, as was proved by its reception. Critics did not need to cast about for an attitude when reviewing it, but wrote easily out of their excitations. And these emotions, being reflected upon poor Ewart again (who in his war-worn state could only just contain his own) helped to bring on his nervous collapse. Darkness gets back again if it can, by many ways.

Way of Revelation is what is called immature in some of its scenes; the author was too near that which had made him suffer to treat the love-theme with the splendid objectivity that helps to make the scenes in France so clear and memorable. Who can forget the march of the Brigade of Guards from Ypres to the Somme in the August harvest weather; the pill-box scene just before the death of Little Percy, the debonair Captain Sinclair; preparations for the attack from Bourlon wood, just before the breaking of the Hindenburg line?

The ending is poor: it was not all Ewart's ending. The typescript of the novel — read and rejected by various publishers' readers on the grounds that war books at that time (just after the War) were of no interest to the public — was cut about and rearranged so much that the author became confused and ill. To help him, a friend suggested that another hand should rewrite the end for him. Ewart, sensitive and impressionable like all men of genius, and easily persuaded (since inspiration is a gossamer that gleams only in sunlight), agreed to this. He saw the new ending in proof. It was then that he had a stroke. The friend, called by telephone, went to see him. Ewart was sitting in a chair, the galleys disordered on a table before him. He managed to articulate, 'I — don't — know — what — this — means.' The ending of the book, as now printed, is deliquescent; it is like a worm lying on a hot tarred road. Ewart was broken-hearted by his experience with 'Rosemary Meynell', the girl in the book who died at the Victory Ball. This was fiction, not autobiography; but we feel that the spirit of truth is in all the foregoing chapters. It is a deeply tragic book, a brilliant and sombre book. Wilfrid Ewart had genius. He was shot, accidentally, by a stray bullet hitting him while he stood on an hotel balcony in Mexico whither he had gone for his health a year after *Way of Revelation* was published. He died on New Year's Eve, 1923.

2

The years go by, and *Way of Revelation* (although sure of a revival) is half-forgotten; and those of us interested in books begin to talk of the appearance of the great war book that shall stand somewhere near *War and Peace*. Barbusse's *Le Feu?* It is said to be one long cry of pain, a protest against unrelieved torture and horror imposed upon military slaves. The English phlegm won't accept Barbusse; he's a defeatist, and his writings those of a man with shell-shock. 'He piles horror on horror . . .' How many times has that been said by critics who have not the chemicals of creation within themselves? And who never got within a mile of the front line?

Here is Henri Barbusse describing what he saw on the battlefield near Mont St. Eloi in 1915:

We are now on the edge of the ravine at the spot where begins the plateau that our desperate charge traversed last evening, and we cannot recognize it. This plain, which had then seemed to me quite level, though really it slopes, is an amazing charnel-house. It swarms with corpses, and might be a cemetery of which the top has been taken away.

Groups of men are moving about it, identifying the dead of last evening and last night, turning the remains over, recognizing them by some detail in spite of their faces. One of these searchers, kneeling, draws from a dead hand an effaced and mangled photograph — a portrait killed.

In the distance, black shell-smoke goes up in scrolls, then detonates over the horizon. The wide and stippled flight of an army of crows sweeps the sky.

Down below among the motionless multitude, and identifiable by their wasting and disfigurement, there are zouaves, tirailleurs, and Foreign Legionaries from the May attack. The extreme end of our lines was then on Berthonval Wood, five or six kilometres from here. In that attack, which was one of the most terrible of the war or of any war, these men got here in a single rush. They thus formed a point too far advanced in the wave of attack, and were caught on the flanks between the machine guns posted to right and to left on the lines they had overshot. It is some months now since death hollowed their eyes and consumed their cheeks, but even in those storm-scattered and dissolving remains one can identify the havoc of the machine guns that destroyed them, piercing their backs and loins and severing them in the middle. By the side of heads black and waxen as Egyptian mummies, clotted with grubs and the wreckage of insects, where white teeth still gleam in some cavities, by the side of poor darkening stumps that abound like a field of old roots laid bare, one discovers naked yellow skulls wearing the red cloth fez whose grey cover has crumbled like paper. Some thigh-bones protrude from the heaps of rags stuck together with reddish mud; and from the holes filled with clothes shredded and daubed with a sort of tar, a spinal fragment emerges. Some ribs are scattered on the soil like old cages broken; and, close by, blackened leathers are afloat, with water-bottles and drinking cups pierced and flattened. About a cloven knapsack, on the top of some bones and a cluster of bits of cloth and accoutrements, some white points are evenly scattered; by stooping one can see that they are the finger and toe constructions of what once was a corpse.

The Germans, who were here yesterday, abandoned

their soldiers by the side of ours without interring them — as witness these three putrefied corpses on the top of each other, *in* each other, with their round grey caps whose red edge is hidden with a grey band, their yellow-grey jackets, and their green faces. I look for the features of one of them. From the depth of his neck up to the tufts of hair that stick to the brim of his cap is just an earthy mass, the face become an anthill, and two rotten berries in place of the eyes. Another is a dried emptiness flat on its belly, the back in tatters that almost flutter, the hands, feet, and face enrooted in the soil. . . .

When you hear of or see the death of one of those who fought by your side and lived exactly the same life, you receive a direct blow in the flesh before even understanding. It is truly as if you heard of your own destruction. It is only later that you begin to mourn.

That is the writing of a man who has sight: and who can translate sight into words. It is entirely truthful: it is as it was. The ordinary writer's methods are no good; he has probably never realized that he has to break down his old self, and rebuild himself entirely before he will have any power or truth. Or, as it was put more neatly and concisely elsewhere, the scales have to fall from his eyes.

Let us examine other books on these shelves. Mr. Masefield's *Old Front Line* and *Gallipoli* are beautifully written, and all old soldiers are surely grateful to him for these books. Mr. Nason's *Chevrons* and Mr. Patrick Miller's *The Natural Man* are fine creations; one lives with the natural or zestful man, the gunner hero, Blaven; and many of the scenes, like that of the preparations for the 18-pounder barrage before Third Ypres, are first-class; but neither book has the sweep and range of *Way of Revelation* or *Le Feu*. Mr. Mottram's *Spanish Farm* trilogy is in the same class as *The Natural Man*, although wider and more representative of the English soldier in France; but the battle scenes are deficient and unsatisfying: they no more recreate actuality than a picture of paper and orange peel on Hampstead Heath or Coney Island beach after an August week-end recreates the life and turmoil of the happy masses. Then Mr. Ford Madox Ford suddenly makes up his mind, as it were, to graft the War upon his Tietjens tree, which has already grown to maturity in one novel, *Some Do Not;* and in *No More Parades* we are given some superb scenes of a base-camp in France during air raids. They are true creations, as authentically created as the storm scene in *The Nigger of the Narcissus;* taken out of Time, and set before us. Then came *A Man Could Stand Up* — a recreation, presumably, of the front line under Kemmel Hill in April, 1918. The first impulse of the German push is over; another is imminent. Second by second, minute by minute, the trench scene is built up. And what a scene! The remnant of a battalion is paraded for the fixing of bayonets in spite of the traverses and fire-bays, specially described a few pages further on. The battalion fixes bayonets to the totally different drill procedure of the unfix; but we have been told already that it is part of the Ragtime Army, and this may account for it. No doubt Mr. Ford would have many excuses for this lapse; he might even give Dr. Johnson's famous answer. Yet, in spite of the original characters, the fresh detail, one remains unsatisfied by the book. This, one meditates, is not what was; it is unreal, it is not 'true but imaginary', it is the ichneumon fly in the wasp cell.

There are other books on my shelves which I read and re-read in order to project myself into the past: *Bullets and Billets*, by Bruce Bairnsfather, is one. It is a good book, only slightly marred by the quasi-humorous references to the 'humourless Hun', (which was, nevertheless, typical of a not uncommon billet-attitude towards the enemy in those early days). It has atmosphere, faithful to the 1914 winter as I knew it — the book of a true sensitivity that may never have completely discovered itself. I remember seeing the first Bairnsfather pictures on the wall of a cottage in the hamlet of Le Gheer; for Bairnsfather was in the neighbouring brigade.

Civilization by Georges Duhamel won the Prix Goncourt, as did *Le Feu*; one feels both will live. Certainly one can live completely in them. Duhamel is a master of simple prose. He is describing a tent in a casualty clearing station behind the Somme front:

> Round the electric arcs, luminous rings were formed by the sickening vapour. On the sides of the tent, in the folds, you could see the flies sleeping in big black patches, overcome by the cold freshness of the night.
>
> Large waves rolled on the canvas, passing like a shudder or violently flapping, according as the wind or gunfire was the cause.
>
> I stepped carefully over some stretchers and found myself outside, in a night that roared, illuminated by the aurora borealis of the battlefield.

I had walked, with my hands held out in front of me, until I came upon a fence. Suddenly I knew what it was to be leaning against the parapet of hell! What a human tempest! What explosions of hatred and destruction! You would have said that a company of giants were forging the horizon of the earth with repeated blows that filled the air with countless sparks. Innumerable furtive lights gave one continuous great light that lived, throbbed and danced, dazzling the sky and the land. Jets of iridescent light were bursting in the open sky as if they fell from the blows of the steam-hammer on white-hot steel. To me who had only recently left the trenches, each of these firework displays meant something — advice, commands, desperate calls, signals for slaughter. . . .

Towards Combles, on the left of Maurepas, one section above all seemed to be raging. It was just there that the junction was made between the English and the French armies; and it was there that the enemy concentrated a tumultuous and never-slackening fire. Every night, during many weeks, I saw this place lighted up with the same devouring flame. It was each instant so intense that every instant appeared to be the decisive one. But hours, nights, and months went slowly by in the eternity of time, and each of these terrible moments was only one intense outburst out of an infinity of them. Thus often the agony of wounds is such that you would hardly think it could be endured any longer. . . .

Morning came. Those who have seen the daybreaks of the war, after nights spent in fighting, or in the bloody work of the ambulance, will understand what is the most ugly and mournful thing in the world.

For my part, I shall never forget the green and grudging light of the dawn, the desolating look of the lamps and the faces, the asphyxiating smell of men attacked by corruption, the cold shiver of the morning, like the last frozen breath of night in the congealed foliage of large trees.

Barbusse has this same power of recreating the past; the divine power of fusing both spirit and letter of reality and casting the amalgam of truth into words. Yet both Duhamel and Barbusse recreate only in short sketches. Lonely towers the mighty Everest in some young writer's imagination. It will need titanic vitality to recreate the lost world of 1914–1918: of which every poor human mole that toiled and suffered and survived those years shall say: This is my molehill, yet it is a mountain, for it is universal, and nearest the stars of Truth! Around those peaks, O surely will the spirit of Wilfred Owen be soaring on glimmering wings — Wilfred Owen, a youth dead in the War, whom men of future ages will hail as the poet of the lost generation

> Whose world is but the trembling of a flare,
> And heaven but as the highway for a shell.

3

A natural companion of Owen's verse is Tomlinson's noble prose of grief. Owen was killed; Tomlinson, the most truthful of war correspondents, lost his job because he saw truth from the human or soldier's point of view, and this directed his writings: he was not 'patriotic'. But let H. M. Tomlinson speak for himself; the book is called *Waiting for Daylight*:

> Yet some of us who watched their behaviour saw the fantastic brightness in the streets on Armistice Day only as a momentary veiling of the spectres of a shadow land which now will never pass. Who that heard 'Tipperary' sung by careless men marching in France in a summer which seems a century gone will hear that foolish tune again without a sudden fear that he will be unable to control his emotion? And those Nobodies of Mons, the Marne, and Aisne, what were they? The 'hungry squad', the men shut outside the factory gates, the useless surplus of the labour market so necessary for a great nation's commercial prosperity. Their need kept the wages of their neighbours at an economic level. The men of Mons were of that other old rearguard, the hope of the captains of industry when there are revolts against the common lot of our industrial cities where the death-rates of young Nobodies, casualty lists of those who fall to keep us prosperous, are as ruinous as open war: a mutilation of life, a drainage of the nation's body that is easily borne by Christian folk who are moved to grief and action at the thought of Polynesians without Bibles. . . . That figure of Nobody in sodden khaki, cumbered with ugly gear, its precious rifle wrapped in rags, no brightness about it anywhere except the light of its eyes (did those eyes mock us, did they reproach us, when they looked into ours in Flanders?), its

face seamed with lines which might have been dolorous, which might have been ironic, with the sweat running from under its steel casque, looms now in the memory, huge, statuesque, silent but questioning, like an overshadowing challenge, like a gigantic legendary form charged with tragedy and drama: and its eyes, seen in memory again, search us in privacy. Yet that figure was the 'Cuthbert'. It was derided by those onlookers who were not fit to kneel and touch its muddy boots. It broke the Hindenburg Line. Its body was thrown to fill the trenches it had won, and was the bridge across which our impatient guns drove in pursuit of the enemy.

Where is that figure now? An unspoken challenge, which charges such names as Bullecourt, Cambrai, Bapaume, Croiselles, Hooge, and a hundred more, with the sound and premonition of a vision of midnight and all unutterable things. We see it in a desolation of the mind, a shape forlorn against the alien light of the setting of a day of dread, the ghost of what was fair, but was broken, and is lost.

Here is *Revolt in the Desert*, by 'T. E. Lawrence', a snow peak climbed by one man only. What would this man have written had he been an infantry subaltern in France? He would have been killed, of course; but had he survived, we should perhaps have had the book of the Somme and Passchendaele which we have been awaiting. 'T. E. Lawrence' is a great poet in thought and action, whom posterity will recognize as a peer of Shelley who achieved where Shelley was frustrated.

Mr. Sassoon's war poems are such that they may be

generally read when Owen's verse is known only by
students: in the sense that Kipling may be read in the
year 2034, or its possibly new equivalent, when the New
Testament may be known only by students. Mr.
Sassoon's war verse would hold anyone, at any time,
by its force and quality of being instantly understood.

For the same reason his *Memoirs of a Foxhunting Man*
will be read for as long as Englishmen care about
country pursuits. Mr. Arnold Bennett, on this book's
publication, stated that English sportsmen would not
care about it; but Mr. Bennett was thinking of Mr.
Sassoon's reputation for 'humanitarianism' perhaps,
and not of the *Memoirs*. The hero was not an ordinary
hunting man — although the term itself needs qualifica-
tion, for what is an ordinary hunting man?

In every hunt there is a small hard core, or backbone,
of men and women who become happy and harmonious
only if the hunted fox dies as he has been hunted — like
a gentleman, as they say; but the majority of fox-hunters
go out to see their friends, and for the excitement and
exultant glow of hearing hound music and the thrilling
ton ton tavern, ton ton tavern, ton ton ton ton ton ton tavern!
and the screaming cheers of the *Gone Away*! Of this
majority roughly one-half do not like to see the kill;
even if they may appear to join in the general satisfaction when, arriving pleasantly warm and excited on
lathered horses among mud-flecked faces and an
occasional crenellated silk hat, they see hounds moodily
baying round the huntsman as he kneels to take the
trophies. And among the more imaginative are a few
solitaries who feel pity for the ragged little tawny beast
which has run so far and so desperately, until — brush
dragging and balled with mud, and stilty-slender legs

moving in a faltering trot, and flacking tongue long and dry, and sight blurred — the clamour of tongues mingles with the bursting of blood in its ears, and a dozen jaws break it up.

In fairness to the author as artist it must be stated that he does not indulge in 'humanitarian' propaganda of this kind; at least he does not spoil his memories of the hunting man he was before 1914 by irruptions of a post-war mood wherein the self-contained fox-hunting attitude became a symbol, for many young old-soldiers, of the Great Blight of 1914—1918. 'They bring up their children to be blooded on the face: has not enough blood flowed on the face of the earth already?' as one of our precious moderns has expressed it. Mr. Sassoon does not go as far as this; his restraint and power to recreate the past days and joys of his pre-war life are such that, considering the prejudices and obscurities of the average writer, his gifts must be called extraordinary. Here is a man who can detach himself from the celestial bees in his bonnet and say just what happened. Only once has the post-1914 Blakian mind interfered with the recreation of what was seen and thought in those days of easy acquiescence.

Soon afterwards the second-whip rode through the undergrowth encumbered with spades, and they took their coats off in the dappling sunshine for a real good dig. The crunch of delving spades and the smell of the sandy soil now mingled with the redolence of the perspiring pack, the crushed bracken that the horses were munching, and the pungent, unmistakable odour of foxes. However inhumane its purpose, it was a kindly country scene.

Well enough I remember that September morning, and how, when I offered to take a turn with one of the spades, Denis Milden looked at me and said, 'Haven't I seen ye somewhere before?' I answered shyly that perhaps he'd seen me at the point-to-points. . . .

That 'however inhumane its purpose' slightly mars the past; for it is an older stranger commenting on history. (And while the above passage is being scrutinized it might be questioned whether 'Denis Milden' would regard the dig as 'real good' — for what M.F.H. likes digging out a 'bad' fox? — and also the term 'redolence of the perspiring pack': the 'redolence' of hounds has nothing to do with sweat, for, like most dogs, hounds perspire through their tongues.)

These are quibbles; but the book is so absorbing and such plain-seeing that these minute points are immediately noticeable.

The style is reader-proof, that is to say, simple and good. It is difficult to imagine any reader, whether narrow-minded, high-browed, broad-minded, red-shirted, black-shirted, true-blue'd, booted-and-spurred, or gentle and feminine and old-fashioned with scales unfallen, being unable to live in the narrative.

4

Real writers are scarce in any age; but those of them who stay the course, which is another way of saying those who keep their nerve, are very rare indeed.

As I see it, a real writer is not the same thing as

a good writer. Good writers exist within the convention of their age. They add much to the fugacious happiness of their time, and occasionally beyond their time; but they add nothing to what is loosely called thought, or the spirit. They do not shock one beyond one's complacency. They do not *see;* their detail is commonplace; they employ what writers with sight (which is the raw stuff of insight) have discovered before them; they are not discoverers; they uncover nothing; they all write the same sort of prose, with the same sort of details. Most good writers have been happy children; nearly every real writer has had a thwarted childhood, something sharpened in him before its time, something which, if he can outlive it, as Hardy did and Shelley did not, will bring him to an honoured and comfortable maturity. Those who don't come to maturity either fade away or never get away from the wilderness; they repeat themselves until the reader gets no more kick out of their stuff. Many Irish writers are like this; they begin startlingly well, and decline thereafter.

Mr. Robert Graves' *Good-bye to All That* has war scenes which are first class, and original. His description of trench life, of Loos and Somme, are the truth—it was just like that, the reader exclaims again and again. Yet Mr. Graves has keen sight but with one eye, as it were. Or his sight is not stereoscopic. His book is the book of a man who has suffered deeply, like Barbusse; but while Barbusse, through pain and mental torture, dissolves into the impersonal horizon of faith and hope, Graves continues the desperate personal search for clarity. With a different environment, one feels that many wounds would have been avoided; the struggle has been to recreate himself by saying good-bye to the past—a natural and heroic struggle to escape from the ranks of the lost generation.

It is natural for a writer to esteem his peer; and Mr. Graves' introduction to *The Enormous Room* is what an introduction should be, an addition to the book it serves, luring the reader beforehand for itself and illuminating its book when that has been read. Having read *The Enormous Room*, which made the coming of bedtime a happiness for seven nights, I turned to the preface and read that for some years the book had failed to find a publisher in England, although sponsored by 'T. E. Lawrence', who found in it:

> . . . a surprising sense of character, and an almost terrifying actuality of imagination in his descriptions! I went through *The Enormous Room* again, after I enlisted, while yet fresh to living in such enormous rooms, and from it knew, more keenly than from my own senses, the tang of herded men and their smell. The reading is as sharp as being in prison, for all but that crazed drumming against the door which comes of solitary confinement. Cummings' party suffered common compulsion, with its abandonment of spirit, to make them as supine as the planks in their prison floor.

What, then, is *The Enormous Room*?

An American Volunteer Red Cross sanitary man, a painter in civil life, had a friend in the section called B, who had written, in the summer of 1917, a letter to America containing statements which apparently criticized the French. The letter was opened by the Censor at the base, and B was arrested by the French authorities. On the principle of birds of a feather, Cummings was arrested with him. After an examination as crude and piffling as Shelley's before the Oxford dons, in which he deliberately chose to follow his friend B to prison, Cummings was taken to a sort of detention compound in a small and dreary French town called La Ferté Macé. He arrived at night, and was interviewed by an official in bed-slippers, whose description is a fair example of the style of the book.

His neck was exactly like a hen's: I felt sure that when he drank he must tilt his head back as hens do in order that the liquid may run down their throats. But his method of keeping himself upright, together with certain spasmodic contractions of his fingers and the nervous 'uh-ah, uh-ah' which punctuated his insecure phrases like uncertain commas, combined to offer the suggestion of a rooster; a rather moth-eaten rooster, which took itself tremendously seriously, and was showing-off to an imaginary group of admiring hens situated somewhere in the background of his consciousness.
'Vous etes uh-ah l'Amê-ri-cain?'
'Je suis Amêricain,' I admitted.
'Eh bien uh-ah uh-ah. We were expecting you.'
He surveyed me with great interest . . . We marched out.
Behind me the bed-slippered rooster uh-ahingly shuffled. In front of me clumsily gambolled the huge imitation of myself. It descended the terribly worn stairs. It turned to the right and disappeared. We were standing in a chapel.
The shrinking light which my guide held had become suddenly minute; it was beating, senseless

and futile, with shrill fists upon a thick enormous moisture of gloom. To the left and right, through lean oblongs of stained glass burst dirty burglars of moonlight. The clammy, stupid distance uttered dimly an uncanny conflict — the mutterless tumbling of brutish shadows. A crowding ooze battled with my lungs. My nostrils fought against the monstrous atmospheric slime which hugged a sweet unpleasant odour. Staring ahead, I gradually disinterred the pale carrion of the darkness — an altar, guarded with the ugliness of unlit candles, on which stood inexorably the efficient implements for eating God.

I was to be confessed, then, of my guilty conscience, before retiring? It boded well for the morrow.

No, the prisoner was there to draw bedding, for the chapel was used also as a store for palliasses.

It is seldom that one can live in a book as one does in reality. This book is a true creation: the reader lives with the author, and comes to know the men he was with as well, or as slightly, as he knew them. Mr. Cummings' sensitive tissue recorded a perfect matrix of his experiences.

He took many notes during the months of his detention in the damp insanitary prison, where men and women of all nationalities, some arrested on the slightest suspicions of small officials, were detained pending arrival of the quarterly Commission which decided who was to be set free and who was to be sent to the dreaded prison at Précigné. Sometimes the text consists of these notes slapped on to the page, a sort of paint-language, but perfectly intelligible; at other times, actuality is recreated in normal, efficient prose. Both methods permit the freedom of the reader's imagination, and are therefore absorbing. They convey impressions of the life as it was lived, with its vivid characters — Jean the Negro, Monsieur Petairs, the Little Machine-Fixer, the Sheeney with the Trick Raincoat, Bill the Hollander, 'Count' Bragard ('who knew Cezanne'), the Wanderer and his lovely wife and children, the Silent Man, Bathhouse John, the Fighting Sheeney, Celine, Renée, Lily, the Wooden Hand, Black Holster, and many more.

This transcription from life is a terrible indictment against a series of ideals which, culminating in war, pervert and ruin the newer, better traits in human nature. Those in authority — from M. le Directeur to the humblest *planton* treating the captives, both men and women, with flourish of revolver, bayonet, roared curses, and slamming doors — are presented, with few exceptions among the war-broken sentries, as creatures themselves fiendishly driven. And they passed it downwards. If a man waved at a woman across the compound wall topped with barbed wire, both he and she – poor innocents — were liable to be taken away and given dark and solitary confinement in a filth-swamped dungeon for many days.

Anyone could point out the insignificant faults of this long and most entertaining book, such as the marring of certain deeply-felt retrospects by a over-muchness of words; but these imperfections we accept, for they are of the richness of the author's emotions. He reveals himself as a man of sensibility and fortitude, and he writes always with such good taste that I do not think anyone, reading his book, could feel otherwise than that it is the work of a rare, fine spirit.

5

This record of entirely personal impressions of war books includes only what I like; an essay could be written on the false, the anti-Christ, or rather, the pro-Barabbas, which infested print during the war, and found expression in the use of certain Jehovah-exhorting verses by Mr. Kipling, and the lesser derivative verse of Mr. Frankau which describes the spirit of the man, shot for 'cowardice', whining and cringing at the door of Valhalla, and being denied by his comrades (Never so, by his comrades. This stuff was not worthy of Captain Frankau, R.F.A., anti-aircraft gunner; whose *Peter Jackson, Cigar Merchant* was a good book). But the record may serve to indicate the quality and texture of a mind which recently has been re-reading a book which on publication was acclaimed by most critics to be the best of the English war-books — *Undertones of War*, by Edmund Blunden.

Mr. Blunden was nineteen when first he went into action; I spent my eighteenth birthday in the trenches. I mention this to show that we were both callow, with minds unformed and receptive. For myself, I have possibly never recovered from certain shocks and terrors experienced in 1914: shock or terror not so much physical as mental, an incoherent sudden realization, after the fraternization of Christmas Day, that the whole war was based on lies, and that, most tragically, the lies were not deliberate, but arose from the obscurity or denseness of the average European's mind. One began to feel the weight of the whole dark world on one's shoulders, without daring even to formulate thought that the War was wrong. After the Armistice, the mental war became acute, the war against the righteous and bellicose attitudes of elderly men and women who had remained at home, whose mental obscurity and denseness not only had made the War but also were preparing the next war. The Versailles Treaty; the monuments to The Glorious Dead; the sanctification of poor soldiers' burden and misery. One was even called traitor for saying that the local War Memorial should be inscribed to the dead of all nations. The years 1919 and 1920, their interior or mental life, were lived in a No-man's-land more bitter than that patrolled and crossed during the preceding years, for they were without comradeship, and the enemy was world darkness which must be created into light. This possibly was hysteria and neurosis; and the statement is made here to show that an impaired mentality is possibly pronouncing judgment on the work of another mind which, if all the truth has been written in it, suffered no great misery. Mr. Blunden was a very young subaltern having in his battalion many friends whose affection saved the immature consciousness from a piercing introspection.

One learns from his book that he first went up the line in 1916, a temporary second-lieutenant serving with the 11th (Service) Battalion of the Royal Sussex Regiment. During a trench tour in a fairly cushy part of the line his colonel (who is usually referred to throughout this narrative by his surname — a small artistic flaw, suggesting a post-war atmosphere) appeared before him one morning with a red and smiling face, having just read a review of his subaltern's book of verse in *The Times Literary Supplement*. The upshot was that Mr. Blunden was given a job at battalion headquarters, together with the nickname of Bunny; and quite probably he owes his life to that favourable review, for although he went through many actions, the job kept him from the mort-blast of machine-guns at close range.

Undertones of War has many fine pages and chapters; some of them are superb — the description of the Schwaben Redoubt at Thiepval on the November night after the successful assault of Beaumont Hamel, and the trench scene during the Passchendaele push. But are even these two accounts creative? They are superb as undertones — but as undertones only. Can any man do more, one asks oneself, while that inner self cries for the truth that shall turn darkness into light. Is it possible to recreate those old turmoils and movements out of Time, to roll the rock of the 1914–1918 Sisyphus over the top of the mighty hill of War is Inevitable in Human Nature? Mr. Kipling, in his *Irish Guards* — has he got that reality, or is his point of view that of the old soldier talking as he leans on his spade?

The human mind forgets and recovers; it does not usually contain its misery. If it does it curdles into madness and shell-shock. Soldiers, unless they were all in, often sang when marching away from a battle, and cheered when they saw a war correspondent with a poised camera; and by these things those at home knew how happy the men were, and murmured Wonderful! They *were* happy, too, marching away from the line: they were often happy, or content, or relaxed, during the pauses in a battle — tin hats tilted, hands under heads, fags in mouth, crown-and-anchor board out, or the frayed pack of cards. But always the undercurrent was there, rising to the surface of their lives in the winter nights, the rain and the cold, the thoughts of never seeing again certain faces and doors and walls and streets and hedges. And long afterwards the men themselves marvel how they survived the terrible martial servitude; and remembering the hectic guest nights and canteen fugs, they say, 'Oh, it wasn't so bad after all. I wouldn't have missed it . . .' But it is the faces of friends they are thinking of, not war.

Mr. Blunden writes with restraint, a necessary attitude for the artist; but too much restraint, like too much tranquillity in a young writer, may result in sterilization; none of Mr. Blunden's men suffered like the men of Barbusse, Duhamel, Ewart, Owen, Sassoon. They (battalion pioneers)

> . . . made themselves comfortable in the cellars, and went to and fro in the exact and ordinary manner of the British working man. One, by turns, stayed at home to cook; the others kept the line tidy, and left no staircase, recess, or buttress unbeautified. They enjoyed this form of active service with pathetic delight — and what men they were? willing, shy, mostly rather like invalids, thinking of their families. Barbusse would have 'got them all wrong', save in this: they were all doomed.

The prose of *Undertones of War* is uneven, and (possibly) a mixture of ancient and modern writing. The bad parts of it may be made up of the letters of a nineteen-year-old poet; precious stuff, a mere exhalation of reality, exquisite perhaps, but weak, like that of the early and very precious Henry Williamson and Edward Thomas.

Mr. Blunden's wounded men are merely wounded; they do not (with scarce exceptions, like the man who moans that he is cold) behave as the wounded guardsmen behave in *Way of Revelation*, where, during Neuve Chapelle,

> Shells were bursting on and behind the road with an accuracy that was evidenced by the loud, child-like whimpering of men who had fallen or were crawling along it. The big sergeant suddenly jumped up with a shout. Adrian thought he had seen a German, and shouted, 'Where?' But the man began groaning and sobbing, his hands clasping his forehead, from which blood poured down his face.

Temporary Second-lieutenant Blunden sets out for France, as a reinforcement officer, at the beginning of 1916. He goes into the trenches near Bethune, and on the way meets a fellow-officer:

> noted for hairy raggedness and the desire to borrow a little money; he now appeared stumping along as though with a millstone about his neck, and, questioned, did not comfort us. The line was hell, he said, and flung his arms heavenward as some explosions dully shook the silence. It was a likely description with him. In the huts at Shoreham, months before, he had been wont to quote soulfully the wild-west verses of one Robert Service, then read by thousands, cantering rhetoric about huskies and hoboes on icy trails . . . the poor fellow was at last killed at Richebourg on June 30th in a hell more sardonic and sunnily devilish than ten

thousand Robert Services could evolve, or wolves and grizzlies inhabit.

That is reassuring, and kindly, although not entirely understanding: it is half-way to clarity. The subsequent description of the first trench tour is good; many young soldiers enjoyed the first time in immensely. 'Got any peace talk?' Sec-lieut. Blunden was asked.

> One of the first ideas that established themselves in my inquiring mind was the prevailing sense of the endlessness of the war. No one here appeared to conceive any end to it.

The young soldier goes through a gas course, and returns to the trenches, south of the 'ominous (La Bassée) canal' — Mr. R. Service probably would have used the adjective *sinister* in addition to *ominous* — and is shelled; a mine is blown up

> The casualties caused by the mine were sixty or more. Cuinchy . . . was a slaughter-yard. My ignorance carried me through it with less ado than I can now understand.

The wish that persists through two readings of this book is that all should have been recreated, so that a youth reading might experience *exactly* what young Blunden experienced at the time. It is much to ask for; it is all; a god-like task of creating. Mr. Blunden has the divine flow intermittently.

> . . . a deluge of heavy shells was rushing into the ground all round, baffling any choice of movement, and the blackness billowed with blasts of crashing sound and flame. Rain (for Nature came to join

the dance) glistened in the shocks of dizzy light
on the trench bags and woodwork. . . .

Was this passage taken out of a 1916 letter? 'Nature
came to join the dance' reads like an extract from
a letter home written in the easiness of relief from
excitation and fear. If so, it should have been quoted as
such: for reality in the line was different from reality
recollected in billet tranquillity.

6

The intimate mental history of any man who went
to the war would make unheroic reading,

Mr. Sassoon tells us in his *Memoirs of a Foxhunting Man*,
and it is this intimacy with the soldiers in *Undertones
of War* that is uncreated.

Mr. Edward Shanks, the distinguished contemporary
poet and writer, uttered the cool judgment in a literary
periodical that my novel *The Pathway* as a whole was a
failure; I don't know what this means, unless it means
that I am not like Mr. Edward Shanks. So perhaps I
should take cover from any back-blast and dig in with the
critical formula, *What has he said, and how has he said it?*

Mr. Blunden has said what he has said in undertone,
and has generally said it well; but in particular
instances, he has not driven himself hard enough
to create. The description of the preparations for
battle for the Schwaben Redoubt, and the evening of the bombardment, are very fine, and in
places tremble on the brink of actuality; this scene
remains in the mind with the more hopeless Passchendaele offensive scene. Here the prose is strong and vivid,

upholding pages of movement and turmoil which are as
fine as any written in Mr. Masefield's masterpiece, *The
Old Front Line*. The lapses are curious, suggesting the
prose of a boy whose poems were published while he was
in the trenches. For example:

> But, prime gift of eccentric heaven, there was the
> evening when Harrison took all the battalion to the
> divisional concert-party performing in the town.
> The roof ought indeed to have floated away in the
> paeans and warblings that rose from us, as the
> pierrots chirruped and gambolled there. In sweet
> music is such art — and never was music sweeter
> than the ragtime then obtaining, if appreciation
> indexes merit.

It is boyish, indeed; it is sweet and innocent writing,
bird-like; but one could not help wishing for a more
workmanlike description. Did the pierrots really chirrup
and gambol? Most divisional concert-parties were
made up of ex-professional vaudeville artists serving in
the ranks, who thanked Christ they didn't have to go into
the line and be killed.

And what was the Menin Gate like? What did Mr.
Blunden *see?* Posterity can see the new Menin Gate;
and wondering what the old Gate was like — whether
entirely blown away, or sandbagged, or reinforced with
camouflaged concrete — will turn to *Undertones of War*,
and find it described as 'that unlovely hiatus'. And of
the town itself, what will they read?

> I had longed to see Ypres, under the old faith
> that things are always described in blacker colours
> than they describe; but this view was a tribute

to the soldier's philosophy. The bleakness of events had found its proper theatre. The sun could surely never shine on such a simulacrum of divine aberration.

One is tempted to comment that, although he might 'have got it all wrong', Barbusse would at least have described Ypres as it was. Yet it must be said that Mr. Blunden shows signs of the power one longs to encounter in books, and finds so rarely: it gleams intermittently in *Undertones of War*, causing our imaginations to dissolve the present, and grow again the past:

> The air gushed in hot surges along that river valley, and uproar never imagined by me swung from ridge to ridge. The east was scarlet with dawn and the flickering gunflashes; I thanked God I was not in the assault, and joined the subdued carriers nervously lighting cigarettes in one of the cellars, sitting there on the steps, studying my watch . . . When I gave the word to move, it was obeyed with no pretence of enthusiasm. I was forced to shout and swear, and the carrying party, some with shoulders hunched, as if in a snowstorm, dully picked up their bomb buckets and went ahead.

Also:

> The men lying at each listening-post were freezing stiff, and would take half an hour's buffeting and rubbing on return to avoid becoming casualties.

Again:

> We also went to a lecture by a war correspondent, who invited questions, whereon a swarthy old

colonel rose and said: 'The other day I was obliged to take part in a battle. I afterwards read a war correspondent's account of the battle, which proved to me that I hadn't been there at all. Will the lecturer explain that, please?'

And there are beautiful descriptive lines here and there, such as:

Deathly blue, sable, hung the pall of the great cold over this battlefield,

and:

We endeavoured to send off a pigeon, but the pigeon, scared by the gunfire, found his way into the dugout again, and presently a fluttering sound under the floorboards led to his discovery.

Some of the verses printed at the end of the prose account, in *A Supplement of Poetical Interpretations and Variations*, partly supply what is lacking in the prose descriptions. If you have done the thing in verse, and then attempt to do it again in prose with an eye upon what must not be repeated, you are handicapping your creative powers. Almost better, one feels, to have cast the coincident verse into the prose. Here are two parallel Interpretations,

A tank officer looked in, asking help to salve some equipment from his wrecked machine, lying just behind our pill-box. Presently the drizzle was thronging down mistily again, and shelling grew more regular and searching. There were a number of concrete shelters along the trench, and it was not hard to see that their dispossessed makers were determined to do them in. Our doctor, an Irishman named Gatchell, who seemed utterly to scorn such annoyances as Krupp, went out to find a much discussed bottle of whisky which he had left at his medical post. He returned, the bottle in his hand; 'Now, you toping rascals' — a thump like a thunderbolt stopped him. He fell mute, white, face down, the bottle still in his hand; 'Ginger' Lewis, the unshakable Adjutant, whose face I chanced to see particularly, went as chalky-white, and collapsed; the Colonel, shaking and staring, passed me as I stooped to pull the doctor out, and tottered, not knowing where he was going, along the trench. This was not surprising. Over my seat, at the entrance the direct hit had made a gash in the concrete, and the place was full of fragments and dust. The shell struck just over my head, and I suppose it was a 5·9. But we had escaped, and outside, scared from some shattered nook, a number of field mice were peeping and turning as though as puzzled as ourselves. A German listening-set with its delicate valves stood in the rain there, too, unfractured. But these details were perceived in a flash, and meanwhile shells were coming down remorselessly all along our alley. Other direct hits occurred. Men stood in the trench under their steel hats and capes, resigned to their fate. The continuous and ponderous blasts of shells seemed to me to imply that an attack was to be made on us.

It reads like an extract from a diary, or a letter sent home; flowing easily in the writing of it; containing a mixture of styles and perspectives, colloquialisms ('determined to do them in'), and creative passages (from 'Our doctor, an Irishman . . .' to 'the German listening-set'), and journalistic insertions ('This was not surprising', 'such annoyances as Krupp', which break the imaginative creation).

Here is the poetical variation:

> At the noon of the dreadful day
> Our trench and death's is on a sudden stormed
> With huge and shattering salvoes, the clay dances
> In founts of clods around the concrete styes,
> Where still the brain devises some last armour
> To live out the poor limbs.
>   This wrath's oncoming
> Found four of us together in a pillbox,
> Skirting the abyss of madness with light phrases,
> White and blinking, in false smiles grimacing.
> The demon grins to see the game, a moment
> Passes, and — still the drum-tap dongs my brain
> To a whirring void — through the great breach
>   above me
> The light comes in with icy shock and the rain
> Horridly drips. Doctor, talk, talk! if dead
> Or stunned I know not; the stinking powdered
>   concrete,
> The lyddite turns me sick — my hair's all full
> Of this smashed concrete. O I'll drag you, friends,
> Out of the sepulchre into the light of day,
> For this is day, the pure and sacred day.
> And while I squeak and gibber over you,
> Look, from the wreck a score of field-mice nimble,
> And tame and curious look about them; (these
> Calmed me, on these depended my salvation).

. . .

And all thought dwindled to a moan, Relieve!
But who with what command can now relieve
The dead men from that chaos, or my soul?

The old soldier reading Mr. Blunden's experiences
in Observatory Wood during Third Ypres will say to
himself, 'Yes, that's true enough!' but when he has
read (as easily he may not) the verses called *Third
Ypres* and *Pillbox* in the supplement, he will realize
what was lacking in the prose descriptions — the
sense of reality in action, verging on the unreal, as
though time were being withdrawn from the world and
the power responsible were endeavouring to substitute a
Fourth Dimension, which was beyond control and
dragging life backwards into chaos. The verse is a true
re-creation, a resurrection of the past.

Prolonged bombardment and physical exhaustion,
several nights without sleep and hope of relief, amidst the
groans and pallid listnesses and screams of the semi-shat-
tered, sometimes produced a bright and glassy delirium
of the senses. As for actuality, what the common soldier
of the line endured in the winter crater zones of the big
battles is not continuously conveyed in any English
book I have read. It can be seen in the unique pictures
of C. R. W. Nevinson: life without horizon or hope, the
will stolen and the body enslaved, unimaginable fatigue
and misery and pain endured through long slow hours
and days and nights ending only to begin again and go
on in rain and cold sleeplessly like that for ever in a world
with no horizon save death and oblivion. A good officer,
as Mr. Blunden obviously was, had some escape through
the feeling of responsibility, and a minor sense of comfort
and freedom; a private (O irony!) soldier just had to do,

and then do, and go on doing, until he died, or until he got what usually he prayed for, a disabling wound.

Until the war novel that recreates the war appears, if it is to appear, we must look for clarity in the Everyman edition of *Under Fire* (not being too critical about the 1905 English prep-school slang translated into the mouths of *simples soldats*) in *Way of Revelation, Revolt in the Desert*, and in the slim volume of Wilfred Owen's verse. The spirit of Truth in these books, informing the mind for the other books (among which *Undertones of War* immediately takes a high place) is needed among *all* men (especially violent pacificists and militarists) to-day, if their children are to remain their children in the universal sunshine.

Postscript I

Since writing the above, I have learned from Mr. Blunden that *Undertones of War* was written direct from memory. 'I had nothing with me in Tokyo to write my book with except a couple of maps which you will remember — Hazebrouck 5a and Lens 11; I had no letters or diary. In quoting my British Working Man passage you make the particular into the general, I think; I defined the instance of the working-party in nineteen sixteen, and they *were* doomed, because nearly all were knocked out or wounded at Stuff Trench a few weeks afterwards, let alone what followed . . . You are quite bound to object to my style if it seemed crude and unlicked. But I should never go to Barbusse or Conrad as tutors; they do not comprehend the use of English words, one because he writes in French (a different task altogether) and the other because he hadn't English in his blood. I learn rather from the Prayerbook and Johnson's *Lives*. Further, although my book looks to you like a rough draft (didn't the War look like that too?), it was not hurriedly written. I was at it from nineteen twenty-four until the final proofs. I tell you that its faults are my nature's; I "cannot daub it further". Life presses on; your "artist" is a hermit adorning his cell rather than a deponent of truth in its normal effects.'

Postscript II

Reality and War Literature was written in 1928, and I have added to it, for this book, fragments of criticism written about that time. Since the essay was published in *The London Mercury* in January 1929, *All Quiet on the Western Front* has swept the world which was waiting for such a book. I do not agree with what so many non-combatants said about *All Quiet;* the spirit of the very young soldier's reality of life in war is there, but not the body. Many of the scenes read like fakes, particularly the battle scenes — 'the tension of imagined dread'. Its enormous success detempered the spring of other writers who might otherwise have attempted their *Old Wives' Tale*; the tide suddenly set the other way. The author of *The Case of Sergeant Grischa* was apparently unable to complete his trilogy, and particularly *Education before Verdun*. Mr. Sassoon's *Memoirs of an Infantry Officer* must have been difficult to complete; and also Mr. H. M. Tomlinson's *All Our Yesterdays*. In 1934, however, was published the first calm novel which is also a great work, in my opinion — *Winged Victory*, by V. M. Yeates, who was an experienced Camel pilot during the war. I beg all who have any interest in any of my writings to read *Winged Victory*.

Postscript III

Books which seem to me to be good are *A Soldier's Diary of the Great War*, which was published anonymously, with a long introduction by me — the author was Captain D. H. Bell, M.C., late of The Camerons and the R.F.C. Bell, Yeates, and I were at school together, and served together in the army for the first few months of the war. Further good books, which I have read, are dos Passos' *Three Soldiers*; *Her Privates We*, by Frederic Manning; Stephen Graham's *A Private in the Guards*; *Nothing of Importance*, by Bernard Adams, who served in the Royal Welch Fusiliers, the regiment of Captains Graves and Sassoon; the *Letters of Charles Sorley; The Secret Battle*, by A. P. Herbert; Bernard Kellermann's *Ninth of November;* Lt.-Col. Roland Feilding's *War Letters to a Wife; 'Happy Days' in France and Flanders*, by Benedict Williamson, a popular and beloved padre; *The Squadroon* by Ardern Beaman, a story of a cavalry regiment; *Pushed and the Return Push*, by Quex; *A Subaltern on the Somme*, by Mark VII; *Four Years on the Western Front*, an excellent everyday account of a territorial transport driver's adventures; *Gallipoli Diary*, by General Sir Ian Hamilton, which has beautiful passages; *An Airman's Outings*, by Contact; *Old Soldiers Never Die*, by Pte. F. Richards, D.C.M., M.M.; *German Students' War Letters*, and their parallels, *War Letters of Fallen Englishmen; R.F.C. H.Q.*, by Maurice Baring; *A Generation Missing*, by Carrol Carstairs; *Marching on Tanga*, by F. Brett Young; *War Birds*, *The Diary of an Unknown Aviator*, which is true although high-spotted, and seemed the best thing written of war-flying until *Winged Victory* instantly towered over it, like a peregrine falcon putting down a sparrowhawk; and other books, which acquaintances and friends have borrowed and not returned, are missing from the shelves. Some were bought, read, and given away, among them *Fix Bayonets!* by John W.

Thomason Junior, and *Warrior*, an autobiographical work by Lt.-Col. G. S. Hutchinson, the overtones of which are indicated by their titles. Mr. Compton Mackenzie's *Gallipoli Memories* is a book to keep and re-read, the story of a staff attachment off Gallipoli, with some moving and exquisitely written scenes; so is the anonymous *Fusilier Bluff*, the occasional trenchant style of which one forgives the author because of his elegiac and passionate protest against human stupidity and sloth. *In Araby Orion*, by Edward Thompson, is a short book, but deep with anguish, an unforgettable story of a poor London soldier's death in Palestine. It is sad to think that in a few years, perhaps, the literature of the war of 1914–1918 will be forgotten, like that of other wars, in a European war arising not because the last war was forgotten, but because its origins and contributing causes in each one of us in Europe were never clearly perceived by ourselves.

Postscript IV

A friend said to me, reading the proofs of this book, 'Why did you write so much about Edmund Blunden's book?' I did not know what to answer; but when verifying some of the quotations in the original edition, an old telegram form slipped from out the pages:

> SRP 11-13 a.m. London City W. Croyde, 6 De 28
> Reply paid Williamson Skirr Cottage
>
> Could you do four thousand words by the fifteenth on Blundens Book to oblidge me
> SQUIRE

PART THREE

AMERICA

S.S. *BERENGARIA*

Sunlight and grey clouds and grey sea by day; darkness and unfamiliar star-groupings above great funnels at night — and always the wastes of the sea.

Gulls followed for the first day beyond the Scillies, soaring effortless and whitely cold above and behind the ship. There is no meaning in the sea's movement; the deep sea that is relict of some ancient flame-writhing power in space.

A small fountain of spray in the distance, another rising near it. Whales blowing. It is in some strange way comforting to think that these ocean wanderers are akin to oneself — sprung from the same flame-writhing power of creation.

Their blood, too, is warm; they are born as we are born; the mother nourishes her young as a woman her child; and they, too, feel love, have hope, taste grief: and their dead sink away into the darkness which awaits us all.

Wind harrying water, the daylong slow lift and fall of white rails against the grey horizon, and an empty sky above. And yet — what can it be? A speck rapidly becoming a dark nervous flicker of wings, a swoop from six hundred feet, a swift curve *cut* against the sky; the bird alights on the truck of the mast aft. Several people taking out binoculars from cases, and focusing on the bird. What can it be?

It has a creamy breast barred with black, like fire-cracks in the grey ash of a half-burnt log; yellow claws and legs feathered almost to the feet; a blue back, a curved beak with yellow skin around the base, and full proud liquid eyes. A peregrine falcon! A voice explains that *peregrine* means *wanderer*, and this bird may easily have flown from Labrador or even Key West in Florida. It was tired but resolute; hour after hour it sat there, facing the wind.

Was it journeying to Spain, or the Azores, or — and fancy held this — to Lundy and the coast of North Devon which one had left, perhaps for ever? For what was it travelling the empty Atlantic skies? It sat there hour after hour; and then with quick rise and wheel and flicker it was gone the way it had been flying — a speck flying towards the sun, and England, sweeping the skies for a wing-flicker like its own, scorning all others.

MANHATTAN

THIS was an island once; wolves lived here. Salmon in bright sea-strength pushed easily into the tides running against them at their own cruising speed. Trees grew among the grey rocks, rounded and smoothed in an earlier age of ice.

Silence, birds piping, the silver-bubble-breaking cry of the loon, the loon-like cry of keen-eyed men brown and half-naked. If trees have memory, then one of the old hardwoods over there, just across the river, will remember it.

The tides swirling around the island to-day are dull-glittering in sunlight with a million million fragments of grey-faced civilized life in dissolution poured from phosphorescent sewer and drain, tipped from truck and reversible barge. It is a *cliché* that New York is the cruellest city in the world. An island! There is a never-ceasing roar; night is day; peaks of buildings stir the clouds. Droves of metallic wolves prowl swiftly on wheels; steam-heat fumes from lids in the streets. All this is as natural, or as phenomenal, as maggots swarming strongly on carrion, as the concrete-protected civilizations of termit-ants. (Three thousand miles away to eastwards the hills of Exmoor lie under the quiet sky.)

What is the use of philosophy? It is a sedentary pastime, like chess or crossword puzzling. Books of philosophy usually emanate from inharmonious men with inferior writing powers striving to prove how life may be lived harmoniously.

Away with philosophy, or sophistry; this taxi-cab is eighty horse-power, electrically warmed, very comfortable, travelling at fifty-seven m.p.h. down Park-avenue, one of five in a line. The driver leans sideways over the seat and with his right hand adjusts the radio to bring in the second act of *Tristan and Isolde* startling, clear and lovely. The lights blink red; and with smooth sinking gliding, as the swooping falcon surely feels as he throws up to his pitch, we are motionless again.

This is the Biltmore; Paul Whiteman's band — essence of jungle sun; this bottle — essence of French sun (we hope!). Laughing lips and eyes, teeth finer than any on the island in those salmon-leaping days. And hark! A bird singing in the pause of the dance music. A real live bird? 'Sure, a real bird. That one always wakes and sings at two o'clock.'

There he is in a cage, and there another, another, and another, all round the room: rolling, trilling — aspiring — to what? Dreaming of the sun over the Canary Islands? Of paradisal love? Where dreams Wagner now?

'These birds don't live long, I guess, in New York.'

Two a.m., Eastern Standard Time. The sun has risen on Exmoor, and the children are waking from sleep.

2

The small sand-martins, that peck their nesting-holes in the yellow bank of the river cutting into the meadow by Brayley Bridge, will have returned now; and the kingfisher which gouges a tunnel also in that bank will just have laid her first egg.

Is the willow warbler singing his plainsong among the alders?

Has the rain come yet for the spate to bring up spring salmon from the sea?

In New York the snow falls, the city roars, and never the sight of a sparrow — although a few do live in the dull plane trees in Washington-square, a block below where this is being written, in the old Brevoort Hotel at Fifth Avenue and Eighth Street. Perhaps the cold has killed them, or driven them South.

Fifth Avenue and the other streets are of dirty corrugated ice, snow compressed by a million rubber wheels rolling swiftly in spite of skids and crashes.

Coming to this room just now, from Broadway — it is early, not yet two a.m. — I saw a cat killed as it was crossing the street. It hesitated a split-second; and the wheel crushed its head.

A passing wop (Italian), scarcely checking in his walk, bent down, picked it up, and went on his way indifferently. He'd cook it and eat it somewhere, said my companion, probably over one of the bonfires of wooden boxes which blaze about the streets at night.

The spirit of Elizabethan London rules the city of New York. One sees small children rooting in ash-cans for scraps of food. They have had a bad time in New York during the Depression. Men with grey faces and thin overcoats, hands in pockets, ask you for a nickel for a cup of coffee. It is no uncommon sight to see a man suddenly fall down in the street, having walked about nowhere, anywhere, for days and nights, starving, homeless. Nobody whines in this city, not even the cat that was run over. It is a city of life or death.

Is this really being written in New York, three

thousand miles away from Devon . . . or is one *really* with the chiffchaff and the celandines, the ring-doves sitting on their raft-like nests swaying in the firs of Bremridge Wood?

And have the crows built this year in Windwhistle Spinney?

I see them all; they are more real than New York. I am in England: and yet in a few hours I shall be leaving for an eight-hundred-mile journey south to Georgia, where they say peaches are in bloom and the sun shines all the time; and there will be strange birds to see, and unknown flowers.

But these things of the natural world are real only when they are part of oneself, of one's vital essence, distillation of sight and scent and sound from childhood and early life.

SOUTHERN SUN

I

HERE in Georgia one sits in March sunshine of power and light equal to that of an English day in July. The sky is a pale azure, and smoked glasses are needed to write this out of doors.

Strange cries of birds score and cross the blue-stained air. Several jays, smaller than the English jays, cry as though petulantly in a China-berry tree. Over my head, in the black oak, a woodpecker tap-tap-taps slowly as she gouges a nesting hole in a dying branch.

A hundred yards away her mate is telling his love in his own peculiar way — by drumming on the steel post supporting power cables. It sounds like the electric riveting of skyscraper girders high up over Manhattan, which I left yesterday by air, flying down the sea coast of the Carolinas.

That was an interesting journey. The monoplane had an open cock-pit. Mile after mile we haared over swamps and derelict cotton and tobacco fields, where among pine trees stood bleached wooden shacks where negro families dwelt.

We flew sometimes only a few feet above the ground, to feel the speed of a powerful engine and the exhilaration of grey-brown grassy earth rushing upon us.

Like a hobby falcon making a point at its own shadow we threw up over trees and glided down again. The soil was reddish-brown for three hundred miles; and after a rest we flew on, coming to a grey sandy land where asparagus and cotton grew. Always the grey-green, semi-ruinous wooden shacks with their sharply defined shadows were beneath us on the flat earth.

At last we came to the Savannah, mark of our destination, a river whose yellow waters absorbed our shadows in its lazy tepid flow past yellow mudbank and yellow-sanded roots of great trees washed down by floods. Beyond on high level ground lay the airport, by the polo ground, where we landed in solitude, over which wheeled in spirals seven small black vultures.

Now one sits peacefully in the sunshine, surrounded by the petulant cries of blue jays, the quiet tapping of female woodpeckers — handsome birds with red-velvet heads and black and white backs — and the arrogant drumming of the males.

Cat-birds call and screak; the mocking bird sings like a nightingale; flights of waxwings pass overhead; and the robins, which are as big as English thrushes with auburn breasts, are about to migrate to the Northern States and Canada. The early settlers, homesick for England, must have seen these birds with joy, for they resembled the birds of home which they had left for ever. *They do not change the sky, who cross the sea in ships,* wrote the old Roman poet. Everyone here is so kind and friendly to the Englishman; they speak in slow, musical voices; the little girls curtsy when they are introduced to one; the tempo so slow and restful. Cardinals with brilliant flush of terra-cotta red fly under the trees pale green with new leaves.

One sits lazily, still a little bemused and strange-feeling, in this chair of hickory wood, the sunshine oozing into one's veins, butterflies lighting on one's hand and resting with damasked wings sensitive to every waft of air. Negroes pass slowly, in deep content of life and the sun; while one by one the peach petals drop to the dust.

2

And here one sits, day after day, smoked glasses diluting the white light of the semi-tropic sky, writing the autobiography: here one sits in the sun of Georgia, watching children still at, or as they say here, in school. A couple of acres of land among the houses has been made into a playing-park.

There is a tennis court, of hard, red local crushed sandstone; a gymnasium, open air, of course; ping-pong table; volley ball court; a horse-shoe pitch — this a sort of quoits.

Black mammies sit about under the mimosa trees, while tiny children play and run around. The attitude or feeling between coloured and white people seems to be a mutual tender respect and affection. This among the leisured class: if America has a leisured class. (Besides the Negroes!)

The children still in school are amazing to me, a quiescent Englishman. They appear to mature so young. This young lady by my side, who looks like Carmen at twenty, lip-sticked, yellow flower of jasmine in dark hair, has just confessed that she does not want to grow up; she does not want to be eighteen. 'Heavens, then how old are you?' 'Thirteen. I guess I don't want to be old. I don't want to have dates.' 'Dates?' She explains that she doesn't want to grow up, eighteen is so old, she doesn't want to have dates with boys. I admire the flower in her hair. With a sidelong smile and glance from long-lashed brown eyes, she gives it to me.

'You have a lot of forgs in England, I guess?' Everyone asks that: England is the land, they think, of sunlessness, fogs, self-discipline. They pronounce many words with the seventeenth-century English pronunciation — dorg, forg, yaller.

These children, boys and girls with a charm of manner that comes only from naturalness, are amazed that in England children go to school in the afternoons. And compulsory games! That can't be much fun, they reckon. And boys are sometimes beaten? Why? They cannot understand. Homework? They have a little, but it's interesting; it's real. Modern life, living stuff.

We play tennis most afternoons. I am becoming a Southerner, the northern core of dream or introspection is being drawn out of my being by the sun. It is an effort to begin to write every morning, although the old world of the past is so real as I recreate its scenes, faces, and the actions of my old self which in retrospect seem so weak and vain and wasteful. Only the outside of me is here: my other, or inner self is disintegrated, scattered away in past desires and hopes and mortifications. But 'if way to the better there be, it enacts a full look at the worst', as Hardy wrote.

In the great white sunlit warren of the hotel nearby, old men from the North sit and watch the Wall Street ticker-tape screen. They have come for the golf tournament, for a holiday. But there they are, out of the sun all day, watching the ticker, nervously fluttering fingers on chair-arms: bearing in their minds great organizations and schemes which are their main life or activity—only the outside of them is down here for a holiday.

The South is different from the North, as heat is different from cold. In heat a plant lives, but to escape the coldness upon itself, it must dream. Several butter-flies have fluttered around me as I sit here under the black oak, while butterflies and moths of fancy flit through my head. *Would you like to play tennis now, sir?* Rather!

3

I spent all this mid-March day under an incandescent sky, at the National Golf Course, watching the tourna-ment. Bobby Jones is the chief attraction, and he was off form, missing putts of a few yards only, many times. He has not played much since his retirement four years ago, and came here out of good fellowship. The rows of negro caddies, waiting in line outside the clubhouse, with their red long-peaked caps and large bags of clubs with burnished metal heads, looked like a lot of coloured praying mantises waiting there. Thousands of visitors, mostly men and women middle-aged. Two dollars for the day to watch, or five dollars for the week. They say the grass (except the greens, which are watered) of this fine course is dry and brown by May-June, when no one plays, it is too hot.

Horton Smith looked like winning — a tall, lean, nervous, shambling figure. The prize is five thousand dollars. His first three rounds were sixty-nine, seventy-two, seventy, very good indeed: long drives and many sand-traps. Lunched at the club and we drank highballs, which made everyone lively very quickly with a sort of hollow-glittering liveliness. Round again in afternoon, and then home to dine with Miss Louise, who told me interesting stories about the crackers or poor whites, and negroes, for whom she has, like all Southern ladies, a deep protective affection. One story was particularly amusing: scene, the local court. A cracker juryman asked to be excused, giving the reason that his wife at home was at that very moment conceiving. 'Don't you mean she is at home being confined?' suggested the Judge. No sir, the poor white maintained his wife was at home conceiving. The poor whites, descendants of original settlers, live in the fields and woods, and usually are uneducated in the academic sense only; and in the atmosphere of a court room, one would feel keenly the effect of a misused word. So the judge replied evenly, 'The juryman will be excused, for whether a man's wife is conceiving or being confined, in the opinion of the Court the husband's place is by the wife's side.'

I wrote some of Chapter Twenty-Four of the auto-biography, the penultimate scene of the Joanna-Julia complication, by the radio until ten o'clock, when I changed into tails and went to the Country Club dance — an informal, enthusiastic, happy-noisy affair which I enjoyed although feeling at first much out of it, being the only man in tails and, as it were, unentailed. People were friendly and hospitable, and after a drink or two of 'corn', from a sedan car parked outside, I felt livelier. I danced with several nice girls, and talked to an intelligent man about books. Walked home alone at two a.m., Sunday morning, liking well this life of work-play-sleep-eat. At twelve-thirty p.m. I got up, had whole house to myself except for coloured servants in background, shaved and bathed, wandered about happily in dressing-gown in garden and palm court, listening to Wagner on radio from New York, had breakfast under white-blossoming dogwood tree — toast, half a pint orange juice, half a pint milk, eggs fried on both sides. Went up to higher ground of airport in afternoon, and watched polo on adjoining ground. Thousands of automobiles parked there. Two unceasing streams of dark sedan cars passing on the road; this the American Sunday. Five hundred closed automobiles for one roadster: the sedans were filled with families, father usually driving and mother, lip-sticked, powdered against grease, looking from open window at the crowds, the unmarried part of herself half-consciously questing among male faces with the diminishing dream of her youth's remainder.

The gardens are now open to the public; azaleas are over; Mr. Horton Smith has departed with his cheque for five thousand smackers; magnolia grandiflora are not yet in bloom. Birds are nesting. White suits appearing. Was bitten by a white Finnish Spitz dog in the morning, right calf: heard myself shouting 'Bloody America!' as it turned and ran away with a wicked look in fang and eye. Next day the owner, a slim little blonde girl about ten years old, apologized to me, and I apologized to her for my nasty temper. I wrote for three hours in the evening, tuning-in in succession to about seven of the nine hundred broadcasting stations in the United States. Their programmes are well-timed, one beginning as the other ends, within a second: every programme is the best of its kind, since they are bought and sponsored by advertisers, who naturally try to get the best for their money.

It is getting very hot, too hot, the sun stands up in the sky like the whiskered spirit of Blake's burning tiger. I did no work the next day. Played in tennis tournament after luncheon at the Pheasant Inn, ninety-three degrees in the shade. Foolishly, against my better judgment, I drank mint-julep with the meal, although knowing it would be fatal to any sustained performance on the hard-court afterwards. Mint-julep, classical Southern drink, is made of crushed ice, crushed mint, whiskey, and served with spray of mint. Hoar frost, instantly marred by finger-touch, forms outside the glass, and confirms the illusion of coolth. The whiskey was Scotch, from New York; fatal derivation. I won the first few games, then dropped away feebly, and left the court feeling as though my veins were running lead.

4

It is past midnight, and the Easter moon shines over the magnolia trees. By its light I see the writing-pad before me, and the shadow of my pen athwart white paper. It is one of those nights, mysterious and warm, which seem a suspension of time, happiness, sorrow. The small life within oneself is released into the life of the night-suns. To-day, or yesterday, the last day of March, the temperature was nearly a hundred in the shade, and to-night it is still hot; the moon with its shine does nothing to cool the earth.

I feel myself a phantom of moonshine, in this white cotton suit. Water falls softly in the pool beside me, and the little bronze Pan contemplates a wavering lunar image.

Until an hour ago children were playing in the park at the end of the road, swinging on the trapezes and turning themselves inside out on the rings; small

children, in age between eight and eleven. Now they are
gone home, and the mocking-bird sings in the sugar-
berry tree.

Everywhere on the hot ground runs the reeling stridu-
lations of crickets; cars pass with their coarse engine-
noises on the sandy roads. Gasoline is cheap in America,
and the engines have not evolved to the English fineness
and balance. Below the garden on the sandy road and
from the distant town, comes the mournful shriek of a
freight train, and the slow tolling of its bell.

Down in the town the cotton mills are working night
and day. The factory windows gleam with a greenish
light, pallid forms move within. Walking outside an
hour ago I saw two old negroes sitting on the grass,
homeless, and apparently content.

Everything in Dixie moves slowly, lazily. Transplanted Europeans called Americans cannot work in the
cotton and corn fields in the summer; only the superior
skin-pigmentation of the transplanted Ethiopians can
withstand the pressure of the sun.

I go inside, and turn on the radio. *This is the Atlanta
Journal calling, the voice of the South. The Atlanta Journal
covers Dixie like the dew.*

Dance music follows. It awakens the mocking-bird,
that imitator of other birds.

Listening, I hear the notes of a thrush — almost an
English thrush, with something of the blackbird's
quality in its notes, but faster in tempo; then the wistful
jangle-cry of the blue jay; the throb of the nightingale
when it cries *teru teru teru*. (Yet there are no nightingales
in America.)

Before I was told about the mocking-bird it puzzled
me, for it sounded as though several birds were singing

on the same bough, all of them hidden in the darkness, and one following the other.

I have been to a barbecue: a pit in the ground holding glowing wood embers, on which were roasted the bodies of various birds and animals, which, when cooked, were eaten around the fire.

The older forms of Southern hospitality are reminiscent of 'T. E. Lawrence's' descriptions of meals with desert sheikhs: vast silver salvers containing many fragments of chickens, my hostess urging me to fill my plate full: legs and wings lifted from her plate to mine as a compliment to her guest, and also in solicitude for the thin face of the foreigner. I retorted in the same playful way, asking my hostess how she enjoyed picnicking in the tropics, and inquiring when she and her fellow trippers were thinking of sailing back to Plymouth? Fortunately this ninety-year-old lady had a young heart and wit, and so the foreigner was not considered merely boorish and insulting. She told me that she liked Englishmen because they resembled Americans: she told me also that I reminded her of Frank Harris, who had been, true to Oscar Wilde's declaration about him, invited to her Northern home — once.

One feels that white people have no roots in this continent, oneself among them. We are transplanted Europeans; the skins of the autochthonous human beings here were red. It is now the beginning of April, but already people are talking of the coming heat. The white hotel closes in three weeks' time, until next year. Fancifully speaking, under this semi-tropical moon, it is a mocking-bird life down here. Here sit I, under this semi-tropical moon, listening to a bird whose song is a mixture of other birds' songs, a veritable American product; and now at the bottom of the garden the two homeless negroes have begun to sing a song based on the literary records of a long extinct nomadic Jewish tribe. So here I end a rootless, mocking-bird bit of writing under the false heat of the moon.

5

One of my new friends asked me if I would care to see the prison, adding, apologetically: 'It's old, and soon will be replaced by a new one.' We were walking at night along Broad Street, with its lights, department stores, and massed automobiles parked at forty-five degrees to the kerb. Crowds of white and coloured people moved easily, at leisure, on the sidewalks. The night was warm and pleasant; this, I said to myself, is the romantic South.

As we approached the brighter lights of a movie palace I noticed they were suddenly dimming; then the smaller boards outside lifted up and were flung into the street. People ran for shelter. It was the beginning of a wind-storm — a small tornado that moaned down the street.

When the cold and distracting funnels had spun away we walked on towards the prison in a dusty fog of street light, our eyes closed against sandy irritation.

The first sight of the prison was astonishing, although many American talkies seen in my home town of Barnstaple in North Devon had given me an idea of what to expect. Behind a large plate-glass window, without blinds or screens, in a brightly-lit room, sat a dozen policemen, playing cards around a hardwood table. It might have been a shop window, and the figures within an arrangement of salesmanship. Indeed, that was the idea: to sell to the public the idea of their civic protection.

My friend was a City Father — equivalent to alderman, magistrate, or councillor in an English town — and we were allowed inside. Cops lounged about within the room, and in the farther yard. All were armed; some carried blackjacks, with short flexible steel handles. Motor-cycles stood there.

My friend said: 'How are you, loo'tenant? This is Mr. Williamson, from England. May we look over?' 'Sure,' replied the officer, easily shaking hands. 'Glad to know you, Mr. Williamson. Not much in to-night. Go ahead.' He waved his hand in salute.

We walked a few yards over the court-yard of trodden earth, and turned into a barrack open at one end. Along the walls were the cells, or cages, in a row. Each cage was a hollow rectangle of steel bars about seven feet high and wide. Bunks of strip iron, without bedding, were fixed to the sides. An earthenware pan, less wooden seat, was fixed in each cell, automatically flushed every few minutes.

In the first cage stood a well-dressed young man, an ordinary whoopee drunk, now half-sobered up. Next to him was a creature with fuzzy hair and dead eyes, mumbling to himself, like an unintelligent gorilla. 'Look, Jake, they're coming down on you! Look out, Jake!' said the cop accompanying us. Jake was often caged there, I learned — delirium tremens; corn whiskey. He held up his arm as a shield against his mental devils.

In the next cage was a slayer, awaiting trial for killing his sweetheart. He asked for a cigarette, and the cop on duty handed him his packet, giving him a light through the bars from his cigar. Another cop was tuning-in the radio, dance music advertising a remedy for B.O., which, the plausible voice confidently explained, was Body Odor. The voice declared that the depression was not always responsible for the loss of your job, your sweet-heart, or your position among the Socially Prominent: were you certain it wasn't B.O.? Somebody's Soap was the sure remedy. Go buy it at the nearest drug-store, and get back that boy friend who hadn't been around so much lately.

A small half-caste negro stood in one of the cages. He had escaped from a chain gang, been caught, and was awaiting transfer to Alabama. He said he had been framed for house-breaking; he didn't do it.

'But the judge didn't agree, did he?' leered the cop. 'I was framed, I didden do it, borss,' said the negro, simply.

In Alabama house-breaking was a capital offence, if anyone was sleeping in the house at the time. This negro, arrested near the house, got twenty years. He had escaped after serving three years, and had just been re-arrested. He wore a new brown suit and new hat. He did not look sad; just very little-boyish, quiet, hopeful.

My friend said they didn't have too bad a time in the gangs; but, gee, twenty years was a long time.

It was a common sight, that of convicts sitting on lorries, striped legs dangling, going through the streets to and from work. Visually they remained in touch with normal life . . . that was something to keep away the Devil.

'They framed me,' murmured the negro, holding to the bars of the cage, and looking at us, superior civilized white men, hopefully.

We went out, and the City Father gave me several drinks of corn whiskey; it was O.K., he said, several years old, and had been inside a charred keg. Some of the corn, he declared, drunken locally was matured only by the time it took to ride round the block from the bootlegger's — for Georgia is one of the states which have not repealed the Volstead Act. So our party did not end up in one of those B.O. cages.

6

Seventy-five miles away is the sea, but the river here is tidal. Not with salt water running up; the land is flat, the water sluggish, returning upon itself twice every twenty-four hours. Dark brown water moves slowly past the muddy roots of cypress trees, where strange crabs move from the shadow of the negro's paddle.

When first seen, these small creatures repel one slightly with horror: for they have but one claw, monstrously out of proportion to the rest of their bodies. They are mud-coloured, the hue of decay and dissolution.

'Fiddlers,' says the negro, 'I reckon them's fiddlers right thar, borss.' I ask how deep is the river. 'Aw, mighty deep, borss. I reckon the ribber is ninety feet deep. Yes sah, yes captin. Ninety feet, boy.'

Obviously he has just invented the information. Later I learn that it is about thirty feet deep in the middle.

The boat in which I sit is called a bateau, in build between punt and canoe. I sit, a little uneasily, in an old armchair, the broken seat stuffed with sacks, in the forepart of the bateau. All bateaux are complete only with broken chairs, for white fishermen. The negro's front teeth are inlaid with gold — not from necessity, but for the sake of beauty — that is, getting girls, or 'tail', as I learn it is called South Carolina.

Rather a terrifying river for a timid provincial Englishman on his first visit; deep green glooms in this creek, the branches of trees hung with moss, a grey lichen which is not truly parasitic, being air-nourished. It straggles thin, airy, and dry; but is strong, the suspensory threads within their grey coverings being like brown cotton thread.

Alligators are rarely seen lying on mudbanks under the trees. Rattlers and deadly moccasin snakes move in the swamps. I saw a red-headed snake swimming a moment ago; it dived when the negro struck idly at it with his paddle. Snapping turtles, their green shells curiously marked in brown, lie by the beds of hogweed, their scaly heads, snake-eyed, poking above the surface.

The act of casting a painted wooden plug for the large-mouthed bass which lie close to the bank by snags and roots, is difficult and exasperating to a beginner. I am unfamiliar with the short steel rod and Pfleuger reel, which tangles the silk line in back-lash: so I rest, and watch the birds.

Buzzards, or black vultures, are sailing far overhead, in the sky which can only be regarded through smoked glasses. Ospreys, called fishhawks (so rare in Scotland) are common here, gliding and slanting with heads down-held for sight of fish: then the plunge, the *splash!* and the brown and white bird flapping up with a mullet or stump-perch in its talons.

Down there, in the open river, beyond the levees or banks of which lie the derelict rice-fields, a lovely white bird is fishing. It is a white heron, and seeing us, it holds its head and beak up at an angle of sixty degrees, looking like an unopened slender snowdrop. It flies up, followed by its mate, and they pitch on the lily pads two hundred yards away.

Across the swamp a crow is cawing repeatedly. Its note is sharper than that of the English crow — a smaller bird, too.

"Coon after its nest, mebbe, yes captin, I reckon that's so, borss,' says my paddler (one dollar fifty cents a day, including information, dubious and otherwise). 'Yes sah. Raised and born on the ribber for twenty-five years, borss. Yes captin, raised and born on dis here ribber, twenty-five years.'

A strange black bird passes overhead, with webbed feet stretching out behind more than its neck and sharp head project in front. It is like a shaped and stream-lined splinter of black glass. It flies swiftly, then glides, flies again, glides.

Can it be a loon? I ask my paddler, who, after spitting for luck on the worm he is using as bait, declares, 'No sah, oh no boy, that's a turkey. Yes, captin. Water turkey, I reckon I call that one, borss. I was raised and born,' etc.

So I say nothing, merely having been borne on the Yemassee ribber twenty-five minutes.

7

It is said that the Southern States of America cannot pay for the roads they have built during the last few years of Prohibition, which might also be described as the Age of Wheels and Ill-health.

Rudy Vallée the crooner, described as Ace of the Air, is probably the highest paid artiste of broadcasting: his weekly hour is eight p.m. to nine p.m. Eastern Standard Time, every Thursday; and this hour is bought, for a coast-to-coast hook-up by a corporation selling a remedy for indigestion.

Bad liquor — wood-alcohol in gin, whiskey, etherized beer — gives only a temporary aetherialized feeling; many temporary New Yorkers — which may be the same thing as saying New Yorkers — feel ill, hollow, rootless, nihilistically philosophical, defeatist, blue, without perhaps fully realizing that these feelings arise solely from a blood-stream polluted by metallic liquor and metallic air.

The annual Old Crocks' Race to Brighton in England is no less quaint and amusing to observe than many of the cars owned by negroes in the South. Flat tires tied to the rims of wheels with wire and rope; hoods tattered as though by shrapnel; exhaust boxes fallen off; a six-cylinder engine with dud plugs, firing on only three cylinders, and being driven like that for weeks.

One morning when we were going fishing for big-mouthed bass in one of the rivers near the Okefinokee Swamp, we stopped at a filling station for gasoline, and the inevitable coca-cola. Coca-cola might be described as the national soft drink of America. Every filling station — even the little one-man shacks in the wilderness — keeps a supply on ice of bottles of this brown aerated liquid, which one buys for five cents, and drinks out of the bottle.

We were having our five cents worth when there was a clattering rattle on the road outside, and a car with four negroes in it came to a standstill. That well-worn *cliché* 'came to a standstill' is an apt description of what happened. It didn't pull up; the driver didn't stop it;

it just came to a standstill. Looking out of the wooden store behind the gasoline fillers, we saw an ancient battered rusty car with burst and faded hood, flapping bonnet, and flat tires tied to crennelated rims with what looked like the remains of several pairs of obsolescent trousers. Apparently the car had no brakes, but it had some gears, which operated through a loose and wobbling prop-shaft, and thus somehow, with ignition switched off, and pistons, connecting rods, mainshaft, clutch, gear-wheels all protesting against motion, it came to a standstill.

It was very hot that day although it was still April, and I did not take much notice of this particular outfit, but returning some hours later and seeing it at the same standstill outside the station, the negroes still sitting motionless under the gaping hood, in almost the same order and postures, I asked the proprietor about them. He said they had no gasoline and no money, and as it was hot and they had some food, they weren't bothering. Sometime, somehow, they would get to Miami, their destination several hundred miles south.

I learned as the days went on that in the Southern States of America this was typical of the wandering life down there. I saw thousands of cars, owned and driven by negroes during my wanderings through Georgia, the Carolinas, and Florida, and almost without exception they were discards of the white folk, and the negroes had little if any mechanical sense. So long as the darn thing goes and the police don't give them a ticket for faulty brakes, the average darkie automobilist, who is usually very poor, doesn't bother.

Everyone has a car. Every small town is black with them, parked at forty-five degrees to the sidewalks or pavements, thus not only economizing space, but also enabling one to back out without pushing or shoving other cars. My various hosts told me never to leave anything that I valued in a parked car, as it would almost inevitably not be there when I returned.

I was driven many miles over sandy tracks with coloured men, paddlers or guides for fishing. One of them, tall and dignified, was the best type of negro. He drove his Ford V8 very fast over sandy tracks and over wooden bridges — bump — crash — bang — with a sure hand, and a high-pitched laugh whenever we were thrown into the air. I feared for the car's springs, but needlessly. The car was built for such country. It was a new car, and well kept. He fished as knowledgeably as he drove, casting his wooden plugs for bass — called trout in this part of Florida — as far as forty yards across the water, with a four-foot steel rod, while standing under tall cypress trees and having less than a square yard of space through which to throw his lure. Like most negroes, he was deeply humorous and content, laughing at what to others might seem trivial incidents — he was a great child, unadulterated, he and I laughed at the same sort of jokes. When we were worm-fishing in a shady bend at the river for red-bellies, and a catfish or a mudfish took the bait — recognized by the way they bored deeply and slowly on the bottom of the river — he chuckled and laughed. 'Another old catfish, I reckon!' he chuckled and squeaked, showing his white teeth and enjoying the joke: for these fish were solemn, scared, sluggish-looking creatures, and their appearance amused him.

I enjoyed being with the negroes; deep contentment flowed from them into myself. There were four of us in the party — two white men and two paddlers. We caught no bass; it was the spawning time, as I learned at the end of the trip, and fish won't strike (or rise as we say in England) when they are laying their eggs. But it was good to be out on the water with my friends.

This coloured man took us about fifty miles a day, and his charge was only five dollars each — including lunch. In the evening, when we were packing up, my friend offered him a drink of corn whiskey, which he carried in a giant thermos flask; but the negro refused politely, saying he never drank when driving a car. He drove well, although rapidly, over tracks that made the going almost like motion on a bronco. We saw turtles on the track, and once a rattlesnake was wrapped round our near fore wheel.

The American engines are of large capacity and coarse feeling after the high revving, economical English engines. But it seems to me that the springing is superior to ours. This good springing is evolutionary, resulting from the state of the roads in America, which are, with the exception of the highways, often rough tracks through logged-off forests, swamps, and prairie. The highways are narrower than the British arterial and main roads, but smoother. They are made of concrete, and often run straight, or nearly straight, mile after mile. When travelling in a sedan — as a saloon car is called — at fifty m.p.h. through the white blazing sunlight, I longed for my own English sports car, laid up on wooden blocks at home; one could cruise all day at sixty to sixty-five m.p.h. and average, with stops for food, fifty m.p.h.

The concrete roads out of the South are superior to those of the North; they lie with often a view ahead of several miles, and go on for hour after hour, day after day, through thousands of miles. Yes, how I wished I were in my own English car, helmet'd and goggled, wind-screen flat, road-dissolving at an easy seventy, sliding past the big Greyhound buses and the orange trucks piled with their lovely yellow cargoes.

One would have to be very careful, of course, when approaching one of those darkie cars with the plumes of steam arising out of the radiators and the wheels wobbling in imitation of one of their own hot dances. And I know now the origin of the so-called hot negroid music: surely it comes not from the swamps, ancient slavery, and nostalgia for the Africas, but from the noises emitted by their crazy automobiles!

8

Southerners, even of the middle generation, still talk of 'the war'; I thought it was the European War, until I realized that the war over the principle of slavery between the North and the South meant for them — generally a quiet, inoffensive, and softly gracious people — the humanitarian, anti-slavery Yankees coming down from the hard winters of the North and laying waste their homes and plantations. The South has not yet recovered from its defeat and the ruthless punitive march of General Sherman's army; older people still grieve in memory for the burnings, hangings, shootings, and the poverty that followed. To the younger generations, it is something that has passed away before their time.

My journey from Georgia to Florida by 'bus was an exhilarating experience despite the heat. My seat was just behind the driver, with a cooling stream from the

open window. Everything was interesting — the palisade
fences made of split boles of trees enclosing fields from
the swamp, no posts, lengths of grey wood laid on top
of each other, zigzag for self support.

We thundered at sixty m.p.h. over old narrow wooden
bridges and modern concrete causeways across swamps.
We watched convict chain-gangs, in their striped clothes,
working beside the roads in the hot sun, under the alert
eyes of guards wearing big straw hats and carrying
rifles at the ready position. We passed avenues of pecan-
nuts with their delicate young green leaves — the pecan
is a soft-shelled nut which tastes so much nicer than
walnut, and with the virtue of the English hazel nut
added.

We passed several of those carts and buckboards which
in Dixie invariably have wheels describing figures of
eight on worn and scrupetting axles, as they proceed
very slowly along the streets, drawn by a mule or a horse
of such fatigued and emaciated frowsiness as would
instantly bring alertness to the eye of any R.S.P.C.A.
inspector in England. Old negroes, in tattered clothes,
often bootless, crouch over the reins.

We passed groves of orange trees, and thoughts arose
of Delius, who in youth came to Florida to grow oranges
— Delius who loved the sun, and dreamed of sunshine,
and those sun-fruits which came from whitest bridal
bloom — Delius whose music is love and dream and
serenity and impersonal heart-ache for starry beauty in
life.

We stopped at filling stations for passengers and coca-
colas. The 'bus arrived at Lacon at four p.m., an hour
to wait before going on south. There were lovely girls
in that town: truly lovely, every one I saw. The sandwich

bar at the 'bus station was excited because one of
Dillinger's — famous bandit, who escaped from prison,
holding up guards with a 'pistol' made by himself of
wood, carved with a safety-razor blade — men came in on
the 'bus, was recognized, and fled, was chased, but not
caught. We went on at five p.m., a new driver and
larger 'bus, he drove quickly, hurling the 'bus about.
I read, dozed, drank coca-colas, chewed gum, dozed,
and it grew darker. We passed a huge truck carrying
ten tons of oranges to New York, lying in the roadway,
overturned in collision with a 1910 Ford two-seater,
looking like half a concertina on wheels; the great
big truck knocked out, the slight little old bewildered
Ford standing near it. A turtle laid on its back by a
cockroach. The driver and I roared with laughter at the
comic sight. 'Look at it!' he cried, 'only slightly
damaged! Just folded up for a quiet little sleep!' We
went on faster than before, swishing past the siren-shrieks
of other trucks, carrying red, green, and blue lights,
which dropped in chromatic whines as they swished by
in the darkness.

All this stimulation for less than a cent a mile.

9

After a rainy journey, we came to this semi-ruinous
hotel, standing in a clearing at the edge of the Floridan
swamp. The hotel was once famous. It was built
before the World War for rich Yankees from the North,
who came here for a cure at the sulphur springs. Made
of wood, the white paint on which is now faded grey, it
stands in the wilderness of sandy soil, among slash

pines charred and maimed by fire, rising amidst the rusty spikes of palmetto grasses.

It is very quiet in the hotel nowadays. The swimming-pool above the creek is deserted. No one drinks at the sulphur springs. No one comes down from the North. The place is slowly falling into ruin. I am at the moment in a suite of rooms which only millionaires could afford during the fashionable days. The suite, with all meals, now costs three dollars a day. I am the only guest in the entire west wing. My two friends and I eat in a vast green-gloomy room; our footfalls echo over the unpolished, uneven floor of the ballroom.

Alone I play a 1909 Edison gramophone, with records a quarter of an inch thick, and scored with such tunes as *Two Little Girls in Blue*.

Walking down the green glooms of long corridors I know by dim whitenesses of eyes and teeth that I am passing one or another of the old coloured women who move so silently about the place. It is said to be haunted. I like to think this. Upstairs in one of the rooms with stained and cracked ceilings there are some old moth-eaten trunks, all that is left of one of the pre-War visitors. He came here to be cured, feeling as all adult human beings feel, that in the future he would be a different person; and here he died; and no one knew who he was, or where he came from, so here he was buried. His trunks remained for years; until one day, when he was almost forgotten, they were opened; and what was left was picked over by the negroes; and now the trunks are empty; lying open on the floor. In the swamp nearby stands the broken casino, home of goats, snakes, and owls, its warping timbers holding what ancient vibration-impressions of love and hope and inner despair?

At night the darkness of the swamp is alive with noises of frogs and crickets: fireflies scintillate, starlike, in sudden turning flashes by the glimmering white walls; the whip-poor-will, that large nightjar, cries with startling nearness from a firtree branch.

My friends said 'Be careful of snakes: black-diamond, rattler, moccasin. The black-diamond's bite is immediately fatal.' Last night, sitting with my two friends in the dining-room, trying to eat grits (maize meal), tough hog, leathery potatoes, and pumpkin (pronounced punkin) pie, I became hysterical with laughter with the black boy who cooks. I fell from the chair, laughing alone at my own Williamson-jokes about food. I was drinking water tasting as though eggs had been boiled hard in it, and then allowed to cool; water which a few years ago was being sold in New York for a dollar the gallon, 'guaranteed for Rheumatism, Indigestion, Dyspepsia, Stomach, Kidney and Bladder Troubles, Gastritis and Skin Diseases'. Scrutinize that quotation; the sulphur water is guaranteed for those ailments. Guaranteed to give you them? Or to rid you of them? *Order to-day at our risk* says the old prospectus. The water could be bought in five-gallon demijohns for four dollars. The creek outside is full of it. I lay on the floor, laughing.

To-night, sitting on my bed and typing, the windows open for the heat, I truly believe the place is haunted. Strange footfalls pad about. It is an effort to sit here with the door unlocked. My spine feels icy cold; the hair at the base of my neck stands up. To test myself against my superstitions, I opened the door just now and walked slowly down the corridor, in absolute darkness and silence, feeling my nervous energy sparking like fireflies out of my body, and walking as in a dream beyond

fear, thinking myself of intense sunlight, and therefore
intangible by any forces of darkness. I walked down the
passage, and back again, my hair bristling and fists
clenched against — what? Those strange fluttering
footfalls? Perhaps the convict from the chain-gang who
got away three days ago? My nerve gave way when I
touched the door-handle, and pushing with my shoulder,
I ran into the room, slammed the door and turned the
key.

Mosquitoes whine just outside the wire-gauzes. The
great-barred owl utters its terrifying bubble-hoot.
Seriously, the place is haunted. There are stories of
negroes being burned alive in the old days. Furniture
is moved about at night. I confess that my door is
locked as I sit on my bed and type these impressions,
while the whip-poor-will cries loudly just outside the
window, and the fireflies flash electrically.

The river is horrible and mysterious. I saw a snake
roll into the water and lie at the muddy edge coiled up,
only its head out. Touched by the wooden paddle, it
uncoiled, loosening a frog which immediately dived
away. Wild goats and hogs — which stamp on and eat
snakes — come down to drink; panthers are here; the
swamp is full of deer. Fish leap before the underwater
rush of alligators; the 'gators revealed only by a rash of
mud-bubbles arising.

I say to myself, This is Florida, this is where the youth-
ful Delius dreamed and planted his orange groves.
To-night another storm of lightning, playing in the east
like gun-fire over Le Transloy Ridge, fireflies crackling-
flashing, high aerial shrapnel. *Whippoorwill! Whippoorwill!* echoing among the pine trees of the swamp, where
this afternoon, riding back on a pre-War Ford drawing

the boat on a trailer, I saw convicts of the chain-gang working.

Is the escaped stick-up bandit hiding here? This derelict wooden palace, with its weed-grown gardens and creepers over windows, would make a fine hiding place. The poor fellow should be warned, however, against eating the grits and the snake-fed bacon, and drinking any of this sulphur water.

10

Why does this country of sand, palmetto grass, thin pines slashed for their life-sap which is made into turpentine, pale grey sky, pale grey sand once drowned by the sea which now foams and murmurs among the shallows of the Gulf of Mexico — why does this land give a persistent feeling of vacancy, of something lost under the sky, a haunting silence in the midst of the sunshine. Since all feeling for Nature comes from within, I wondered if it were solely of myself, an exile in a strange land, one whose deeper thoughts are always of England.

Yes, there is a remote sadness, a vacancy in the sunshine. Day after day, as I sit in the light of the high silver-burning sun, wearing only shoes, cotton trousers, and dark glasses, writing while the small and concentrated shadow of a cabbage palm moves so slowly towards my chair, the feeling comes upon me, and I find myself suspending all thought and hope in order to listen with the mind's ear.

All things are simple when they are known; as simple as their source, which is the sun in the sky.

For days I have been travelling on concrete roads and

sandy tracks to rivers, lakes, and creeks, threading a way on wheels through thousands of square miles of flat, sandy land. Everywhere the same sight: league upon league of rusty palmetto grass, often burnt; a few poor slashed pines standing thin, and seldom straight, against a sky bleached of all colour.

Sometimes our car passed through areas of scrub growing as though hesitantly among the stumps of great trees. Only the stumps, grey and crumbling; never any great trees. The earth we traversed was almost as open as the sky.

I asked my companion as we were eating lunch by a creek if he felt anything vague, strange, melancholy, about the country. He was an American, a world traveller in search of big game; one whom I secretly envied, as he appeared to be, while yet remaining sensitive, a wholly happy man.

He enjoyed life to the full, he wrote stories which were read and appreciated by millions and paid for accordingly, and he was, so far as I could see, without any of that penetrating morbidity which is present in writers whose works are generally disapproved by nice old ladies.

Was this feeling, I asked my American friend, merely an emanation from my slashed and melancholy self? To my relieved surprise he replied that he always felt the sunshine of Northern Florida held the ghosts of great trees which were 'brutally logged off' during the last century.

'Some of the species are now extinct,' he said. 'The lumber kings got concessions for next to nothing from the Government, and they went through the whole country, clearing everything away, big timber and small stuff, treating the forests as the bison were treated, not giving a damn so long as they got the dollars.

'Old chap, this country still bears the wounds and death feelings of those trees. You may think it strange, but I feel myself that the tree spirits, or the Tree Spirit, were so shocked and wounded by the clearing that they or It just ceased to be. Trees won't grow here again for a long, long time.

'It may be sentimentality, it may be merely an anthropomorphical identification with the trees, it may be transposing effect and cause, that you and I just hate to see the unending bleakness of this sandy country, the decaying stumps, the weak scrub growing up as though it knew it didn't have any real right to the open sky.

'It was so cruel, so damned senseless, the way they logged off everything . . . And I kind of feel that even when we begin, as we are now under Roosevelt, to think of afforestation and planning things in a way that will be good for every *thing*, if you understand, as well as for every man, well . . . perhaps we'll be forgiven, and trees will grow again down here once more.'

II

My visit is over, and it is time to leave for the north again. The day after to-morrow I shall be in New York, and after a few more days there, on my way to Montreal and the St. Lawrence seaway home to England. The red spinners will now be over the bridge at sunset, and the trout will be in fine condition, golden-brown and with vermilion spots. How high will the grass be in the hilltop field? I am excited, for all the current of my being is set towards the east, to England.

The bags with the zip fasteners are packed. Oranges, two hundred large Florida oranges, are in that sack — they cost a little less than a farthing each. I shall tip them all out on the lawn by the cypress tree, and cry to the children, 'Help yourselves!' In the other sack are soft-shelled pecan nuts, five pounds for a dollar. That duffle bag holds several pairs of white cotton trousers striped with various dark colours, of the kind worn only by negroes and crackers down here, costing seven shillings a pair. My hostess was amused by their purchase — I, an Englishman, buying clothes in America, and such cheap clothes, too! Nevertheless, it is beautiful material; the pockets set aslant, a watch-fob in the waist-line, and the cut is of a pleasing spareness, no bagginess or loose folds in the seat.

When the sun is in the sands of Crow Island and Vention I shall wear my cotton trousers, and lie and dream of this phase of my life that now is about to end. The invitation to visit the South came just at the right moment; it was a sick man who travelled from Waterloo to Southampton on the last day of February, feeling worn to the verge of death. Now my body is soaked with the sun, colour has meaning again, and Night is beautiful, tranquil for sleep once more — the lovely southern nights with their soft, unflashing stars. When the cold river mists hide the trees in the valley of my Devon cottage I shall think of the brilliant sparks of the fireflies, little Sirius-flashes; the reedy dry rattle of frogs; the terrifying great hooting of barred owls from the cypress swamps in the darkness as we stopped the car by the wayside one evening, alert for approaching footfalls, since we had been warned of bandits in the woods who shoot and rob. And shall I ever forget the first cry of the whip-

poor-will, and its association-memory of my childhood —
for my mother gave me a whip-poor-will's egg when I
was a very small boy, the egg which she brought from
America as a girl. I put it under my pillow that night,
and it was smashed. And when I was older, and an
enthusiastic egg-collector, I blamed her regularly several
times a year for giving me that egg when I was so young.
The South for me in memory will be the little cracker
boy who paddled us one day, clad in the usual blue
overalls and barefooted, and he could neither read nor
write, but was so polite and naturally a gentleman; the
hanging moss in the cedar swamps; the misty blue
eyes of the old and drunken 'poor white' in the woods
who hired us his boat — he shaking and half-dissolved
by corn whiskey.

And I shall remember the forest creek on the banks of
which I had been sitting for days in forest solitude,
writing *The Sun in the Sands* when suddenly a hundred
girls and boys from the school in the neighbouring saw-
mills town appeared, and the swimming bath behind the
hotel was alive with cries and colour and splashing
laughter. I wonder what will happen to the yellow-
haired girl in the red skirt whose passion was the stars,
and whose dream was to be an astronomer, she told me,
while the mandoline played and I felt myself to be
sixteen again. Will the stars betray her? Or her feeling
for them? And when I see vipers on the paths of Bremridge Wood, I shall remember that rattlesnake swimming
across the river, holding its tail out of water, to keep the
buttons, which made the rattle, dry. And the white
light of the sky, the high silver blaze of sun, the white
egrets fishing by the riverside — the nesting females
no longer slain for partial reappearance on the heads of

young ladies at the Courts of Buckingham Palace. And
so much else to remember — the Negro morality play
staged in the Negro church, with the Devil in red, an
attractive Devil with his capers, grins, winks, and offers
of whiskey, lipstick, and children's toys, to tempt to
destruction the heaven-bound souls of all ages. The
success of the play was assured by roars of happiest
laughter! And that white preacher who came to the
town and took seventy-five hundred dollars away after
a week's exhortation — some of it over the local radio in
this manner, 'Friends and brethren, the Lord has spoken,
the Lord has awakened one of us into the Light — my
friends, at this moment Mr. Richard Lowry is praying
for guidance whether he shall send for the Lord a
cheque for fifteen hundred dollars, the sum due for my
life assurance, which I have not, as I have taken no
thought for the morrow, but have got goodness organized
for this Drive against Sin — hold it folks! — a telephone
message just received at this broadcasting stoodio,
saying Mr. Richard A. Lowry is mailing that cheque
right now — the Lord has answered his prayer —
Hallelujah, Hallelujah'. And the name of the preacher,
of whose sanctity and Christian unselfishness many old
ladies assured me — his name, folks, was HAM . . . but
here is the car, my friend is waving, and I must go.

12

Entering the cavernous station from the brilliant
sunlight without, I was given that feeling of trepidant
doom that amateur travellers feel just before the commencement of a long journey. It was strangely quiet in

the station which was without platforms, a place in which parallel lines gleamed dully.

Walking over the rails followed by the coloured porter wheeling my baggage and bewildered by my cheap cotton pants and forty-nine cent shirt I came to the Dixie Flyer which every day runs its thousand odd miles between Florida and New York.

The coaches, each with its name painted on the side, were longer than English coaches, which are still cautiously faithful to the old horse omnibus.

The pleasures of travelling in the Pullman were increased by the thought that at the end of them I should reach the port of embarkation for England. England! Now that I was about to leave the South, I found myself wishing that I had done more things, instead of sitting about in the sunshine so many hours, and writing of what had happened about ten years before. Why hadn't I gone with Miss Louise to see the azalea gardens and houses of Charleston, and that fine writer, Herbert Sass? And why hadn't I explored the Okefinokee Swamp, where frogs confronted by snakes puffed themselves out and made faces at the reptiles — usually in vain? Too late now; England in May was drawing me, as it drew the swift and the nightjar from this line of latitude through Africa.

The negro followed with my luggage on a trolley, eyeing meditatively first the trunks and then the cracker pants — but seeing the label for England, his brow cleared.

Under my arm were fishing rods, in one hand a type-writer, in the other an ice-water bucket of the kind which everyone used in Florida. The strip of tickets was round my hatband. This seemed proper. Had I not been in the coach to Boston, containing two hundred Yankee souls, all of them men, and I the only one who fumbled for my ticket when the collector came round deftly taking tickets from hats engaged in contemplation of Wall Street or *The Saturday Evening Post?*

At the doorway of my coach stood a big and silent negro. He smiled pleasantly, and took the things from my hands while the strip was tactfully removed from my hat. The negro led the way to my seat. I sat down, suddenly weary. He took my hat, and put it in a large paper bag beside me. Over my head the coach roof was smooth as though with mahogany. We started almost without awareness of motion. I was going home to England.

The attendant reappeared after awhile in a white coat. I spoke to him about cotton fields, and instantly he was bending over me, and giving knowledgeable answers in a soft voice. He was a type; every Pullman attendant I had encountered in America had the same personality, alert, attentive, unobtrusive, and restful: fine creations of the sun.

After dinner I returned, and found the coach transformed. Where were the seats, the smooth mahogany curves overhead? I saw the last set of seats being converted before my eyes. The attendant pulled, there was a click, and a bed came out of the wall. He pulled again, and a green curtain, with net for underwear and coat-hangers shook out and fell into place. He pulled again, and another bed was suspended under the top bunk. When I came back from the Rest Room, where one may smoke, wash, drink from paper cups, and deposit safety razor blades in a special slot in the wall, the coach was a dormitory, with a narrow gangway of green hanging curtains concealing bedrooms. Shoes, hairy shanks and sock suspenders were visible; but never a film star's slender leg.

Now I am snug in my bed, curtains drawn and buttoned, and reading Hemingway's magnificent *The Sun Also Rises* by the light of the small corner lamp. It feels late, although not yet ten o'clock. I switch off the light, and settle to sleep; but sleep is intermittent, I waking and drowsing off and waking again to see lights and streets and stars through the window. It is a comforting feeling, to be in bed, and moving all the time towards England.

After breakfast next morning the dormitory had vanished again, and the coach was as I had entered it nearly a thousand miles away. I read and stared through the window; and then the familiar yellow reeds and dumps of the swamps outside New York were moving backwards. My old battered hat is withdrawn from the paper bag, and handed to me with a bow. And then, as I leave the coach, the negro produces his little dusting brush, and strokes my shoulders with it, receiving with discreet gratitude half a dollar into the pink palm of his faithful hand.

TO ENGLAND

ONLY four more days to wait.

Turning from Fourteenth Street into Fifth Avenue, I found myself in the midst of a series of processions or progressions — loose battalions of people passing with banners bearing anti-capitalist slogans and devices. Mounted police escorted the processions. Most of the marchers were young, hatless, wearing unusual clothes, sunburnt; the older comrades were usually pale, and many wore beards. A city wind blew red scarves and ribbons and ties; and when they had passed with their shrill religious songs the empty wind was whirling bits of paper in the deadly street, skidding peanut shells and silver paper and food cartons in the dry gutters — the litter left by these apostles of the new clean civilization.

Eddying city air and deadly street remained. The street was dark with rubber and grease, uncountable wheels being urged forward, for the swifter pursuit of the means to escape from that place of deadly streets. The Communists were striving to remove deadness from the streets, to bring to the sidewalks an azure air of dream. The dusty human passing gritted my eyes, the sunset was mortified by the city's noise and fume. Were the stars now wavering in the deep water below the bridge, and had the spring salmon moved down at twilight from under the white waterfalls to the tail of the pool, leaping out and smacking down on their sides, playing and rolling gravely around one another now that cool darkness had come into the water? And had the moon risen yet above the fir plantation of Bremridge Wood, watched by a grave little face through the bars of the cot in the eastern room? I thought of the moths over the quiet grasses of my hilltop field, of candlelit peace in the hut, and the white owl floating over the mice-runs in the hedge . . . so I hurried to the Radio City music-hall, seeking the azure air of serenity within that lofty building, and there I sat with seven thousand others and forgot wheels being urged forward and the harsh noises of human striving.

Rows of heads in front of me diminished and grew smaller and smaller towards a soft yellow light illumining a seated orchestra of two hundred players slowly rising to the stage. Bands of greenish light glowed in the lofty barrel of the roof. I sat half-way down the hall, yet the trombones looked no bigger than tiny golden hairpins. I looked about me and marvelled at the genius of the American builders, akin to that of the ancient Romans: they conceive on the grand scale, their heads are truly in the clouds. The four initial chords of Wagner's *Dreams* started tears in my eyes: and I saw the summer waves curling on the sands of the estuary, and was released and dissolved into the blue air, beyond the thistledown drifting in the sky from Labrador.

The floodlit building rose high and tranquil above the night-fire of New York. I said good-bye to William Rose Benét, and walked down town to the Brevoort.

Only three more days to wait.

A swift visit with friends to Connecticut, where wind blew through shining sunlight from the icefields of the North and trees were not yet sure of the spring, where the body used to Florida's heat was dismayed, and the spirit or imagination was driven in upon itself to think of Europe and its political torments. All those truthful war-books burned in Germany: the lost generation lost in vain. I sat in a canoe with a boy of fourteen and a girl of eleven, rejoicing for the poise and surety of these American children which was as the flight of swallows; and wished that all fathers were natural as this friend of mine, for then there would be no fortified frontiers, gas-factories, super-furious aeroplanes, and other manifestations of mental fear.

The clear ice-wind, holding down the sap in trees which had endured the bitterest winter of the century, ruffled the dead waters of Farmington river, the waters polluted by mills and factories, so that never a fish or a fly rose from its streams and eddies.

New York again: only two more days.

My younger self used to scoff mentally at the idea of men who before death wished to be buried or their ashes thrown in particular places; but for many days now I had known poignantly the desire to be home, which comes from the deep instinct in man, and bird, and fish, and seed borne under its Maker's marvellous small parachute. I was desperate to return to England, which had been all my thoughts since leaving Southampton three months before.

The final day came, a swift visit to an old friend in Eighty-sixth Street, his warm friendliness and handshake of good-bye; and so to the subway opposite the German *brauhausen* and the express to Fourteenth Street, down to the Brevoort, the luggage coming up on the elevator. And at last the taxicab was filled with ice-water jar for hut, sacks of pecan nuts and oranges, toys for the children, rods, bags, typewriter, boxes, trunks, fifteen pieces in all, an appalling pile of stuff — and the lights of Fifth

Avenue were opening wide upon my sight and passing swiftly large past my temples as I sat up and anxiously counted the streets mounting to Forty Second: and the yellow cab was turning swiftly, and I was giving away silver half dollars to porters in red caps after the checking of the heavier luggage, then following others through the yellow lava-stone hall of Grand Central Station, with the zodiacal signs on its roof, and down the slope to the Montreal train, where stood ebon sentries by doors of dark-green coaches, silent, serene strength of service.

The minutes ticked away in my wrist-watch. It was almost half-past ten. I was glad of no one to see me away, for there was nothing of me to see away; none of me had really crossed the sea. Waiting in the corridor, I heard the deep rolling thrilling warning, 'All-l-l-l A-boo-ard'; and the train was imperceptibly moving, and I was going home to England.

Once again the rods and grips and sacks and water-bucket and duffle bags of nuts and oranges were counted; then after washing and a smoke in the Rest Room the green curtains were drawn over the Pullman couch, the corner light switched on, I got into bed and read more of the proofs of Victor Yeates' *Winged Victory*, one of the very best of the war novels, a beautiful and balanced transcript of reality. The title of this story of a group of single-seater pilots was originally *A Test to Destruction*, but no one seemed to know what that meant except the author and his friends who were human flesh and spirit tested to destruction. Everyone looked blank when they heard the title *A Test to Destruction*, so it became *Winged Victory*, which if the reader is an old pilot of the R.F.C., will seem ironic enough.

I relived the scenes in mess and ante-room during the

heated August days and nights, when 'the sky had turned to brass', and then, wearied out by present desire and need and by old memory, I put out the light and listened to the wheels rolling northward to the great seaway of the St. Lawrence.

At sunrise I looked through the window, half expecting the landscape to be English, since this was now Canada. Then, with other passengers I was in Montreal Station, watching for and claiming luggage; a dash into the street to buy a bottle of Canadian rye whiskey from a government store served by officials behind wire grills; toast and marmalade and coffee in a cafeteria, and back to the fifteen pieces guarded by a redcap and into the 'bus and down to the docks, and up the gangway and down to C deck aft and a little cabin.

A jazz quartet played briskly on deck, a boy went round with paper whizzers, a few were thrown to the dock below. I went back to the third class deck. A girl in drab clothes was trying not to sob, as she stood alone and sometimes looked at what appeared to be her parents, poor French Canadians, standing silently together by the sheds. My companions for the next ten or eleven days seemed suspended in life like myself. A young dog was dragged, four feet protesting, off the gang-plank to the deck. I went below to my cabin and poured the rye whiskey into a silver hip-flask bought in New York — being a traveller from the New World, it seemed right that a return home should be made with a hip-flask. I had a pull at the flask, wondering why it was called a pull. The spirit after sixteen years guaranteed in an oaken cask, bit my throat, although bit seemed a curious word. Unable to think only of the word burn as an alternative, I swallowed some more, screwed the cap, pushed the cold curve of silver against my hip, and went out again to see the paper streamers multiplied and fluttering and to hear the siren blowing as we cast off. The girl was now sobbing unrestrainedly, and so was her mother below, and her father's arm was sadly round the woman's shoulder, as he stood beside her, with bent shoulders. The wind blew coldly across the water, and my ulster coat was in the heaviest trunk in the baggage room.

Dutifully the decks of all three classes were walked, with determination that there should be no seasickness this time. Quebec, with the Chateau Frontenac on the heights, dropped astern. The channel was marked by buoys and floating lighthouses — little red and white cottages that swayed to our bow-waves. Dark blue were the mountains against the northern twilight gleaming on the widening seaway. My table in the dining-room had been selected in the far corner, apart from the others, an eyrie for observation and detachment; but now at dinner a stranger was seated beside me. We said good-evening, and ate in silence. Afterwards the shore lights seen from the forbidden A deck shrunk smaller on either shore; the last light was absorbed by the water. Nine more days, and then England! I went to bed, after washing in the lavatories where in seven languages I was exhorted not to throw my unwanted property down the pans.

Next day at luncheon my table-mate after telling me that I was supposed to be a writer, asked me if I knew what a vespasian was. A vespasian? No, I didn't know. He said that the civic authorities of Montreal had built one, and not liking the sound of the usual names for it, had called it that, and moreover had cut the letters

VESPASIAN two inches deep in the rock over the principal entrance. Inside, the vespasian was very luxurious, and the authorities were about to install the radio, at a further cost of thousands of dollars, to broadcast from the vespasian, when it was stopped. I listened patiently, and then I was asked if I knew what a vespasian was? No, I didn't know, but now that my interest was aroused, I said I hoped he would tell me sometime. Sure, he would tell me. And he would tell me right now. But first, did I know what a vespasian was? I looked at him. He appeared to be about forty, although he had told me he was over fifty. Perhaps he would tell me another time? I suggested, rising to go. Wait à minute, he said. Couldn't I answer a plain question? I waited. He wanted to ask me a plain question, Did I know what a vespasian was? Well, did I know who he was? Who was? I asked. He repeated, Did I know who Vespasianus was? He would tell me. Vespasianus was a Roman Emperor, who erected the first public conveniences in Rome. Now couldn't I make a story out of that, he inquired.

This man was a pathetic figure, not happy at home, at odds with his grown-up children, and he was losing his sight because he drank too much whiskey: sometimes a hundred ounces a day, he told me. He was taking a trip to England, which he had left twenty-five years before, in the hope of curing himself. So I wouldn't press him to share even a bottle of wine, would I? I told him he would be all right, and he grew suddenly very cheerful at the thought of seeing England again after twenty-five years.

The next day we passed into the open Atlantic south of Cape Race, and ran into fog, for icebergs were beginning to drift south. The air was bleak, inhuman.

Rise and fall and rattle, creak and uninteresting same-
ness of everything and nausea made me remain in my
bunk. Singly and in twos and threes the large oranges of
Florida were lobbed through the port-hole as they went
rotten. I swore to myself and the cheerful steward that
never again would I cross the Atlantic. 'What, still in
bed, sir? Why it's like a millpond.' The white of a wave
swished past the port-hole. 'Lovely on deck, sir. The
ozone, you're missing it. What, only dry toast and honey
again? My word, what you've eaten so far wouldn't
feed the smallest fish outside.' I told him that was my
intention.

The next day I saw an iceberg through the port-hole,
pale white sightless peak without purpose in the grey sea.
There was some satisfaction in keeping my watch at
Eastern Standard Time, for, when the suspension of life
became unbearable, I could assure the inner uncontroll-
able self that England was nearer in time-space than the
mental set of the mind's endurance. Eventually there
was a credit of five hours, and mid-Atlantic, with its
miles of uncaring deep blue depth, was being left behind
the eternal thump and shudder of the screws.

Dressing-gown journeys to the salt-water baths of
morning were no longer an ordeal: had I acquired sea-
legs while lying down? The oral adjustment to false
walking had been made painlessly. One need never be
afraid of seasickness again: the cure was to lie down
and rest until the balance adjusted itself. Assured of
this, I got up and dressed feebly but determinedly, and
went into the dining-room, to be greeted gladly by my
table-mate, who said he thought I was the one who had
jumped overboard. Had someone done that? I asked.
Apparently one of the passengers had been missing for

some days; the ship had been searched, and he was not in it. How about a bottle of wine, he suggested, to celebrate the nearness of England. He was very friendly, and I fear my aloofness or apparent unfriendliness may have disturbed him, for that evening he was to be seen drinking glass after glass of whiskey in the smoke room, an expression of secret enthusiasm in his blank eyes. Was he thinking of England, and the good life of the future, when he had cured himself of weakness, and was happy again, as he had been years ago? I thought I understood him; but without words.

Now the five hours could be conceded easily, and deep draughts taken of steward's ozone. In the company of some young men from various Canadian universities, travelling steerage for adventure and economy, we trespassed on the select decks and rooms forward, and we told each other our adventures, theirs seeming so real and substantial, such as crossing the Atlantic on cattle boats, working their passages; and driving sledges with teams of huskies in Greenland, feeding the dogs on frozen salmon, and enduring blizzards: while mine were only rearing trout from eggs in a single tray in the runner at the bottom of the garden, digging out wasps nests and feeding trout with them while standing hour after hour on a small eighteenth-century ornamental bridge over a small West Country stream; reading books; planting sapling trees; sheltering from a storm in a linhay on the downs; and listening to the river sounds at night. They said it must be grand to live in Devon, and I thought to myself it would be grand to have them visit me, but I knew from experience that my words were one thing and my actions another. We were together all the time, it seemed, and I almost lost the feeling of being older and slower than they were. Had one ever been so young and carefree as these youths? Was one young and carefree in nineteen fifteen? Memory was so easy a deceiver. But what was that light on the port bow? I saw it first. The Bishop Light? Could it be? We all ran to the rails. There, far away over the sea, shone the first light of England!

A Boy in Kent

C. Henry Warren

New Introduction by G.R. Warren

C. Henry Warren belongs to that line of writers which includes H.E. Bates, Adrian Bell and John Moore. In *A Boy in Kent* he recreates the countryside of his childhood and his pages sparkle with supreme joy.

> We'll talk of sunshine and of song,
> And summer days, when we were young;
> Sweet childish days, that were as long
> As twenty days are now . . .'

This dedication, quoted from Wordsworth, sets the scene for what is to follow; a world of meadows and fields, the village pub and in particular, the village shop seen through the eyes of a child. Everyone was a neighbour in the village. It is true that the village rambled over several square miles, but all told the population numbered only some eight or nine hundred and it was next to impossible for any one family not to have some kindred feeling about any other family. And the author brings them to life in this vivid and beautiful memoir.

Sovereign
160pp   198mm × 127mm
ISBN 0 86299 137 4 (paper) £4.95

Men and the Fields

Adrian Bell

Illustrations by John Nash

The drawings of John Nash perfectly match the country scene as described by Adrian Bell in this highly acclaimed portrait. In chronicling the life of the fields the author, with a sure touch and in beautiful prose, evokes a bygone world of farmers and shepherds, land owners and countrymen.

A new year's eve party in an old farmhouse yields a host of memories. As the year's hours grow fewer, the older people do the talking, the younger ones listen, and an England far older than the passing year is resurrected. One old lady tells of how the river was used for bringing chalk and coal to the farms. Another storyteller recalls how they used to go to Christmas parties in the country when he was a child. And so on, through the months of the year – the seasons unfolding in a highly personalised way as man and nature come together in a book to keep and to treasure.

Sovereign
160pp   198mm × 127mm
Illustrated
ISBN 0 86299 136 6 (paper) £4.95

Among the Quiet Folks

John Moore

First publication in the United Kingdom

Here are fourteen stories by the author of the Brensham Trilogy, each of them one of a kind.

There is evocative simplicity in the title story, there is unforgettable malice in the powerful vignette, 'A Cold Wind Blowing.' 'Mr Catesby Brings It Off' is a delectable comic invention and in a boisterous tale entitled 'The Octopus,' four inebriated Frenchmen, survivors of Verdun, get themselves trapped in a wild midnight escapade aboard a carnival ride.

Most of John Moore's books are set in the English countryside but in his short stories he ranged further afield. Whenever he took a trip or a holiday he brought back a tale. 'Tiger, Tiger' originated in Andalusia, 'In Gorgeous Technicolour' on a West Indian island, 'The Octopus' in Normandy and 'Mr Catesby Brings It Off' in the Welsh mountains.

Sovereign
216pp   198mm × 127mm
ISBN 0 86299 146 3 (paper) £4.95

The Country of White Clover

H.E. Bates

In the heat of a clear April morning in the countryside somewhere between Valence and Auxerre, H.E. Bates had the desire, as always at some time every spring, to stop the flow of bursting bud, of fresh shoots, the brilliance and richness and let it rest there. For nothing of later summer could ever in any way, be more beautiful than this. In England more than half the beauty of spring is its length, its long four-month course draws out slowly, uncertainly, with repeated moments of exquisite and infuriating change.

These contrasts suffuse a book overflowing with love for the countryside; a rustic world of trees and flowers, of birds and animals, unfolding seasons and characters such as Messrs. Kimmins and Pimpkins, and where every village contains its Victorian survival, man or woman, who over the years has never made a trip to the nearest town and, in typically stubborn or placid way, never wants to.

Sovereign
192pp   198mm × 127mm
ISBN 0 86299 142 0 (paper) £4.95